Customers

Strategy

Business Outcomes

I0015833

ONE IT, ONE BUSINESS

KEVIN J. SMITH

Customer Success

One

Our

Our
IT

Our
Business

Customers

Strategy

Business Outcomes

ONE **IT,**
ONE BUSINESS

KEVIN J. SMITH

Customer Success

One

Our

Our
IT

Our
Business

Outskirts Press, Inc.
http://www.outskirtspress.com

Paperback ISBN: 978-1-9772-0909-2
Hardback ISBN: 978-1-9772-1239-9

Library of Congress Control Number: 2019901290

Cover Photo © 2019 www.gettyimages.com. All rights reserved - used with permission.

Outskirts Press and the "OP" logo are trademarks belonging to Outskirts Press, Inc.

PRINTED IN THE UNITED STATES OF AMERICA

AUTHOR DEDICATION

To Julie. You continue to amaze me every day.

ACKNOWLEDGMENTS

My sincere thanks to Steve Daly and Steve Morton for their support of this project and for their commitment to the continued improvement of Information Technology (IT) organizations everywhere.

To the talented and passionate people of IT with whom I am so fortunate to work every day across hundreds of global market-leading organizations of all sizes, each of which is committed to the exciting future of our craft. These same organizations are now experiencing the rebirth of IT and unification of every action across IT and through this journey embracing a bright new future.

This is the essence of One IT, and this same essence brings to life One Business. Although not commonly understood today, it will become a vital part of the next decade, when a new model for Business will emerge, the profile of which is woven through the pages of this book.

The professionals at Outskirts Press have been a joy to work with throughout the publishing process, and my thanks for holding to a uniquely aggressive schedule and bringing the book to life.

My appreciation goes out to my patient and talented illustrator, Julie Felton, who once again was called on to recraft my many all-but-illegible pen and paper sketches into something far better.

FROM THE MANY, ONE

PREFACE

The professionals of Information Technology (IT) today are enjoying a remarkable rebirth that will cause us to think and act differently in virtually every dimension of IT. This transformation is underway today, not an abstract series of events yet to occur somewhere in the future.

This rebirth of IT is both an exciting opportunity and a responsibility we all share. A responsibility to embrace this change, to enrich it and to carry it forward in order to ensure a brighter future for every aspect of IT.

Remarkably, this rebirth is only the beginning—the beginning of a new era for IT and one that looks very different than the past thirty years.

The accelerating reality of the simultaneous rebirth and unification of IT is the compelling upside and equally compelling downside of IT not rising to this historical challenge. The upside is a new, agile, and innovative IT that will fundamentally change the business. It will become widely understood in the next decade by market leaders of the future that technology is now strategic and not just a corporate resource.

*Those organizations that leverage technology
as a fundamental element of corporate strategy
will thrive and all others will fade away.*

The downside of any inability to unify IT will be the gradual dissolving of the IT organization as we know it today, or even worse, the very real risk of an implosion of IT and a rapid dispersion of IT elements into the functional organizations. As IT professionals, we must recognize this is a valid scenario: the needs of the business can't be denied, and if IT is unable to rise to the challenge, the organizational organism must and will adapt.

*We simply can't let this happen, as we will have
failed IT and failed the business. In this model,
the business will be weaker and diluted.*

But let's take a step back for a moment. In my previous book, The IT Imperative, I described the eighteen elements that are driving this transformation and will ultimately bring to life the strategy and operating models of IT for the next twenty-five years. While this evolution will certainly change virtually all that we do, it is not enough. Not nearly enough.

Beyond these elements that are shaping the future of IT, there is a singularity of purpose, a unity of action that must occur in IT and the Business. This unity and singular focus will ultimately separate the organizations that have simply transformed themselves from those organizations that will emerge as the new market leaders and those organizations that will change the world of business forever.

*This book explores the future of IT in more
depth by taking a look at the strategy
of a Unified IT and an equally Unified
Business as a unique and singular path to
a successful and thriving organization.*

The urgency of this unity is not an exaggeration. This is quickly becoming the new reality of IT and of Business. Better is not good enough. Good is not good enough. The IT organization must be strategic and must be great in order to secure our future. Even further, the only path to business success travels squarely through the unification of the IT organization.

> *This is a critical concept—the transformation of IT will not stop or slow at the boundaries of IT. It will quickly influence and then transform the full Business.*

Lines will be blurred, functions will come together, and people and organizations will unite, all with a single, clear, and unified vision, strategy, and operating model. This singularity of the many becoming one will unlock value and create leverage simply not possible before.

We will revisit this notion of leverage throughout the book as it is so fundamental to One IT and then to One Business. Leverage is an organic force that is under our control and put simply brings us a greater return on an equal or lesser amount of resource expended. Think in terms of faster, better, and cheaper in every regard. This is, of course, a great simplification, but it gets to the heart of this book.

With singularity of purpose, thought, and action, we unleash a value that has yet to be tapped in the rich history of IT.

> *What I'm proposing is not only that IT becomes a better organization to support the business, but that IT becomes a powerful engine of innovation and operating excellence that redefines and leads the full organization, the full business, forward.*

Yes, I know, this is surprising, and many people would find the idea of IT leading the business into the future anywhere from unlikely to controversial to absolutely crazy. That's okay. This is to be expected and should not discourage us. Great leadership often comes from the most unlikely of places, and history has taught us this lesson repeatedly.

If anything, this should increase our resolve to take up the challenge and complete the transformation of IT, understanding that this is not the final result, but rather the next critical phase in the journey of our business. The stakes around the rebirth of IT are higher than ever in that this transformation in many cases is the only action that can save the future of the business. The relationship between IT and the business is critical and must be better understood by all IT and business professionals. Again, some will question this given the history of IT as a somewhat tactical and slow-moving organization.

I see the evidence all around us of this being possible and, even more so, of this being needed and vital. One only needs to thoughtfully consider how our world has changed and how business has changed over the past ten years to begin to see a rapidly growing body of facts that support this strategy.

It is there for those who take the time to look. The following pages will lay out a model for this unification of IT and of business, including a mix of the vision IT must carry forward, a set of strategies to make the vision a reality, and then a number of operational elements to support the strategy. The scope of this model will include culture, people, the role of technology, customers, the organization, and much more.

As you read through the book, you will quickly note that much of what we do today in IT must change, and the very fabric of what the IT organization has been assumed to be and not to be must be questioned from within.

This is another critical point that is central to a Unified IT—IT must ask of itself the toughest questions and hold itself accountable at the highest level.

This simply can't come from outside of IT. By then it is too late—far too late—and to some degree the business has been weakened and damaged, which can't be reversed.

We must embrace the idea of questioning everything we do in IT and opening our minds to where this will take us in order to achieve a Unified IT. This scrubbing of every minute of effort expended and every work product delivered must be conducted by IT and only by IT. The implications of this are deep and broad. <u>IT can only lead the business into the future by first getting its own house in order</u>.

Then, everything becomes possible, and in the process of renewing IT, we create a powerful machine of innovation and speed vital to the future of the business.

This powerful machine born in IT becomes inextricably linked to the full organization to the extent that IT and the business become one.

Singular in everything we do, unified in every action, and absolutely focused on the same strategy and in executing every action necessary to drive the unified strategy every day.

TABLE OF CONTENTS

CHAPTER 1

WHY A UNIFIED IT

Why a Unified IT? Because it is the only way to enable a successful business, the only way IT can be great, and the only way to ensure IT will have a future.

Yes, there is much at stake here, including the very survival of IT.

The upside is huge and the downside is equally big. By unifying IT and ultimately the business, we have the opportunity to change everything. But if we are unable to rise to this challenge, the IT organization we know today will cease to exist. The reason for this is simple—in order for the very heart of the business to survive and ultimately to thrive, big change must occur. And this is fundamentally and inextricably connected to IT.

These big changes can't occur without big changes to IT because technology and data are now strategically linked to the business, linked to the strategy and the operations of the business.

We are constantly reminded of the context of today. The pressures and demands of the global marketplace and the resulting expectations and requirements brought to bear on the IT organization are causing us to question everything we do. Every thought and every action alike. All IT professionals must accept that the long-standing strategies and operations of IT simply can't keep up with the demands of the business, much less allow IT to work proactively and ultimately to lead the business.

It's critical that as we remake IT, our goal can't be to simply keep up with the demands of the business—we must build a new IT that realizes the vision of being strategic, of being proactive, and to ultimately lead the business. This is a higher bar that we must set for ourselves, and nothing less will do. So much is at stake.

Now, with this in mind, we can get to work on rebuilding IT from the inside out, driven by the new vision that can only be realized through unification of IT and the singularity and focus that come with this unification.

When thoughtfully reviewing the IT organization of today and what we must create in the rebirth of IT, one thing stands out—we can't meet these challenges and successfully achieve the rebirth of IT when working as a fragmented and divided IT organization. The IT functions of the past create fundamental inefficiencies and challenges that are not exposed.

> *These limitations keep us from working with the speed, agility, and leverage we must have for the future of IT and the future of the business.*

There is so much that is exciting about the remaking of IT and the unification of IT.

This singularity and unification that we will discuss repeatedly throughout the book and from many different perspectives is so many things rolled into a single dramatic change. It is a maturing, a refinement, an elegance of motion, a shift from strategic to tactical, and a full remaking of the culture to name but a few.

We can only achieve the leverage and value by pulling together, to the same cadence, every minute of every day across all of IT.

What does this mean? Well, that is exactly what we will explore in detail throughout the coming pages.

THE SURVIVAL OF IT

Let's come back to the fascinating upside and downside of unifying IT. The real opportunities and consequences of One IT should be clear.

We will spend the balance of the book on the exciting upside of a unified IT and how we make this powerful model a reality. But we also need to explore, if only briefly, the downside of not unifying IT so all of us in IT clearly understand just how serious the consequences can be if we don't rise to the challenges in front of us.

What is at stake here is not just a marginally better IT, not just IT creating leverage for the business and ultimately changing how the business works every day, but in fact the very survival of IT. The pressures coming to bear on IT today are massive and unstoppable. The pressures originate from everywhere—from increased competition, to a global marketplace, to the mobile lifestyle, to the blurring of work and personal time, to an always-on culture, to ubiquitous access to information, to impatient and demanding customers, and this is only the beginning. These pressures will continue to build and certainly will not slow down or recede. If we are waiting for that to happen, it is time to abandon that notion for good. Our world is transforming before our eyes, and this change is unstoppable. Nowhere in business will this pressure and these changes be more evident than in IT. Why?

Because IT is now the living intersection of technology, data, and the business. This makes IT unique in every organization today.

We now understand that business can't be great today and in the future if the business is not able to strategically leverage technology to create a competitive advantage and to make this technology a seamless element of the business strategy. The companies that have done this successfully are the market leaders of today and have become the world's most valuable companies as well. The short list of these companies would include Apple, Google, and Amazon. The companies that have not managed to embrace this duality of business and technology have failed or will fail in the next ten years.

It is as simple as that, and this truth is inescapable.

Having said that, it is important to understand that a vital transition occurs while the business is struggling to understand, appreciate, and then adapt this powerful union of technology and the business model. The tension that occurs during this transition is remarkable, and there will an unconscious or very conscious awareness of a void in the business that must be filled. This void will be the ability to connect technology to the business strategy as a necessary transition and to then over time create an engine of innovation that can be sustained into the future and create a pipeline of product improvements, new breakthroughs, and ultimately a competitive advantage.

This transition and need then creates an opportunity for IT that must be met from within, or a dramatic compensation/adaptation will occur. This adaptation is only necessary if IT is unable to meet this challenge. The adaptation can take two forms:

Outsourcing of IT in its entirety

*Breaking up IT elements and dispersing
them into the functional organizations.*

These changes are not a desired outcome for IT nor a desired outcome for the business but could become necessary should IT not
fill the void that has been created in the business.

As IT professionals we can't let this happen. This is bad for the future of IT and for the future of the business. The good news is that
this is fully under our control, and if we take the necessary actions
and drive the necessary changes, the compensation will not be
required.

Only IT can ensure the survival of IT.

One key action to a stronger future for IT is the unification that
brings us so much leverage, a singularity of IT that changes everything. This is another reminder that One IT both creates a strong
IT and a stronger business but at the same time ensures the very
survival of IT.

Beyond any selfish concerns we might have, it's a difficult transition for the business to make the two changes above. Remember,
these actions would only be taken if IT was unable to provide the
business what it needed over the next five to ten years. So, we have
a little time, but not a lot. Whether it is the outsourcing of IT, or
moving pieces of IT into the functional organizations, either of
these changes will take several years to complete, and we are then
left with a sub-optimal model. In the case of outsourcing, the new
service provider will face a learning curve, and it could be a long
one depending on the nature of our organization. They don't know
the business the way IT does.

Beyond the learning curve, this outsourcing requires a significant investment of capital which will grow over time. There is a significant investment to create an RFP and then go through a partner evaluation and selection process. Remember, this is under our control, and the business would only reach this stage if IT was not providing what the business required.

The second scenario is the distribution of key IT functions into the other organizations of the business. This creates a different set of challenges, including a skills gap, a loss of leverage and natural efficiencies, and the transition time required to reach an equal level of capability. Once again, this would only occur if there was a perceived lack of leadership and execution on the part of IT. I'm confident this will not be necessary for most organizations. We highlight these issues as another sobering reminder of how the business needs IT more than ever. Not just the daily work of IT, but the strategic role and thought leadership of IT.

With so much at stake, we must get this right. The best path is a unified IT, the power that One IT is capable of bringing the business.

A SINGLE STRATEGY

In many IT organizations of the past thirty years, the daily operations were conducted in the absence of a clear strategy. The focus has been on operations and tactics out of necessity, to keep up with the daily demands of incidents and escalations. With resources under pressure, the many pressing demands of IT made it difficult to look beyond today and tomorrow. This fostered a tactical and responsive lifestyle that became the accepted norm over the past three decades. This was just how we ran IT.

Yes, there might be a corporate vision and strategy in some form, but this was not alive and clear in the IT organization.

**Strategy has not been given much
thought by traditional IT.**

To some degree this strategy would not translate well due to the siloed and fragmented nature of traditional IT. Each of the functions of IT was focused on the localized needs of the particular element, and strategy was not seen as a need and certainly not a critical need. This propagated the view of IT from within IT and across the organization of IT being tactical in nature and very much responsive.

With the transformation of IT into a unified organization and with a new emphasis on the singularity of our daily work, it will be clear that a strategy for IT is absolutely critical. We simply can't accomplish our goals for the next decade without creating, validating, and communicating a clear strategy for IT.

Note that this is an important collision of something fundamentally new to IT and something that is absolutely critical to the future of IT and without which we simply can't complete the unification of IT and then the unification of the business. These things are inextricably linked, and each enriches the others.

The good news is that the timing is perfect—
we now must have a clear strategy for IT
to serve the needs of building a unified IT
organization and ensuring we think and
act differently every day across IT.

This is not possible without a clear strategy for IT that directly supports the corporate strategy and at the same time speaks directly to the needs of IT specifically. This is a very powerful thing and will change not just how we work in IT but fundamentally change the culture.

There is another dimension to the strategy to IT. While it is certainly true that having virtually any basic strategy is a big boost for IT in itself, this is an opportunity to create a single strategy that directly supports our singularity of action across IT and in making the vision of One IT a reality. This changes everything and, when done correctly, brings us the leverage that is so critical to the future. So, the timing is good in that we need a strategy in many cases for the first time, and this gives us the opportunity to create a single strategy that provides the context all of IT needs to plan and then execute for the next decade.

I will reference the next decade throughout the book because this is a good and reasonable intermediate timeline during which we should expect to complete the rebirth and unification of IT. This won't be possible in the next two to three years, and both IT and the business need to see real change as soon as possible due to the new demands of customers today and the fundamental changes of the global marketplace. We can't wait fifteen to twenty years make these changes a reality. Everything is different and the clock of business has changed forever.

One of the keys here is identifying the key elements the strategy must address, and defining those elements in a language and in terms that make sense across all of the elements of IT. This is fundamental to One IT, creating a strategy that encourages and directly supports this coming together.

The very best IT strategies of the next decade will include a focus on some combination of a few things:

The customer

The user experience

Sustainable innovation

IT agility and scalability

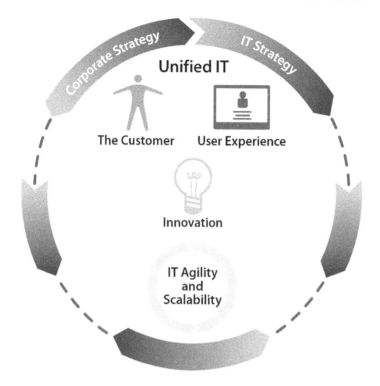

Figure 1.1 IT Strategy

Of course, these will be different for every organization, but make no mistake: The future of IT and of our singularity must be linked to the customer and sustainable innovation. This directly supports our shift from the traditional inside-out thinking of IT to one of outside in, naturally creating a focus on the beginning and end of our future—the customer. We can't go far off course by creating a new focus across all of IT on the customer. Then, One IT makes much more sense, and this focus brings us the clarity that is so vital to our future.

TEAMWORK

One of the wonderful and natural benefits of unifying IT is a new focus on teamwork—a very powerful part of both the daily operations of IT and the cultural change that goes hand in hand with how we work every day. Again, this has not been natural to IT, but it is a change that reaches through virtually every element of how we plan and work every day. Teamwork needs to be encouraged and enabled, and the unification of IT clears the way for teamwork.

Teamwork is a powerful force in an organization and a culture. But we need to give our people some help in making this happen. It can start with a very small step and then the good work accelerates throughout the work done across IT. People are quick to recognize something good and something that comes naturally, and teamwork falls squarely into this category. When we begin to put the pieces of a unified IT into place, all kinds of good things start to happen.

> *The singularity we create will then*
> *enable teamwork to not just happen,*
> *but to be successful and thrive.*

Even with a desire to improve teamwork within the traditional model of IT, it would not be easy. We would quickly discover that many natural divisions, many natural gaps, would slow us down or make this teamwork all but impossible. This segmentation and partitioning of IT has put a fog over IT for decades. A unified IT begins to lift this fog, to improve the clarity of everything we do.

All of these adjustments in how we plan and how we act across IT will nurture teamwork, and then anything is possible. It is best to begin the transformation of teamwork within the existing elements/silos of IT. This is a quick and natural step that will allow us to make some quick progress. It might seem like a small step backward, but it's not. There is more here than meets the eye. What we will find is that even within our existing IT silos, the work performed every day is localized to the degree that there are often several mini-silos within an existing IT silo. We need to melt away these mini-silos to fan the flame of teamwork from the bottom up and to build some momentum to drive our larger and broader teams in the future. Even the dilution and melting away of these mini-silos is a big step forward. This work also allows us to build a model for the broader teamwork that will occur as a natural next step.

> *As a clear and simple action to get started,*
> *we need to think in terms of all the work done*
> *in IT going forward being driven by teams.*

These can be small teams, medium-sized teams, or large teams but always in teams. Always in teams.

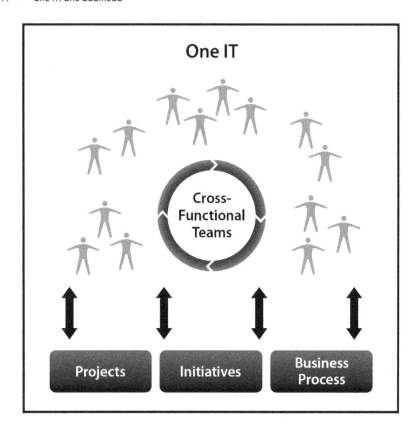

Figure 1.2 The Teams of IT

Teams can be mobilized quickly, given a simple charter with deliverables and the necessary authority. Our good people know what to do and only need the opportunity. This is a cultural shift and must be supported by and enabled by IT leadership. It becomes a very natural model and then it is just what we do. This teamwork model has been very effective in other markets and other organizations, including the military. In fact, IT and technology have a lot in common with the military, and so we borrow one of their best organizational disciplines here.

Closely related to teamwork is creating a new cross-functional model for IT. These two things are unavoidable and fundamental to making lasting changes to IT, for unifying IT, and to ultimately unify the business. Another wonderful case of simple but not easy.

This new cross-functional model complements teamwork and will change how we get work done. We will begin to appreciate that every new project, every new initiative, will be mobilized with a small to mid-sized team, and the team will include cross-functional skills. This is simply the fastest and most effective way to get work done. There are many reasons why this was not the commonly accepted model in the IT of the past, but no need to get into all that now. We will focus on how we go forward, and we will quickly begin to appreciate how One IT, agile and small teams, cross-functional skills and collaboration are the model of the future. Likely seen as very non-IT in the beginning, this will become a model that role models the best way for the business to work in the future.

> *This teamwork fundamentally changes both the culture of IT and how effective the results are that we create across IT.*

ADAPTABILITY

Adaptability brings so much more than meets the eye to IT.

When we create a focus around adaptability, we are able to shift the mindset of IT from one that lacks a focus on rapid and successful change, to one that makes managing change a competency. We will recognize that this brings real value to the business and when executed well can make adaptability a competitive advantage.

This concept drives a wonderful cultural change as well. When we anticipate change and design our processes and the organization to embrace change and do it well, we naturally create agility and speed throughout everything we do. There is another important result here—and that is the shift from a reactive organizational model to one that is proactive. This has always been something the traditional IT organization coveted, but in most cases IT was not able to make it a reality. That is changing now and it is very exciting.

Note the strong connections between the following elements of IT:

A focus on strategy

A new teamwork model

A proactive IT culture

Formation of new cross-functional teams

Dramatically improved agility and scalability

Considering this for a moment, one could see it as a good mini-model for the IT of the future, and all of this as only possible with a unified IT. It really is a strong combination of common sense and a realignment of IT that creates a powerful engine of change for the business.

Each of these elements complements and enables the others. At the same time, if there is a void in one of these areas, it makes it much more difficult to bring the others to life. We are so much stronger and so much more dynamic with these small changes that are fully under our control. Even better, making these elements part of IT every day does not require new budgets, new hiring, or big capital spending. These things are fully under our control and can be executed in most cases with the people and budgets we have today.

> **With small cultural changes in the beginning,**
> **bigger IT changes come quickly and then**
> **the business transforms around IT.**

All of this of course is quickly disabled—paralyzed, if you will—from within if we are operating a slow and rigid IT that struggles with change. This is not too dissimilar from the traditional model of IT that was constantly buried in tactical requirements and reacting to escalations, outages, and the like. We were always behind, which put us even further behind and trapped in the reactive lifestyle.

Let's get back to adaptability for a moment with some specific examples and actions we can take to improve it. But first, let's clarify what adaptability refers to.

> ***In this context, adaptability is the ability***
> ***of our systems and people to complete***
> ***technology and business-related***
> ***changes quickly and successfully.***

Note that these changes must include growth and the related implications to scalability.

Now, back to our to-do list for adaptability. A few things for the IT agenda of the future along with actions that can be taken over the next twelve to twenty-four months:

1. Review and rate all current IT systems on a scale of adaptability. Keep this simple, something like a scale of 1-5.
2. Add an adaptability requirement to the build/buy criteria of all future IT systems. This becomes a top priority for how we develop and source future IT systems and can be used as a key tie-breaker.
3. Assess the current IT software/hardware/technology roadmap with regards to adaptability.
4. Form a small "Adaptability Tiger Team" to drive these evaluations, reviews, and assessments. This team can put a face to the adaptability initiative and be agents of change.
5. Proactively communicate with key business owners outside IT with regard to adaptability planning and future needs. These stakeholders will likely provide insights into new requirements and be happy to work more closely with IT going forward.
6. Evaluate board of directors/CEO/CFO goals for the next twelve to twenty-four months with an eye toward the implications for adaptability of technology and IT systems. This brings us important strategic insights.
7. Realign the strategy of IT with these corporate and executive findings.

SIMPLICITY

The power of simplicity is remarkable and yet unappreciated by many. All highly advanced and powerful systems seek and achieve a high level of simplicity. By high level, I mean simple and elegant. This is the ultimate evolution of a system of any type that achieves its intended purpose over a period of time. Simple yet powerful. Simple is not simplistic. Just the opposite. Simple is thoughtfully robust. Mature and proven systems evolve to an advanced level of simplicity.

They do, because they have to.

Simple scales...

Simple is reliable...

Simple is agile...

Simple is repeatable...

Simple is understandable and relatable...

Simple is cost-effective...

Simple is serviceable...

Simple upgrades well...

Simple is fast...

You get the idea, and this is only the beginning.

With these unique attributes of simple, we should recognize this principle has a place in the future of IT and represents an important advantage of a unified IT. As we take on the need to unify IT, the simplification of all things IT goes hand in hand with this effort. A simpler IT is at the same time a more unified IT, which is, of course, a faster and more agile IT. These highly desirable attributes are closely related and inseparable.

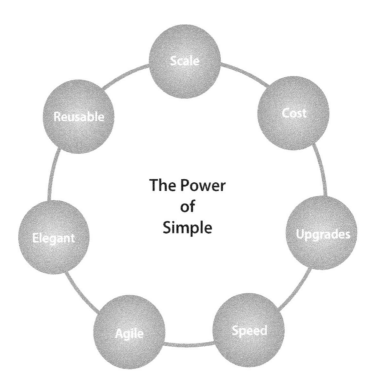

Figure 1.3 The Elements of Simplicity

These relationships then create the synergies of value that together create a singularity of IT, a unified IT operating in a superior manner in virtually every regard.

It's simply not possible to accept the
goal of unifying IT and then take
off. It just won't work this way.

Creating One IT is a practical and step-by-step process. Yes, of course, we need to embrace the vision of a unified IT and recognize the many benefits it brings us, and then we begin the journey and process, which is very much methodical. Methodical is good. Methodical is disciplined. And this approach is what we discuss throughout the book in order to provide a framework for how we create One IT that will last.

One key in this framework is to be dedicated to the strategy of simplification, which helps us in so many ways.

Complexity is a natural enemy of One IT.

When we look closely at the balance of simplicity versus complexity, we find that simplicity has many advantages. But this is a good thing because in most IT organizations, the opportunities to simplify are virtually everywhere we look—but not because our people have done the wrong things or have been negligent in any way. The presence of complexity is more a matter of it accumulating a little bit at a time, bit by bit, over the past thirty years. So let's see this as a good thing. We can likely make progress very quickly when we begin the cleansing of IT, and this naturally leads to simplification.

We won't address this process now; that is the stuff of later chapters. For now, we put forward the idea of simplification as being powerful and strategic. Trust me on this if you are skeptical.

You will come to appreciate—all of IT will
come to appreciate—the power of simplicity.
It is thoroughly a beautiful thing.

Simplification should be an early step in the move to unify IT, to deliver to the business and IT our vision of One IT. As we highlighted earlier, there are many benefits of simplifying IT, including three themes that will repeat themselves over and over throughout the book. Simple is fast, simple scales, and simple is agile. These attributes go hand in hand with the future of IT and are at the core of the benefits of a unified IT. The unification of IT is descriptive, as we should see One IT as our vision for IT—a vision that directly pulls us into One Business.

We cannot and should not do one without the other. A higher performing IT organization that does not influence and then change the business is not good enough.

Back to simple. This is a great place to start, or a great next step to take in the remaking of IT. I really like this idea of simplification because it is something fully under our control, to the benefit of IT, and will have an immediate impact. This is an initiative we can staff with IT resources (yes, a small cross-functional team is a great way to get this done) and we can then review the existing systems of IT with an eye toward complexity, asking the tough question "how can we make this simpler" over and over again. Question everything and anything that is complex, inflexible, and expensive. We really need to go after these systems because they will hold us back and slow us down in the future.

This review should be done for all existing IT systems, and it will have an immediate impact in both how we operate today and how we can automate many of these workflows and business processes. This automation work will be on our two- to five-year IT priority list because we can't unify IT and unify the business with highly manual processes.

This just won't work and won't scale.

Remember, it is far better for IT to ask the tough questions of ourselves and to crawl through these systems carefully than to have an outside organization or consultant do this for us. And make no mistake, if we don't get our own house in order, somebody else will. That is not what we want, for many reasons.

If a simplification or leaning-out of existing systems is in your plans today, then great. If not, this should be added to the IT plans of the next twelve to twenty-four months. It has lots of benefits, both short and long term.

CHAPTER 2

IT SILOS NO MORE

The current forces driving IT are a combination of many things. And these forces have not appeared suddenly—they have been building, although somewhat unnoticed, for some time...in most cases for years. Now, we are able to recognize many of these forces, and increasingly understand the good they bring us. A big part of this good is the blueprint for the transformation of IT. It is there if only we look carefully and are thoughtful about all the facts unfolding in front of us.

An important part of the IT rebirth is a mindset, a willingness to accept new ideas and to change: taking a step back, being objective about what IT is and is not, and then being open to new ideas and making changes.

This change is not easy, not natural for many people.

But holding on to the past, holding on to the traditional models and concepts of IT will not serve us well and could make the difference between successful change and the very survival of IT. I will call attention to this concept throughout the book—the very real risk of the IT organization not surviving the next ten years. We should all be clear about this risk and be reminded of it frequently because there is so much at stake here. This point can't be overstated, so we will come back to it from time to time.

Everybody in IT should understand exactly what we are playing for. To take this thinking and strategy one step further, the fundamental and traditional model of IT has been built up over time around domain experts, experts on technologies and services, and the organization has evolved to what we know today as the silos, or functions, of IT. This model made sense and was very much a product of the IT evolution, but today's global landscape, the modern business, and the IT of today and the future have fundamentally changed with fundamentally different requirements. A few things are at the heart of this change and as such will be mentioned throughout the book in order to keep our ideas in order and to clarify the few things driving this wonderful and comprehensive change—One IT and the many good things it brings us. One of the wonderful things about One IT is that in making this a reality, we create an unstoppable momentum and build a model that won't and should not stop at the boundaries of IT.

> *This simple and powerful model then*
> *becomes a living and working example for*
> *the business and then naturally and quickly*
> *brings a strong influence to the business—*
> *One IT, One Business then comes to life.*

Back to the few core strategies for One IT, one fundamental element is the transition away from silos. This is not something we mandate, but rather the silos of IT melt away when we begin to make other changes. This is a great thing because trying to eliminate the silos of IT as a stand-alone initiative would be lacking the strategy to drive the outcomes that are necessary to transform IT. We will explore those elements throughout the chapter, and we will come to understand that by creating the right strategy and making the right changes in how we work every day, the silos of IT will naturally fade away. But as this begins to occur, it is important that we let them go and are open to change.

From time to time there will be a natural and very human tendency to hold on to the traditional model and avoid change. Many people are uncomfortable with change. But that is okay. We need to understand that the silos are blocking our path forward and we need to remove any roadblocks that can slow us down. We need to be ready to address any concerns that come from our people and teams as the changes are made.

To keep this simple, we must accept and embrace over time that the silos of IT will go away because they are inhibiting the fundamental changes that are coming to IT and then to the business. These changes, these remarkable improvements are simply not possible with the fragmented and disconnected organization of IT. We will discover the amazing simplicity and speed of the new IT, which is closely linked with One IT.

A single team working toward unified goals.

A remarkable thing to behold.

THE MISSION

The elimination of silos must have a face, a purpose, a mission for us to rally around and to create a sense of energy and purpose for what lies ahead.

This is not just about the elimination of silos. Putting silos behind us is an outcome, but this is not our strategy, and as such this is missing the point. The elimination of our beloved IT silos is simply a natural byproduct of a strategy and the tactics that bring the strategy to life. If we get this backward and pursue the elimination of silos as a mandate, as a strategy in itself, we are risking the fundamental outcome we must achieve. That then brings us back to the mission and the strategy.

People do their best work when they have a mission to believe in.

The fundamental mission behind eliminating our silos is very simple.

The future of IT can only be realized with a singularity of purpose and by bringing all the people of IT together to drive improved business performance and by creating happy customers every day.

These outcomes shift from the internal goals of IT to be aligned with key business outcomes. This is at the heart of the elimination of IT silos, allowing us to shift our focus to working in step with the business—something that is just not possible when we are working within IT silos and focused every day on the local goals and tasks that come from a particular function of IT.

The silo sustains the silo by creating daily work product that comes from the silo and requires us to work in the silo model, and then the cycle repeats itself. We never find the time to raise our heads and think differently. The silo keeps pulling us back into the tactical needs and deliverables of the silo. It never changes and it never gets better. We know at some level that something needs to change, but we are never able to get beyond the silo, or rise above it.

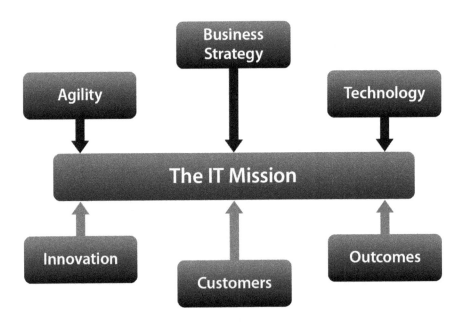

Figure 2.1 The Elements of the IT Mission

With the elimination of silos, something so simple becomes so powerful.

It is absolutely necessary to unshackle our people in order to focus on the business and our customers, to focus on innovation. But this won't happen when we are continually pulled into the daily demands of single IT functions—consumed by these demands, really. The silos of IT are selfish and demanding. They won't leave room for thinking and working differently.

It will become completely unacceptable to continue working in our silos because our understanding of what is required of IT has changed. Continuing to work in our silos and accepting the silo model will sabotage our future, ensuring that IT remains tactical and in some cases that IT has no future.

The silo model can directly contribute to the IT organization ceasing to exist. It can block the path to our future. The survival of IT is at stake as we discussed earlier, and we will touch on this point throughout the book to make sure we are all clear on just how much is at stake—everything!

So our mission is clear: building the future of IT to drive the business and innovate, to bring change to IT and the business from within. From the very core of the business and those good people who are stewards of our tools and our data. These are the key enablers of the business, the backbone, if you will. To make IT strategic, to make IT proactive for the first time. Now is the time, and this change is long overdue. Part of the remarkable power of this model is that it's about so much more than IT; it is about creating a momentum as we make these changes to IT and they then carry into the business and fundamentally change the business. This is a very important element of our mission.

Change IT and then change the business.
This linkage is very powerful.

This is so fundamental to One IT.

The mission must then be defined in terms of key business outcomes, including improvements in how we serve customers. There will be variations of this from company to company, depending on maturity and the current state of the business. But this mission should be crafted by IT leadership and then communicated to all our people—ensuring that everybody in IT understands this call to action.

Our people and our teams across IT will be united in working toward this common mission.

This makes all the difference and creates yet
another powerful force in the organization
that pushes our silos into the past.

Remember, this must come from IT, and it must be done in the pursuit of a strategic outcome. It then becomes clear that the silos are slowing us down, our teams adapt quickly into integrated and cross-functional teams and then move forward quickly together. Soon, we will look back on the traditional silos of IT and be amazed they stayed with us for so long.

CROSS-FUNCTIONAL TEAMS

Cross-functional teams change everything.

It is very simple really.

This is a natural way of working, and small to medium-sized teams are agile and able to make quick adjustments and adaptations in delivering the work product required by the business. By adding the dimension of a cross-functional team makeup, we change the perspective and the mindset of the team. We have domain experts working with domain experts, and we create a different discussion.

> *This becomes a multi-dimensional view that dramatically improves the quality of our work and improves the integrity of our deliverables.*

We just see things differently. We ask different questions. We create better answers.

We should see this as an all-star team of sorts, working together to change IT and bring IT closer together. Cross-functional teams have better discussions, consider topics differently, have better debates, and make better decisions. There is another wonderful thing that happens with cross-functional teams, and that is the education and training that occur over time.

*Every team member learns more
about the full scope of IT.*

Every member of the team gains access to information that was not readily available before, creating a cycle that brings IT close together and broadens the perspective of all our team members. Our discussions, our processes, and the quality of decisions are improved.

This cycle of improvement was limited or not possible previously. The silo focus kept our thinking, discussions, and decisions localized and did not encourage the quality of discussion, investigation, analysis, and decisions we should expect from IT in the future. It was just not possible except in those isolated cases where our teams took the initiative and connected to other domain experts and other teams across IT. But this was the exception versus the norm. A very big difference.

*What we need is a reproducible model,
a scalable model for how we work.*

In thinking about this, it does seem like common sense, and that is true, but despite that fact, we did not create cross-functional teams as a standard and accepted way of working in IT.

The specific action we take from this discussion is to change how we get our work done. For most IT organizations, work is done by individuals and focused on very specific deliverables—often a standard set of deliverables that are the responsibility of the functional team and delivered on a regular cycle, whether weekly, monthly, or quarterly. We tend to continue to deliver these work products to the existing schedule as we always have. We have individuals who were trained by individuals who were in turn trained by individuals in the same ways. The cycle then repeats.

Our takeaway here is to break the cycle.

All new IT initiatives going forward should be mobilized by forming cross-functional teams. These teams should include, where possible, one member from each of the primary functions of IT. Depending on the nature of the initiative, it might include two members from a key team. Security, for example, has many connections to IT strategy today, as does Service Management. If a project is already under way today and is only staffed by one or two functions, we need to look at adding members to the team to increase the scope of the team's skills.

This team makeup is critical not because we are simply trying to make people feel more involved and more empowered, which is certainly a benefit, but because we are trying to enable our teams to think differently, act differently, and to deliver superior results.

Results that have a bigger impact on the business and stand the test of time. This is how we design and deliver more adaptable, robust, and scalable solutions.

IT leadership needs only to make this initial shift, the shift to our commitment to working in cross-functional teams in everything we do, and all the people of IT will quickly recognize this is a better way to work and a better model for our culture. Then our people will embrace this model and take it forward.

The full IT organization will enthusiastically join in and be happy to participate in this new team structure. As with other elements of One IT, other parts of the business will be influenced by this model and are likely to adapt the same model, bringing a more balanced, thoughtful, and united culture to the business.

IT leading again from within.

A PROACTIVE IT

The IT organization has held a desire to be more proactive in all things IT and across the business for many years. But it has been difficult if not impossible to make the change from reactive to proactive while working in the traditional IT and silo-based organizational model. One of the challenges the silo model creates is fundamentally poor visibility of IT and the business, which then in turn all but ensures we will work reactively every day. The combination of very localized work, very localized knowledge, and poor visibility beyond a single function locks us into a tactical and reactive work model.

This is all we know and all we can see. It propagates each day with little opportunity to change. Each day of reactive work all but guarantees the next day will be the same.

The good news is that a change in this model is closely linked to other changes we must make, and we will realize the many benefits of these changes, including a shift to a more proactive model for everything in IT. In the beginning it will be small things, some of the more routine deliverables of IT, but then quickly we will see other broader and more strategic initiatives and deliverables will be reshaped by our proactive thinking and work.

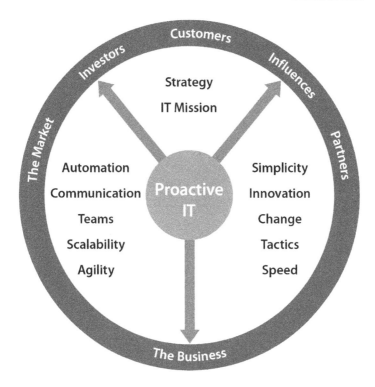

Figure 2.2 The Motion of Proactive IT

IT will begin to ask questions of itself that have never been asked before. IT will begin to ask questions of the business that have never been asked before and to pursue answers that will change our future. Remarkably, this will come from IT and it will surprise many business owners across the organization. This is important to the business, even vital to the business, and that is what is most important—reshaping the strategy and performance of the business itself, which enables us to better serve our customers. Of course this is the primary benefit, the ultimate result always tied to customers, but another benefit is the changing perception of IT. IT will begin to see itself differently. We can think of this as a big boost in IT self-esteem. A big boost in the confidence of IT.

This will bring some swagger to IT—
something that is greatly needed.

But then another amazing thing happens. IT will be viewed differently by the business. IT will be viewed differently by executive leadership, by the CEO, by the board of directors. This then emboldens IT to move even faster, to lead us forward.

There are several factors that enable IT to take more proactive action, all closely related. Each of our cross-functional teams, a dedicated innovation task force, and a commitment to automation are included here. Each of these streams of action then allows us to take more proactive action and gives us the information required to even consider the shift to proactive. It's not possible to leap directly to working more proactively while skipping over some of the building blocks required to make proactive possible.

For example, reaching the standard of 90 percent automation for standard IT work product (reference the chapter on the 90/90 rule) frees up our capacity to think differently and plan differently. Automation also means that tactical work is completed more quickly so we are not living hand-to-mouth and always a step behind. When we are able to compress the standard daily deliverables of IT, each minute we earn back is a minute we can reapply to proactive actions every day, and every minute matters. In a short time, automation will bring us hours of savings and then days of savings. These time savings will free our teams to extend the horizon of planning, to look further into the future—maybe just days in the beginning, but then weeks or months become possible. This then extends the content of the discussion to include:

How do we complete a deliverable more quickly?

How do we simplify a specific work product?

Is it possible to reduce the resources required to complete a deliverable?

What new requirements will the business have of IT in the future?

How can IT improve the quality of the user experience?

What current IT initiatives are not supported by a cross-functional team?

Considering these questions and others like them changes both the internal perspective of IT and the perception of IT across the business—a very simple but very powerful thing.

The questions naturally dovetail into our commitment to innovation. Some of the same questions in fact lead us through the innovation process. And so it goes, one element linked to another, linked to another.

Suddenly, a proactive IT is a reality and then we can see the next level gain in performance. Our confidence grows, our visibility grows, our communications improve, and then we take another step forward with our proactive commitment.

> **Proactive both in terms of visibility into the future, the scope of activities we govern, and connecting to key business owners to open new discussions and consider future plans in a way that has not happened before.**

Once these connections are made and our scopes are increased, we open yet another door.

With the new discussions and planning sessions that occur around innovation, and the looking-ahead mindset of planning, this discipline and hard work shift the world of IT to proactive. Day by day, bit by bit. This then enables us to raise IT to another level in the business, and a wonderful momentum that becomes unstoppable

One more thing on a proactive IT—it's time for IT to start the right discussions, not just be part of them. Yes, joining the discussions that occur every day across the organization is important. This in itself is progress and is important. But it is not the leadership needed across the organization.

By starting the right discussions, IT begins to lead. IT is getting ahead of the business. IT is a catalyst. IT is provoking a different way of planning and acting. The business needs this and in many cases needs this desperately. IT is not where this leadership is expected to come from, but that is okay. All that matters is that this shift is happening, and by driving the right thinking, IT will change the daily motion of the business. This is just the beginning.

SINGULARITY

The elimination of silos is much more a case of the powerful pull and natural synergies of singularity than it is about running away from something bad. That is certainly not the case.

Our transformation to One IT, to a unified IT organization and people, is about the power of the good that comes from bringing our people together with one mission and as one team. This is a remarkable and primal thing that we are all drawn to.

> *Together we are stronger, together we are smarter, together we are faster, together we are more empowered.*

This is the fundamental truth of One IT and what underlies so many of the changes in IT we must make over the next decade.

So how do we make this happen? I mean it sounds good, but exactly how do we make these changes? These are natural questions.

It can only begin with a common mission for IT and a strategy that supports the mission. This mission will be different for every organization, so it must come from within, in many cases from the CIO or COO or VP IT, and should reflect the core values of the organization and the strategic needs IT are able to fulfill.

Normally this mission will make sense for the people of IT, who should be able to understand it without any explanation, and it should be connected to the strategic agenda for the CEO and the board of directors. When we do this right for IT, all these elements are connected. At every level of the organization, the daily motion of IT is then connected in a new and fundamental way to the business.

This is the beginning of our singularity—a simple mission and strategy.

With this mission now in place, we are off to a good start. It is then communicated to everybody in IT—posted in public places and reviewed in staff meetings and team meetings. The next step is to mobilize small teams and to ensure the composition is cross-functional. All our work product in IT should be driven by small teams. This could be part of the current culture and this is great; the needed changes are under way. If this is not part of the current culture, we need to make this change and use small teams to drive all our new initiatives. And, if existing initiatives are being driven by single individuals, it might make sense to put a few additional people on that assignment and convert an individual into a small team.

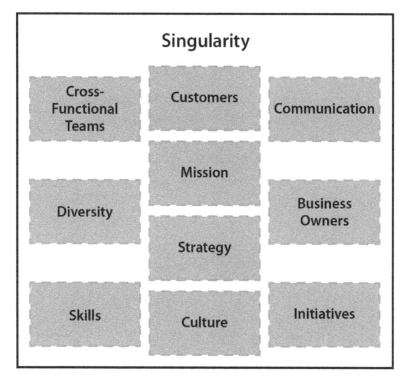

Figure 2.3 The Building Blocks of Singularity

Then, all new work projects going forward will be driven by small cross-functional teams. Even further, consider staffing these teams with individuals who have little or no experience working together. This creates so many good behaviors and drives all the right changes.

This team model does not just bring us better results on our projects and initiatives; it also drives cultural change, which is perhaps even better. We plant the seeds of cultural change, and get projects completed more quickly and with better results. How good is that? With these actions, creating our mission for IT and mobilizing our cross-functional teams, the silos fade away and we begin to build singularity every day. People will embrace this model and know instinctively it is good and want to be part of it.

In the beginning our people might be members of several teams, and that is okay.

> *Take some care to ensure that most*
> *if not all people are members of at*
> *least one team. This is important, as it*
> *supports singularity for everybody.*

Always err on the side of being inclusive. This is important to enable our people and create the cultural change we need. Don't underestimate the sources of great ideas and how we advance our focus on singularity. These great ideas can come from the most unlikely of places. Sometimes the very people you think are the least likely to bring forward the next great idea—the idea that changes everything—are the very ones who surprise us. Give people, all our people in IT, the opportunity to contribute.

Key people or our most senior people, perhaps people with unique skills, can be members of several teams, which makes sense. This can help to call our attention to skill areas where we need to invest. This, too, is good because we know these needs are out there, and the sooner we can find them, the better.

Building a sense of singularity will increase our transparency and our communication naturally. Bringing people closer together will do this. Creating this alignment will call attention to where our skills are deep, and where we need to develop skills. This is a great thing and can get us to a fuller and more complete organization more quickly.

Our people and their skills are our most valuable resource. Achieving the right mix of skills and expertise only enhances this value.

CHANGE FROM WITHIN

As IT professionals we must first embrace change, and then recognize we can't wait for change to come to us. The change should begin here. This is important for several reasons.

By embracing change and knowing it is ultimately good, we can get started on making this change sooner, saving us precious time. And time is becoming more and more valuable as the cadence and motion of the market and our business are fast and getting faster. Speed is becoming a competitive asset, and will be a key characteristic of future market leaders. What organizations can move the fastest, adapt the fastest, and deliver the fastest? These are the emerging leaders in any market.

Speed is now strategic.

Embracing change is now strategic.

Starting our local changes, the changes we know must come to IT now will save us precious time and increase our speed. IT must be comfortable with change, must have a process for change, and must become good at change. Change must be a competency, and there is no better place for this to originate from in the organization than from IT.

This is not natural for people or for an organization—people are naturally not comfortable with change. But there is a lot at stake here, so we need to push ourselves, step outside our comfort zone, and call IT to initiate the changes that are necessary for the future.

Darwin said something to the effect that the species that survive are not the biggest or strongest, but those that adapt best. This has proven to be true, and very much true for businesses and organizations.

Organizations not willing to change will die.

IT organizations not willing to change, or
slow to change, will cripple the business.

So, we are faced with a choice in IT: becoming great at change and turning this into an organizational strength. Or, denying change or being slow to make changes and risk impacting the business—actually, more than impacting the business. The truth is that this could fundamentally prevent the business from succeeding.

The people of IT and IT leadership can't wait for change to come from other functions in the organization. IT can drive this change. IT can lead in this important category.

Taking a step back, this makes a lot of sense. Nothing is changing faster in our markets and in our global economy than technology. Organizations that adapt to this rapidly changing technology landscape and identify how to best leverage technology will be creating a sustainable competitive advantage and far more likely to be successful. Because IT teams are the stewards of technology and closer to technology than any other organization, the people of IT find themselves in a unique position—resist change and slow down the organization as the people being closest to ground-zero of technology. Or, be a leader of driving change, push an initiative around planning for change and planning to scale, and in the process drive a new mindset across the organization, ultimately pushing the business to a new level of change readiness.

The choice lies with IT: resist or lead. Slow down the business or accelerate the business forward. Embrace change as a cultural improvement, a cultural shift, or deny change and risk everything. This is quite a contrast. At the same time, it is quite a remarkable opportunity for all of us proud to be associated with IT.

Which will it be?

Most of you will agree this is an exciting opportunity, a unique opportunity, and we have a limited window in which to take action.

This is our time, and we will be up to the challenge. We are reminded again the business needs us more than ever.

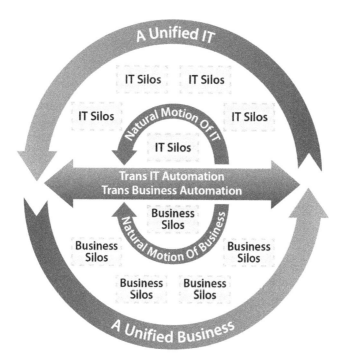

Figure 2.4 A Model for Unified IT

INTEGRATIONS

Integrations are an artifact of the traditional model of IT. Something born of the time when integrations were a necessity, but a model that is now outdated for many reasons.

Integrations are fundamentally flawed in that they require a hand-off of information from one system to another. From one technology to another. Whenever this handoff occurs there is a very real risk of problems and delays. There is risk here that simply can't be completely eliminated, so our charge is not to improve integrations, or to optimize integrations. Our goal must be to completely eliminate integrations. This is the only acceptable outcome. This goal is very much in line with core principles including speed, scalability, singularity, and reliability. All of these things are achieved by eliminating integrations and queues. An additional benefit but certainly not the driver for this important improvement to IT is breaking down our existing functional elements and silos.

> **What we will often find is that the systems
> between which our integrations occur
> are a mirror of the silos themselves.**

We have seen an evolution of sorts across IT where domain experts are aligned with our systems, which in turn are supported by other tools and organizational elements that further reflect our traditional silos. This is evident from top to bottom in IT, from left to right.

By recognizing the risk, slowness, awkwardness, lack of agility, and cost that comes with integrations, we can launch a new inspection and review of all existing integrations and queues (any waiting or delay included in a business process or workflow) with the intent to eliminate every one. Only those with unique requirements or verified value with no opportunity to be removed can be allowed to continue forward. In those cases, we should use the review to improve the integration to the greatest degree possible.

In particular these improvements should focus on simplifying the integration, reducing the risk of failure, increasing the speed of performance, and improving the ability to change the integration when upgrades or new technologies dictate a change. What we are trying to avoid here is the classical integration risk—the integration failing to work properly when either of the systems engaged in the integration are upgraded, or changed in any way. This continues to haunt many IT organizations everywhere. Another improvement for integrations is the ability to be automated. The integration should execute when needed, in a reliable and scalable way. There should be little or no manual interaction required.

This effectively transforms the integration into a much faster, reliable technology, something very much unlike a traditional integration that is manual, slow, and prone to error. Of course, an investment in improving an integration should only be made when every possible effort has been made to eliminate the integration altogether, because a greatly improved integration is a big downgrade from no integration. We need to be clear on that point.

An additional benefit to eliminating integrations is the incrementally reduced silo model for IT. Integrations have been part of the fabric of IT and have reinforced and propagated the silo model.

*In many ways the integrations across
IT form a map for the very web of
silos across the IT organization.*

Where we found an integration, we normally would find a boundary for a silo. The integration would represent the transition from one IT function to another, from one silo to another.

With the elimination of an integration, we are not only creating a more scalable and more reliable model for our systems; we are chipping away at the silos of IT. Step by step this is a far superior model and brings us many benefits. Never underestimate the little improvements and changes we discuss throughout the book. Alone, they might seem meaningless and not possibly capable of making a real change. But this could not be further from the truth.

The real and lasting transformation of IT, the new unified IT, is all about the little things. It is all about the details. Yes, we will create a new mission and strategy for IT that will unite us and show us the way. But the real substance of the changes we will make in IT over the next ten years are all about the hard work of the small improvements. This is what creates our new culture and what creates superior systems.

In this case, we must systematically review, question, and scrutinize every integration. This will take time, but it is an important investment. As we have highlighted, an integration is about much more than a small application or script. It is a reflection of the very fabric of IT and the shift we are making from the past to the future.

From manual to automated.

From slow to fast.

From segmented to continuous.

From fragile to robust.

From limited to scalable.

From rigid to agile.

All of these characteristics are embodied in our old integrations and so we reap the many benefits for each integration that is eliminated or improved. In many organizations there are hundreds of these. It's a remarkable opportunity where we might not have seen one previously.

CHAPTER 3

AGENTS OF CHANGE

The leadership of IT in the future—and the ensuing unification of IT and the business—brings with it a few key principles, a few key shifts in our mindset.

One of these is the role of change in our future. Much maligned by IT in the past as a disruptive force that just makes our job harder and more complicated, change was seen as something to avoid, something to be delayed, something we all but ignored.

The simple fact is that change is here to stay, and by most measures, the pace and scope of change are growing. Change hits a business with no warning and with significant implications and consequences.

Whether IT recognizes it or not today, it soon will—those organizations that are great at change and embrace change will survive and thrive. Those that don't will struggle and perhaps fail altogether.

It might be that there is no place in the future for a business that has not thoughtfully designed a strategy and capacity for change. Of course, this is different for virtually every business and every market, but the key is finding the right model for change in your business and one that is adaptable.

> *We must plan for change within the*
> *very process that plans for change.*

Think about that for a moment. This is an advanced concept that will become increasingly important to all of us...central to the future of IT and to the business.

So, we are left with the realization that we must first come to an understanding of just how important, how vital change will be in the future of IT. Then we must thoughtfully and carefully design a process for how change is evaluated and executed in the organization. Then we take it one step further. We must design a process for change against the core change processes across the business. This effectively gives us a self-governing process within the process.

All of this then begs the question—from where will change leadership come?

There are many considerations, but I will make the argument that the best although unlikely source of this leadership is IT.

Looking more closely, there are many good reasons for this source of thought leadership for IT in the beginning and then for the business.

IT OUTREACH

There are many benefits of IT leading a new outreach strategy across the business, and this is yet another example. In this context, the outreach will be to drive a new discussion around the role of change in IT and in the business, assessing the current state of change readiness in IT, with the systems of IT, and across the business.

It is best to start this assessment with IT, complete a round or two of this assessment, and then have a strawman plan in place for how we improve the adaptability of IT to change, and what process we will use to update our process over time. With this experience, we will have an idea of how best to manage the assessment going forward.

Then, we take another step in engaging the business in the discussion. It is a good idea to start with key business owners, to invite them into this discussion and the process. IT initiates this discussion and brings a set of ideas to get the process started with some structure and guidance.

Just a few of these questions would be:

How do we manage meaningful change in the business today?

How do we anticipate change today, or are we purely reactive?

Do we have mechanisms in place to identify likely changes early?

Are we limited to an internal view only or do we have market sensors in place?

How do we identify changes that are worthy of investment?

What types of changes should be delayed, or put on hold?

What technologies in the business today handle changes well?

What technologies are problematic with changes?

What can IT do to better enable your organization to successfully address change?

No need to create a fully comprehensive list. We are simply looking for IT to get the discussion going and to get the right people engaged. Our talented people will quickly take the discussion forward and bring many more questions to the table along with lots of great ideas.

> **With this process started and the right discussions taking place, IT will be a leader, a catalyst, and IT will be perceived differently. Very differently.**

IT begins to assume the role of leader, of driving strategic thinking, and of being proactive with the business.

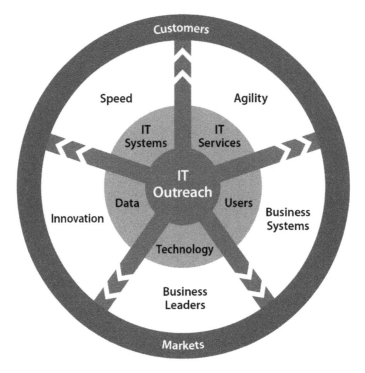

Figure 3.1 Motion of IT Outreach

Beyond this single discussion, which is an important one, the outreach of IT is building a foundation for the future. We are building relationships with key business owners and leaders in the business, and this relationship will serve us well for the future discussions that become necessary. The process we establish—managing change in the business and improving how the business plans for and executes changes—is a process we can use again and again.

By IT leading this outreach and discussion, the perceptions of the people of IT begin to shift. This does not happen overnight, but bit by bit. That is okay, because this is a perception that was created over twenty-five years and so we can't change it in a day or in a week.

We are talking about the old perception of IT being slow, of being reactive, of being tactical, of being a laggard, having little business acumen, having a limited or no view of the market, and more. By driving the outreach around preparing the business to be great at change, the perception of IT becomes one of IT being proactive, of driving strategy, of being a leader, of understanding market dynamics, and of having a good grasp of the business. This is good for everybody and very much needed—good for IT, good for the business.

And it all begins with IT shifting to this model of reaching out across the business to drive the right thinking and right actions.

A LITTLE BETTER

When taking on the subject of change, of making real changes to IT and to the business, it can seem overwhelming. It can seem as though we can't possibly get there, we can't possibly be successful. There is just too much work to do.

This is very natural and all great changes will include some level of this doubt. This is a time to remember that great things happen by taking small steps. By getting just a little better today, and then a little better tomorrow. Then in a little time, we can look back at how far we have come and be surprised at the progress we have made.

For the changes we will make in IT and for the changes that will come in the business, we need to constantly remind our people and all the people we work with that we are just trying to get a little better. The really big changes ahead of us can seem bigger than they really are, bigger than life, which can be discouraging. We need to be ready for that, so it helps to get ahead of this issue by reminding our teams that it is good to have the goal in mind, to understand what we are working toward, but to be grounded.

What grounds us is trying to get just a little better today. Then we will evaluate where we are and try to get just a little better tomorrow.

This mindset in our culture will help keep our teams positive and encouraged. When we focus on the progress we can make today—the small piece of a big problem that is achievable—over time we can accomplish anything.

Take small steps toward a big, ambitious goal.

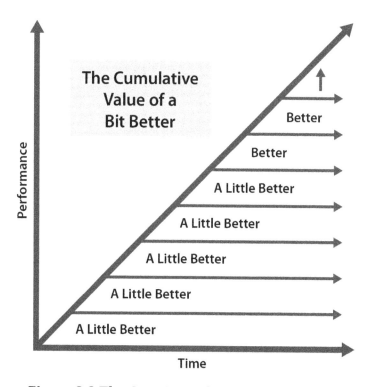

Figure 3.2 The Growing Value of a Little Better

It also helps to recognize key milestones and celebrate along the way. We need this validation and this fun to keep us going. A little recognition goes a long way.

You will also find that creating this mindset of a little better every day, or a little better every week, is very empowering for our teams. It takes a bit of the pressure off while at the same time keeping the drive to improve alive. It is good to reinforce this approach every chance we get and to discuss and brainstorm the big ideas and little ideas, even the simplest ideas that can help us get a little better. When we encourage this thinking, the thinking of getting better and every idea is a good idea, it builds a momentum in the culture that everybody wants to be part of. Ideas for improvement will likely come from just a few people in the beginning. These will be our experts, the people with the most experience, and the people who are naturally vocal. All of this is good. But as the ideas come and the discussion around how we get better grows and continues, others will begin to participate. Everybody will see this is a good and healthy thing, and then want to be part of it.

> *This is a very important shift—that is, welcoming participation from every person in the organization in the process of getting better and raising the ideas that will bring us the next great idea that can change the business.*

Don't assume the next great idea will come from the established experts and leaders. That is not always the case, and we can't risk suppressing the participation of others, the very people we need to be part of this process. The very best ideas sometimes come from the most unlikely of places, which is something we need to always remember.

Be inclusive, be welcoming, be open-minded.

Encouraging ideas on how we get better is another element (we really can't have too many) of the leadership that IT can create. This mindset, of small steps of progress, can start within IT and we can then watch and enjoy the advances we begin to make. With some of this experience in place and some of the progress in the culture of IT becoming real, we can take some of these ideas into the business.

Think of IT as a launching pad for not just technology improvements, but cultural improvements that benefit IT and then spread into the business. Virtually every business today needs more of this thinking and more of this leadership, and why not IT.

QUESTION EVERYTHING

The process of change is demanding. It requires us to do things that we are not comfortable with. It requires us to leave our comfort zone and to do things that challenge us in many different ways. The path to this change always includes a critical review, an inspection if you will, of the current state of things. An inspection of everything we do, large and small.

There is no other way—we simply can't create the changes and improvements that will shape our future without this critical and careful review of what we do today, of everything that makes up the average day across IT.

A careful inspection is inevitable and long overdue. The key then becomes IT performing this review ourselves—initiated, driven, and completed from within. Demanded by IT and executed by IT.

This is important for many reasons. First, if this review is initiated and conducted by resources outside IT, that will change everything. The process and the tone of every discussion become different. Every step becomes more difficult and the role of IT becomes closer to hostile witness than what any of us want. The outside resource, often an independent consultant, is looking for problems, looking for shortcomings in IT. That is understandable if we let the process get to that point—another reminder of how important it is for IT to be proactive and to embrace this initiative and launch it by IT.

The second reason this must come from IT is that this initiative will reinforce the leadership of IT, sending a message to the full organization that IT is becoming something very different. It's a living example of IT thinking strategically, of acting proactively, of leading versus following.

The best possible way to send the message of IT leadership is through action. In this case an action that is self-critical and completely transparent. All that matters here is getting to the truth and building the best possible plan for the future.

Our inspection of IT will look at many things, including:

Any form of waste

Any obsolete work, data, or systems not attached to a current requirement

Any form of waiting or delays

Highly manual work business processes

Special deliverables including reports

Legacy systems that have not been upgraded in over five years

Any system with a high annual cost of ownership

Any system with a poor track record of availability

Inflexible systems

Any system with poor user feedback

Poor scalability

Any integration and in particular highly complex and costly integrations

High volume tasks

Systems with a large administrator requirement

These are just a few areas to question, and you will surely have many more. Remember, we are questioning everything; nothing is off limits.

We are looking for every possible opportunity to improve the performance of IT with a particular eye toward automation opportunities, speed of execution improvements, and any opportunity to eliminate waste and simplify what we do every day.

The simplification concept is an important one.

> **Simplification is far more valuable than what might first be apparent. Simplification helps us with scalability, speed, automation, and agility. It is hard to fully capture the true value of simplification.**

Making any existing process or system more simple, more streamlined, shorter, is a good goal to have when reviewing any system or work that is in place today. The best outcome is to eliminate work or a process altogether. But when that is not possible, virtually every process with very few exceptions can be simplified. Removing only a single step, a single element of any business process or workflow, is good progress. Every small improvement helps. Every simplification helps us with the next important steps. Remember, our goal is to automate a minimum of 90 percent of the business processes that exist in IT today over the next five years.

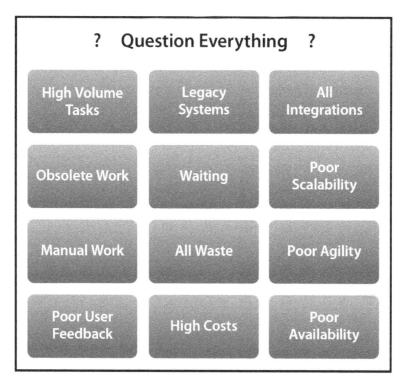

Figure 3.3 Question Everything

So, this process of questioning everything has many benefits. It is a process of renewal.

We receive the immediate benefit of eliminating work and saving time when that is possible, which is always our first priority—eliminating a deliverable or task completely. We discover these actions or products are no longer required and simply a legacy that was carried forward from the past. This brings us a savings of work, resource, and time. All of these are valuable, but ultimately the savings of time might be the most impactful. Every second we shave from any business process or task is important.

When elimination of work altogether is not possible, we look for the opportunity to simplify. Unlike the complete removal of a work process or delivery, which is not normally possible, it is possible to simplify to some degree virtually all of the work that occurs in IT today. Every simplification will allow us to better automate the process, will save resource, can save money, and will save time.

Time savings could be the most important savings of all. This is strategic and has a direct impact on the performance of the business and our customers.

> *In many cases the ultimate evolution of a market is a race to determine who can deliver a good or service to a customer the fastest.*

Not something we commonly think about today in IT, but this could become a top strategic priority in the next five years.

Ultimately, the initiative of questioning everything is about getting our IT house in order as we prepare to transform so much of what we do every day. We are eliminating unnecessary work, eliminating any form of waste, and saving precious time. But beyond these more visible benefits, the value of holding ourselves accountable to a detailed and critical review and the perception of leadership this creates for IT is a big added value as well.

DELIVERY DEBRIEFS

The process of change is demanding, and one important opportunity to learn and improve is right in front of us. Even more than an opportunity, it is a continual source of unique and valuable insights. This is the process of performing a debrief following the completion of any meaningful initiative or major milestone in IT. Make this a part of our culture and how we work every day.

There is so much to be learned, and this process takes shape naturally, including a few questions that get us quickly to the heart of any lesson:

> *What was the overall result?*

> *How would we rate the performance of the team that completed this milestone?*

> *How does the customer/user rate the overall result?*

> *What went well?*

> *What did not go well?*

> *What are our key takeaways?*

> *What changes will we make the next time this work is performed?*

Is there an opportunity to simplify or streamline the delivery process?

Are there any business stakeholders we should follow up with?

Any members of the IT team who should be further debriefed?

Any members of the IT team who performed exceptionally and should be recognized?

Remember, we are learning from the good and the bad. Both are important and we need to avoid the temptation to focus on the bad.

Keep this in balance, fact-based, and direct. Never miss an opportunity to recognize a person who did great work or went above and beyond the call. People will notice and want to be part of this. Hard work and recognition are highly contagious. People know a good thing when they see it. This is role modeling from within and in the very best form.

Likewise, if we came up short in any areas, that feedback must get to the right people. Again, keep it simple and keep it direct. People appreciate honest feedback, and the best people thrive on this and will want to get better.

We build the new culture of IT one conversation at a time, one action at a time, one day at a time. We then become what we do every day. This process, this habit of performing debriefs on deliverables, projects, and initiatives, reinforces that culture. It's a simple process that includes the following things at the heart of our new culture:

Open communications

Timely information and feedback

Recognition for good work

Fast action

Direct customer engagement

Honest and direct critical feedback

Transparency

Alignment with results

Alignment with the business

Remarkable really how much our new IT culture overlaps with some of our processes, although at first glance they might seem very limited in scope.

STRATEGIC INITIATIVES

Very much counter to the traditional culture of IT, strategic initiatives can be identified and launched from within IT. Yes, born in IT, driven by IT. No longer can IT wait to have initiatives and, in particular, strategic initiatives launched elsewhere in the business and then simply join the process in-flight and react as needed.

> *IT is in a unique position to see real customer needs, real business needs as they live and as they often operate close to the systems and data of IT. This is a powerful cycle of proactive and strategic action that then generates innovation.*

Organic innovation is perhaps the most valuable inside action of all. The use of the word "inside" here means this action can be born inside the organization and under our control, albeit with strong outside influences beginning with real customer needs, market dynamics, and expected future customer needs. This is a powerful mix of influences and insights just waiting to be tapped. A wonderful thing that continues to give.

This fountain of innovation is our future, the lifeblood of the organization, and when we can create an engine of innovation that is growing inside IT, it becomes a remarkable source of renewal and value. This is a natural element of our IT transformation because so many ligaments of the business now run back to the systems, tools, and data of IT.

But let's go back to the beginning of this discussion for a moment.

Every organization is different, and certainly some businesses have IT creating and driving strategic initiatives. This is, however, the exception today. We are trying to create a new standard for IT, a new template for the culture of IT that becomes the norm, and one that should be expected by the business. The key stakeholders in the business should know that IT has this, will deliver innovative ideas and technologies to the business, and is losing sleep every night thinking about this stuff and making it happen.

It will become clear that this source of innovation goes hand in hand with strategy, customer engagement, and a Unified IT.

All of these plans and actions bring us back to how IT must transform in order to meet the precious challenges in the business. A unified IT is central to this transformation, and a segmented, fragmented, disjointed, and tactical IT simply cannot rise to this challenge.

> *A unified IT is naturally aligned, communicative, and cross-functional, and the powerful characteristics lead us to proactive action and strategic planning as a continual cycle within the model of transformation.*

The historical model for IT is fundamentally incapable of driving the innovation process.

In stark contrast, the transformed IT organization is now fully equipped and able to drive the innovation process to the extent it becomes natural—a simple extension of the many elements of One IT.

For example, IT-driven activities—including standing up a new server, upgrading an application, delivering laptops and mobile phones to employees, and implementing updates to a governance process—are all necessary but not strategic. What we are called to provide in the future is the connection to corporate strategic initiatives and then IT getting out ahead of the business and taking the necessary steps to be a catalyst in leading the business toward the necessary solutions. This could be opening a new country to business and all the considerations this brings, hitting a revenue target for the business, or working to improve customer satisfaction. These initiatives are typically growth, corporate performance, or customer related. Not limited to the traditional boundaries of technology and purview of IT.

Even with a focus on revenue, growth, earnings, and customer satisfaction, these top-line stories are supported by and enabled by technology and data.

> *The distinction here is a top-down view of the business embraced by IT and proactively engaged by IT to meet the strategic goal by deploying technology, tools, and processes in direct support of the strategic goal.*

This is in stark contrast with IT being pulled into these initiatives by the business after the initiative has begun, often late in the process, to upgrade or deliver a system or technology that meets a specific requirement in the project.

This is a big difference, a very big difference that can't be lost on us because this shift changes so much.

Once again, we are reminded of the contrast of:

Strategic versus tactical

Proactive versus reactive

Top down versus bottom up

Moving fast versus moving slowly

Business-focused versus technology-focused

Leading versus following

IT is in full control of this shift. And so much of our success is connected to our acceptance of this mission, of this new role, and a constant search for how we connect the talented people and technologies of IT to the strategic needs of the business and then take proactive action to form agile teams that drive the business forward. Ideally, we are connected with key business owners and always connected to the needs of our customers and committed to performing at a new, higher rate of speed.

> **This simple micro-model applies so well to virtually all of what will shape One IT and then One Business over the next ten years.**

There is wonderful and powerful consistency here that runs through virtually all of the changes we will make and how we will plan and perform every day.

BUSINESS OUTCOMES

IT today and the formation of One IT will create a new connection, a new focus: one of business outcomes. This is another important dimension that expands our view of the business and brings a more complete balance to our daily work.

It is something of a lifestyle change—after all, this perspective is important in many ways and helps all the teams of IT to make better decisions, to have clarity around priorities, and to be better connected to the business. When we start to think about business outcomes, many new questions are created and we begin searching for a connection to the business in everything we do.

> *Curiosity is a wonderful thing—in life and*
> *in business. Many important discoveries*
> *were made possible by simple curiosity.*

Curiosity drives us to look and to learn. To question why things are done and why they are done the way they are. Curiosity will cause us to look far beyond IT and to seek answers to many questions. A few questions that are natural when we begin to look at business outcomes include:

Why are we doing this?

Is this work really necessary?

Who will benefit from this work?

How will they benefit exactly?

Is what we are delivering everything they need?

Can we improve what we are delivering?

What are the big benefits of what we are delivering?

Can we improve on these benefits?

Do we have an active engagement with those who utilize what we deliver?

Have we asked these people for feedback on our products/ services?

Is it possible to deliver our work faster?

Is it possible to improve the quality of our work?

How often do we validate the requirements around what we deliver?

Each is a simple question, but we will learn so much in the process of both formulating the questions and the search for answers.

> **Business outcomes are always there, waiting to be discovered and understood. They bring color to the business, bring the business to life, and are the reason we do what we do every day.**

But this search to understand business outcomes has not been common in IT. These outcomes were understood and managed by key business owners but obscured or altogether missing in IT.

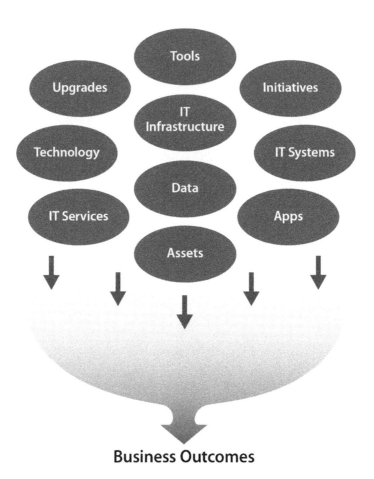

Business Outcomes

Figure 3.4 Focus on Business Outcomes

Let's not view this as a problem or a shortcoming of IT but rather a compelling opportunity.

Curiosity is another positive behavior that is contagious. When we see curiosity in action, we take on the same mindset, and it changes how we think. All people have a natural desire to learn, and curiosity is a powerful engine for learning.

Curiosity and the questions it will create will be a fuel for the unification of IT. The more we learn about the business and the outcomes we need to drive, the more it becomes clear IT must change, IT must transform, IT must execute differently every day. All of these things are connected. All of these things will bring us the realization that working together, working to the common mission of serving our customer better, and working as motivated and agile teams can best be achieved as One IT. We are far better and are stronger working as One.

This is our only future, and we must begin that transformation today. One IT is superior in virtually every regard, and when we begin making the changes described throughout the book and embrace the thinking and the model we describe in our many reflections, the rate of change and our commitment grow. When we get a taste of One IT and then One Business, we will want more and want it to come quickly. We know this is right, and we know this is a better way to live.

By making IT agents of change, we embrace our future and become a catalyst in making it real, in creating our future each day. This is as powerful as it is unlikely, and this should be embraced.

Let's enjoy taking on this responsibility. Let's enjoy surprising the good people of IT and across the business, and take great satisfaction as we begin to enjoy the wonderful results.

CHAPTER 4

A NEW CULTURE

The journey to the transformation of IT and what will become One IT is very much about a thoughtful redesign of our culture. New processes come and go, new technologies come and go, but the power of our people and the culture they work in every day is central to what IT will become in the next ten years.

There are so many things that are important to building One IT, but three things lie at the center:

The customer

Our people

The right culture

By recognizing this vital triune, anything becomes possible. Everything we do begins and ends with the customer, and then all else, every thought and action, is carefully designed to serve the customer. This is best done through our culture with empowered people. Yes, innovation must be a vibrant part of our culture, and a culture that does not include innovation will not succeed long term.

Culture provides us so much. Our good people are unable to thrive unless surrounded by the right culture. This is the very reason our culture exists—to provide a healthy and exciting environment in which our people can grow and thrive.

This is the future of IT and the future of the business. Wait, you might say, I thought you said our future is about creating happy customers? Yes, exactly, so let's look at this a little more closely.

Extending our focus on and passion for our customer, there is a chain that must be understood and appreciated. The customer is our beginning and our end, but there is a chain of value and action that connects this beginning and end.

That chain of value consists of four primary elements:

> *Technology*
>
> *People*
>
> *Culture*
>
> *Innovation*

Each of these four things complements each other and creates our ability to serve the customer. This then effectively creates a cycle that begins with the customer and understanding customer needs, which becomes the catalyst for the application of technology, piloted by our passionate people. Our people are nurtured by the right culture, enabling them to be at their best every day, and a commitment to innovation sustains our work every day. This combination brings us back to the customer with an innovative solution to the needs and requirements that launched our journey within a journey.

There are, of course, other elements that build the culture that creates this fertile ground for people to grow and flourish. These elements are each important and help to make the other possible. It's a wonderful thing when this culture begins to grow, take shape, and thrive. We will explore these other elements throughout this chapter dedicated to culture, and this broader view of culture will help us to shape a strategy and plan for IT that is focused on culture. It can't be an afterthought. Culture is worthy of a strategy all its own, and this very action is a good reminder that IT is changing.

Not a focus in the history of IT, culture now ascends to a place on a very short list of the things that are capable of changing IT, then unifying IT, then making IT great.

Taking this a step further, a new culture helps to create a transformed IT, which then enables us to create One IT, which in turn is necessary to the journey that then creates a unified and energized business. As the elements of IT are related, so we begin to appreciate these same elements are part of our journey to a unified and improved business. Looking at the topics of the book more closely, we begin to appreciate that the powerful and undeniable synergies within IT are in many cases the same priorities and synergies that will fuel our improvement of the business.

> *The priorities of a unified IT are very much*
> *connected to and empower a unified and*
> *stronger business. Each needs the other. Each*
> *makes the other renewed, better, and stronger.*

None of this is possible in the absence of the right culture.

COMMUNICATION

The health of a culture can be traced to a few things. One is communication. This is not necessarily about the quality of communication, the frequency of communication, or any other measure. It is more about the organizational commitment to communication and understanding that this is important, this is part of who we are. With this commitment, the pieces will fall into place.

The good news is that we now have a lot of help. The tools that help us communicate have improved, and the style of communication has evolved significantly in the past decade. These factors combined can launch the organization forward when the will to communicate and communicate better exists.

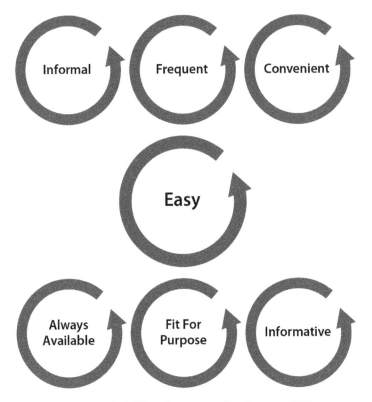

Figure 4.1 The Communications of IT

Where more formal communications have been the rule in the past, tools including weekly activity reports, regularly scheduled management reports, long staff meetings, and the like have become less common for a number of reasons. What we have learned is that communications, much like other aspects of our work, are best when they are framed in the following model:

Informal

Frequent

Convenient

Easily created

Easily updated

Always available

Fit for purpose

Many things have influenced this model, including the rise of social media, text messaging, chat, email, and much more, bringing a strong influence from our personal communications into the workplace and business.

This model brings a near constant and easily consumed stream of communication into the business, which is good for everybody— both the people providing the communication and the people consuming it.

All the model needs is a little nudge, and off we go.

The communications grow, our people will recognize this is valuable and easy to create, and then more people are willing to contribute. This contributes to the changes in IT and brings IT closer together, because our people have better and broader visibility across all of IT. And when people feel informed, they feel included. It brings our people closer together. This directly supports our growth toward One IT.

It is also true that as IT communicates better, both IT and the complete business benefit. Another form of leadership that can come from IT and begin to influence how the full business operates.

There is no downside to better communication. Today, this is no longer a labor-intensive, somewhat painful, and time-consuming process. It is easier and faster and more flexible than ever. When it is easier to communicate, we all benefit.

*Communications can come from anywhere
and should come from anywhere,
because the different views across IT
are valuable in different ways.*

We want to encourage people to participate, how and when they can. Every bit of information helps. We do need to be aware that communications are not natural for many people. But their participation is important and so they need some encouragement. A big advantage of making communication faster and easier and more convenient is the broader participation of our people, which in turn increases the quality and usefulness of our communication.

Communications can include just about everything:

An important project milestone completed

A great deed done by a member of our staff

A reminder of the IT Mission

An update on new initiatives launching

Recognition of an IT initiative being completed

A customer success

A successfully resolved security issue

A closed customer escalation

A new employee starting

Everything helps in one capacity or another to bring our people closer together and to keep them informed and up to date. A unified IT will always include more frequent communications.

Email is okay, but not the best medium. An IT community portal or something similar is a great tool, and we will take advantage of new communication forums as they emerge. And new ones will certainly emerge. Some organizations are using group texts as an easy and convenient tool.

This is common in our personal lives and so a natural for business.

PASSION

Is there anything more precious and more powerful than passion in a culture? If there is, I'm not sure what it would be.

Passion can do much more than just change us. Passion can heal. Passion is contagious and can transform a culture that is struggling with apathy, a culture that has stagnated as so many IT cultures have, into a healthy and vibrant workplace.

Passion includes the following characteristics:

Belief in a common purpose

High energy

Sense of optimism

Desire to be part of something bigger than ourselves

Willingness to help and mentor others

Positive outlook

A natural affinity for the customer

High desire to succeed

A good teammate

Readiness to go beyond the normal boundaries of a job

Virtually any culture, no matter the current condition, can be transformed. This happens one small step at a time, and from within. This is fully under our control and only needs our attention and a consistent effort. No magic here, just faith and some hard work.

As with other elements of our culture, a growing passion in IT will be a natural complement to our vision of One IT. As we see passion grow, people will come together. Our best people will role model for all others and bring people along on the journey. All people with few exceptions want to be part of something good and are drawn to passion.

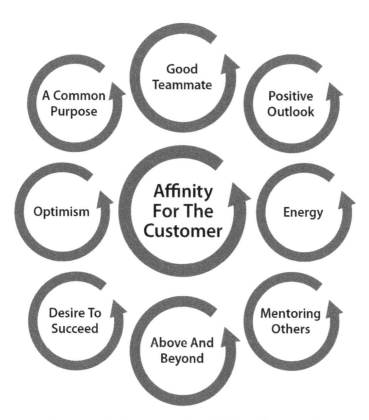

Figure 4.2 The Wonderful Passion of IT

A spark of passion is highly contagious. Passion is charismatic. Passion pulls people in.

Given the choice of working with a person filled with apathy and a person brimming with passion, what do we choose? Of course, passion every time. So, we just need to get started.

Don't think for a minute that passion is simply an emotional thing.

Passion brings with it an innate ability to do our job better.

Passion carries an intensity and clarity of thought along with an urgency of action that together create a more effective worker. This then in turn influences others around us and begins to change the results that we achieve in the business every day. A single person with passion and planted in the middle of an organization of any size will then begin to grow the passion of every person. Passion calls others to share in this wonderfully positive force.

It is true that some people will be unable or unwilling to elevate their level of passion. These people become easier and easier to identify over time as passion grows in the organization.

Apathy stands in stark contrast to passion. It is not hard to find either.

But we need to encourage these people and give them some time to respond. Most people will rise to the challenge, and this is good for everybody. But those people to whom we have given every opportunity to take on a passion for their teammates, the IT organization, and the business, and they are simply unable to make this transformation and leave apathy behind—those people must be coached out of the organization. This is best for them in that they should find a place they can be passionate about, and it is best for IT in that we can't transform the organization with apathy in our teams. It goes against everything we are trying to create.

Back to this idea of passion and how we grow this across IT, ultimately helping us to unify IT. A few things really help:

>*Recognize passion and commitment when we see it in our existing people*

>*Make every effort to promote our passionate people and bring them more responsibility*

>*Provide spot-bonuses to these passionate people when possible*

>*Assign passionate people to lead small teams*

>*Make passion a priority when hiring new people for new positions*

>*Make passion a top priority when back-filling for a staff departure*

>*Add passion as a characteristic to be valued in performance appraisals*

What this creates is an ability to grow and nurture the people we have today who possess passion and to then bring more passion into the organization every chance we get. Hiring—even if it is limited, which is the reality of IT—is a wonderful opportunity to infuse passion and diversity and diverse skills into IT. We need both.

>***Diversity brings us nontraditional IT people with nontraditional backgrounds and training. This includes more women in IT, which is very much needed to build a brighter future.***

Of course passion as an attribute in these people is even better.

With these small adjustments in how we manage our people and how we hire, we will see passion grow and grow and we will enjoy the wonderful benefits that accompany it.

Passion then becomes a fuel to bring IT together, to unify IT, and to then pull the business together as well.

FAIL FAST

Fail Fast is an empowering strategy in an IT organization where failure of any kind at any time has been foreign to us.

> **This is a big shift and about as non-IT as anything could be.**

We simply can't change the culture of IT, transform IT, and then unify IT without embracing some risk-taking.

This is not about reckless behavior; this is about calculated and thoughtful risk. About doing some things completely differently and bringing some crazy thinking to IT. In some cases the big improvements, the big innovations, the breakthrough ideas we need for the future can't take flight without some risk-taking.

We are, of course, not talking about risking critical systems or critical services but about working in a safe testbed of sorts to try new models and new ideas.

What we need to foster is the ability to try new things, to prototype ideas that might be very different than what we have done in the past, and to try these ideas in a fast and agile environment. This could be a new IT test environment where we have access to the tools we need to create prototypes quickly and in a way that does not impact our production environments.

> *This test environment can be a fertile*
> *proving ground for new ideas that ultimately*
> *feed our pipeline for innovation.*

IT can create a process that brings forward new ideas which are then reviewed by peers. If they pass the peer review from IT leadership, the most promising ideas are promoted to the IT Innovation/ Test environment, where we build a fast prototype to determine if the idea should be investigated further.

Even the act of bringing an idea forward for review is a good thing. Even better is making it to the IT Innovation proving environment. This is fun and fulfilling for the individual and an important pipeline of new ideas for IT.

These innovation ideas can include:

An improvement to an existing IT system

An improved user experience

An all-new new IT system that complements existing systems

A targeted technology to support a key business owner

An improvement to a customer-facing system or technology

An automation technology that replaces a manual process

A new solution that replaces a legacy system

A new AI technology that improves the user experience

A system enhancement that improves speed of performance

It could be anything really that improves how IT performs every day.

In the interest of failing fast or proving value fast, the design of the prototype must be agile and able to be completed in just a few weeks.

We can't have prototypes that take six months or more to complete; it's just too slow and too costly and goes against everything we are trying to achieve with this process. Possible exceptions could be major new initiatives that take more time to prove, or a second-phase prototype that needs to be investigated further following a successful first-phase prototype.

Good areas to focus on with the prototyping environment are automation, AI, and improving the user experiences. All of these are high-value technologies, and providing a test environment that encourages advancements in any of these areas is important to IT. This encourages the strategic focus of IT and encourages innovation. Once this process has begun and new ideas take flight in the prototyping/test environment, IT needs to give the business visibility of this work and encourage feedback.

Previewing the most promising prototypes with the business is a great idea for many reasons.

The business will appreciate this and will see the innovative work being done by IT, further accelerating the changing perceptions of IT. Even better, it will encourage others with ideas to bring them forward—everybody will want to be part of this process.

This is not about IT driving innovation autonomously—this is about IT pulling the business together as the innovation facilitator.

A key part of this cycle is to reinforce that all ideas are good, and it's important to bring new ideas forward. Every idea helps. When we do prototype or investigate a new idea and it does not work out, that is okay. The next idea could be a big breakthrough, and if that idea is never raised, we have done the organization a disservice. Participation is important, more is always better, and proving that an idea is not what we need at this time is fine. It is what we need. The key here is agility with new innovation possibilities and the ability to prove or disprove them quickly.

Speed is at the center of this process.

Heck, it will even make IT a little more fun, a little more exciting.

TEAMWORK

We would be remiss in having any discussion about the culture of IT without discussing teamwork. Yes, teamwork comes up a few times throughout the book, as it should—this is really important to the future of IT and to a Unified IT!

There is no possibility of a Unified IT without a commitment to teamwork. This is natural to unifying IT—the strategy of bringing people together both to work better every day and to rally around a common cause.

> *Teams are powerful, dynamic, healthy, and empowering. Form a small team with a clear set of goals, and then stand back and watch amazing things happen.*

Any talented individual can contribute as an individual. But there is no leverage in this model. This is a model of brute force and almost certainly a tactical lifestyle.

> *This individual focus is the hero lifestyle of traditional IT and has no place in our future.*

This individual model does not scale nor does it nurture happy and healthy employees.

When we put a talented individual together with a few other talented individuals, we have created a remarkable machine. This is leverage—a case of the team creating far more value than the sum of the individuals. It may seem a little uncomfortable in the beginning, but this feeling will pass quickly. Experts working with other experts is exactly the team we need to transform IT and to unify IT. There is more than meets the eye in this model and in particular when we bring the stars of individual silos or functions together with the stars of other silos.

Another wonderful thing that happens here beyond getting more work done is making people happy. We are enabling our people to enjoy their jobs and want to stay with the organization for a long time. The loss of an experienced and talented staff member in IT is difficult.

Retaining our people for longer, making them believe this is a place they want to be for years into the future, this is building the IT of the future. It begins with our people and building a motivated and happy workforce...not always a strength of IT.

Forming teams is completely under our control and is something we can begin immediately. This has so many benefits in terms of culture, improved productivity, the transformation of IT, and creating a Unified IT. Remember, when we reach a Unified IT, we have created a wonderful momentum that then rolls into the business.

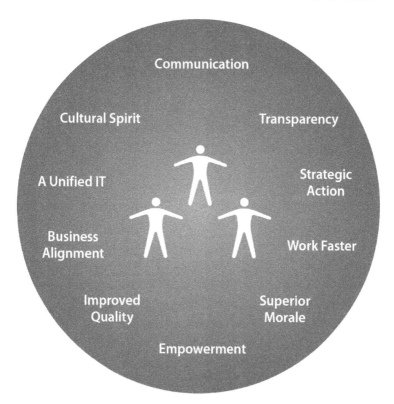

Figure 4.3 The Teamwork of IT

Yes, it is possible that the business is already undergoing the transformation required for the full organization, but my experience has been that these dynamic organizations are in the minority today. There might be some growing realization the business needs to change and some desire to make it happen, but the clear and visible actions to make this a reality are not there. Desire is good, but there must then be some growing sense of commitment that precedes real action, and for most organizations that real action, that real change has not occurred yet.

This is okay, but IT can now become the catalyst, the leader that brings real change and real unity to the business. After all, it really does not matter how this happens, only that the changes begin to occur.

For IT and for the business, teamwork is
simply one of the powerful elements of the
cultural changes that lie at the heart of One
IT and One Business. Some things are nice,
some things help us in the journey, and
some things are core to our transformation.
Teamwork is one of these core building blocks.

Yet another wonderful characteristic of teamwork is the boundless improvement model it brings us, something that makes sense for every part of the organization, top to bottom and left to right. Everybody can be part of this and everybody can benefit from the model.

Teamwork can make an organization better and stronger without spending money, without hiring new people, and without waiting years for a return on investment. Teamwork can make us better overnight and can be mobilized in an instant.

It would be a fair question to ask—how do we get started? Very simply, we want to use small teams in support of all new projects or programs launched within IT going forward. Every organization is different, but small teams are normally in the range of three to five people in number, and we want to ensure these teams are cross-functional and not simply staffed by a single department or single function. We want a minimum of two functions or organizations represented, and three is even better. Put another way, we should not drive any significant undertaking in IT without a cross-functional team in place. This is the model for anything but the simplest tasks, and it is far more powerful than what its simplicity might suggest. Just a few benefits of small cross-functional teams include:

Better communication

Better transparency

Faster work completion

Better decision making

Improved cultural spirit

Directly supports a Unified IT

Elevated morale

Encourages better strategic action

Better aligns IT with the business

More likely to avoid costly mistakes and delays

Improved quality of work results

More empowered workforce

Of course, there are many more benefits of teamwork.

After we have committed to assigning small cross-functional teams to drive all new projects, we need to take the next step, which is a review of all current work under way to ensure legacy or current work is also staffed with the right teams. If that is the case, great, and if not, then we make an adjustment as needed to form the same type of cross-functional teams for the work in-flight as well.

These two actions will realign how all work gets done and become a natural part of how we work every day across IT and then across the business.

Once this model has gained some traction, everybody will be amazed that we ever worked any other way, and we look forward to a more unified and brighter future.

ENTREPRENEURSHIP

Entrepreneurial spirit is another important dimension to the new heartbeat and singularity of IT. The thinking created by this spirit is unique and powerful—virtually limitless in the good it can bring the IT organization and the business. It simply changes how the people of IT view the work that is performed every day, how we plan, and how we think about strategy.

At the heart of entrepreneurship is a set of very simple reflections and questions:

> *The success of our customers is more important than anything else.*

> *The success of our business is only possible by creating happy customers.*

> *The success of IT is only possible with the success of the business.*

> *Every individual in IT must be focused on our shared success.*

> *How can we in IT make the customer experience better every day?*

> *How can IT better empower our business colleagues to work better every day?*

How can we improve the performance of every system in IT?

How can we anticipate the next big change in the business?

How can IT be proactive in enabling corporate strategy?

With these reflections and questions, we can frame all the planning and execution that happens every day across IT. Every minute of every day.

This is our context. These points bring us clarity if we ever lose it for an instant.

This context also creates a fundamental shift from technology to one of business, further creating a natural alignment between IT and the business and between the people of IT and the business owners across the organization. It creates a common focus and a common vocabulary. A wonderful thing to drive change.

Taking this shift a step further, by thinking about these key points and asking these questions, we can mobilize the resources of IT to be better aligned with strategy and with the business. And this is just the beginning. This thinking will drive us to connect to our business colleagues and our customers and creates a natural curiosity that sends us in search of answers. In most cases these answers can't be found within the walls of IT.

These answers can only be found in the market, with our customers and across the business.

This is exactly how it should be. This thought, search and discovery will have a remarkable influence on everything we do. It is also a process, a lifestyle really, that once begun won't stop and can't stop. It becomes how we think and how we work every day.

The people of IT, very much technology aware and technology capable, but now with a new awareness of the business and operating with the best interests of the business at heart—even more, the success of the business and the success of our customers foremost in mind every day.

An entrepreneurial spirit has not been common in the IT of the past, but it makes so much sense today when we consider the new place technology and data have in the business and how technology and innovation are now so closely linked to future business success. Remarkably, IT can be the catalyst for these discussions— a driver across the business to help elevate our awareness and search for answers.

> *This is an important distinction—the*
> *difference between IT simply participating*
> *in the planning and discussions that must*
> *take place in the business every day versus*
> *IT initiating and driving these discussions.*

IT taking on the role of catalyst, of facilitator, to rally the resources of IT and the business to bring our very best people together in a new and united model to equip the business for the future. Then, to equip the business for future success.

This evolution is timely and benefits IT, the business, and our customers.

NEW SKILLS & DIVERSITY

The expanded thinking and execution of IT will require a new mix of skills and people, leading to an exciting expansion and enrichment of the IT workforce, organization, and culture. With new skills and a few new people, we can take on a more extended and deeper set of responsibilities in IT. This will change IT itself, and also how IT is perceived by the business. Even more importantly, it will change what IT is capable of doing. This is effectively a shift in the DNA of the IT organization in the best possible way.

Adding skills and diversity creates a more capable, diverse, skilled, and talented IT workforce which then creates another level of benefits, including:

New IT career paths

A new IT compensation plan

New IT recruitment priorities

Key corporate initiatives assigned directly to IT

More diverse IT workforce

New customer-facing skills

New business-oriented skills

Deeper relationships with customers

More effective engagement with the market

New partnerships with market influencers

More diversity within the teams of IT

Better IT engagement with the business

All of these benefits and more are made possible with a new set of skills hired, developed, and nurtured across IT.

> **These new skills will bring a new feel and a new look to the IT organization. More diversity, more energy—more balanced and more complete in everything we do.**

Yes, we will forever be IT in our hearts and we will always be technology savvy and technology skilled, but we now balance these technical skills with new and complementary skills that allow us to better leverage the value of technology expertise.

Think of these new skills as magnifying and clarifying the real and equally important, the potential impact of IT. A few examples of the new skills across IT:

Communications skills

Customer-facing skills

Budgeting and financial skills

Program management skills

Creative skills

Team leadership skills

Innovation skills

Automation expertise

AI expertise

Social media skills

Mobility expertise

Cloud expertise

Note that these skills are a broad mix that reflects the broadening nature of IT itself. Some of these skills are business-oriented, including financial skills, customer-facing skills, and leadership skills. Other skills are very much focused on our need to communicate more effectively. Additional skills are in support of technology that will reshape the future of IT and for which we have limited expertise in IT today. Yes, this knowledge is growing, but so much of what we do across IT and the business will be shaped by Cloud, Mobility, AI, and Automation over the next ten years that an investment in our expertise around these technologies is critical.

Figure 4.4 The New Skills of IT

The business will need IT to enable the full organization to leverage AI and Automation, for example, as it appears in an increasing number of business functions. IT will be an important adviser to the business in how we best leverage AI and Intelligent technology.

New skills will naturally bring improved diversity to IT, but diversity goes much further. Building a diverse and healthy workforce for IT will include a conscious commitment to nurturing, supporting, and hiring additional diversity. One example here is bringing more women to IT. Current metrics indicate that women in the IT workforce represent about 10 to 15 percent of the IT organization, and this seems to be accurate today based on my experiences. It is simply unacceptable for the future.

Women bring so much to the reshaping of the IT culture and so much advancement of the many skills we need to complete the transformation of IT. Of course, the diversity needed in IT goes beyond a growing workforce of women, but this is a good example that needs our immediate attention.

> *Broader business experience, global cultures, and expanded educational backgrounds are just a few examples of how we will enrich the diversity of IT.*

The leadership of IT, including the CIO, CISO, and VP, will understand this need and will provide their full support to the immediate and ongoing improvement of diversity alongside our growth of new skills.

Skills and diversity go hand in hand, and each makes the other better in that we are growing the strength of our knowledge, our culture, and the quality of our business.

OUTSIDE IN

The history of IT has been very much one of inside-out thinking and execution, very much an inside-out culture. The "inside" of this pair is technology and systems as managed by IT. The "outside" of this pair is the marketplace and customers. What we will do for the transformation of IT is turn this model upside down—shattering many of the traditional conventions and biases of IT.

Taking a step back, the concept and strategy of "outside in" are a focus that is rooted in the market and our customers and then extends back into the systems of IT. By making the marketplace and customers the origin, we then qualify everything we do in IT based on beginning with markets and customers. These markets and customers provide the context and clarity we need. Marketplaces and customers are very clear and what is important and why. These sources of requirements and priorities are the ultimate truth and are not watered down, diluted, biased by organization preferences, cost, feasibility, artificial limitations, or any other internally driven factors.

Customers in particular know what they want, why this is required, and are typically passionate about these requirements. They find it easy to be passionate because the success of their business often depends directly on the quality of systems provided by vendors/ partners and by IT.

It can be said that if we are ever in doubt
about requirements or priorities or why a
system or capability is necessary, just ask
a customer and the fog will lift quickly.

This is a good mindset to live by for both the transformation of IT, our unification of IT, and then the singularity of the business. The customer truly is the best single unifying force to bring IT together and then to bring the business together.

This is likely the single biggest element of One IT and One Business—a newly elevated focus on the current and future needs of our customers and in delivering consistent innovation to our loyal customers. This in turn keeps customers engaged longer, creates more happy customers, and these customers seek to invest even more with the products and companies that stand apart.

The cycle of customer engagement
becomes more natural as we move the
trigger for our processes from the internal
anchors of today to the customer.

The customer and the surrounding marketplace then provide a description of current and future needs through requirements, use cases, or some other means, and these descriptions are translated into more rigorous requirements for the systems and data of IT.

IT is about the business of developing or sourcing solutions to address these requirements, then moving through the process to deliver these customer requirements in a manner that solves real business problems and enables the customer to be more successful. This creates a system that is triggered by customer needs, then connects to systems and solutions development, which is validated by ongoing customer reviews and engagements and then is completed by the delivery of a product or service to the customer, bringing the cycle full circle by concluding where we began—with the customer. The outside-in process regulates itself by maximizing customer communication and engagement. In most cases, frequency is important to ensure our investments and work products can't go too far astray.

> *Ideally, customer transparency would approach 100 percent, meaning the customer has a depth of visibility into our processes that matches our own.*

The right customer can see everything at any time and provide comments, clarifications, and additional information when required and as required, which is highly productive when we get it right. It is productive even when the process is not perfect, because the simple involvement of and focus on the customer can make up for many mistakes.

As we move toward a unified IT, the model of One IT, we should think of the customer as a natural part of this community. All the teams of IT, of course, should be included but also the customer in some capacity in most of our activities and work product. This model then extends even further into the next important step, One Business.

It is simply not possible to unify IT and to unify the business without placing the customer at the center of our orbit. This brings so much balance, clarity, and value to all our work and benefits everybody. Not easy of course and not natural for many, but when we begin to make this change and create this focus on the customer, so many benefits begin to emerge.

Our commitment will then grow and the pace
of our changes will quicken. The outside-
in model will gain momentum quickly
and become muscle and mind memory,
and we won't need to give it a thought.

Outside-in becomes how we do everything—where we start and where we end.

EMPLOYEE DEVELOPMENT

The creation of our new culture for IT centers on our people and on the customer. These things go hand in hand in that our good people will naturally recognize the customer as our very reason for being in business, and they will naturally rally around this cause enthusiastically. Our customers will in turn embrace the idea of working more closely with our people across the business and the people of IT, and this becomes very much a mutual admiration.

Taking this further, this focus and engagement with the customer will create happier customers inevitably and build customer loyalty and tenure. Customers of the future will invest in products and services that provide value, and the model of One IT and One Business is very much about building a strategy of value and then operating within this model every day.

But there is another very important element here, and that is the longevity and loyalty of our employees. Our very own people can't be forgotten. This is part of the circle of customer loyalty and value—the longer we are able to retain our people and in particular the key people of IT, the more value we are able to deliver to our clients. The ongoing investment in our employees makes a lot of sense but has not been a strength of IT in the past. As such, employee tenure in IT has lagged the best-in-class numbers for other organizations.

Most experienced managers know well how to manage and develop employees. This is not the issue—the issue is that IT has not been one of our best organizations at retaining and developing talent. The technology focus of IT and other cultural forces have pulled our focus in IT away from our people.

> *We need to turn this on its head and build IT into one of the best if not the best employee retention organizations in the business. This will be to the benefit of the employee, IT, and the business.*

Even better, our customers will benefit. The service of a knowledgeable and experienced and motivated employee is a powerful thing for every person they come in contact with every day. Employee development includes a few things:

New and enriched career path, clearly defined

Annual investment in training and education

New assignments aligned with the business

Working more closely with customers

Engagement in innovation activities

Annual budget to attend trade shows that are business- or innovation-focused

Recognition

Improved compensation plans including incentives

It's beyond the scope of this book to take on each of these elements in detail, but it is most important that the IT organization create a new employee development plan specifically for IT. A plan for IT will not exist in most organizations today, but it just takes a bit of focus and a commitment to make this plan a part of IT growth and the unification of IT and the business.

> *We will likely find Human Resources a very willing and capable partner in making this happen. Beyond the ideas we bring to this discussion, HR will no doubt have other great ideas to help us accomplish the goal of developing and retaining the stars in our IT organization.*

Note that a lot of this development is under our control, including recognition, working more closely with customers, and engagement in our innovation brainstorming and prototyping activities for example. The HR team can help us with some career path planning, including new titles, the compensation plan, and a training and education plan.

Begin with identifying a few of the top talented and uniquely skilled people in IT and focus the first wave of this program on those people. This will allow us to get to our very best people first, our best all-around athletes and the people who can drive the new agenda of IT, help bring IT together, and help bring the business together. With an employee development plan in place for these key people, we have validated the model, helped to secure the key people in IT for the future, and can then broaden the participation of the plan and reach the next group of our most talented and skilled people.

This makes a big difference. We are helping to secure the leadership role of IT and the value we can deliver to customers. Never underestimate the impact a few talented people can have.

These key people also become mentors for other staff across IT, which then further secures the future of that broader circle of people in IT and in the business. Note these very same people are likely to be key to our innovation, automation, and speed focuses as well. All of this is strategic and only possible with the improved retention of our key people.

It is not possible to drive these strategic activities with inexperienced and junior IT staff.

We need our best and most experienced people, the experts who have the content and this unique insight into IT and the business. There is unique leverage with these people, and we need to unleash them on IT.

CHAPTER 5

SPEED IS STRATEGIC

Speed is ascending in its value and importance to the business. It is important to appreciate just how vital speed will become to the success of the business, and as such we must rely on IT to enable the raw speed business requires. The systems of IT are an important part of the speed equation. This is where speed begins. With this in mind we can drive the speed of the business through a focus on speed for all infrastructure and systems across IT.

Think in terms of the common business life cycle of taking an order, processing the order, and fulfilling the order, which includes the good or service being delivered to the customer. This is a system-intensive process and one that can only accelerate, and then accelerate significantly with the leadership of IT. It is not unusual in business today for this simple cycle of order-> order processing -> order fulfillment to take days or even weeks. But this cycle must be compressed and compressed significantly. This compression will take us from days down to hours or minutes and from weeks down to hours.

This is not about simply trying to go faster—
this is about creating a strategic advantage
in the business and creating happy customers
by delivering what customers need, and in
a fraction of the time possible previously.

There is another important relationship here we need to address. The connections of speed begin inside the business with our employees. The IT organization must increase the speed of our internal systems and of our employees first, which helps our employees better serve our customers. There are so many connections of systems and technologies across the business, and by increasing the speed of performance for each of these technologies, tools, and systems, we are bringing improved speed directly to the customer. This is a wonderfully powerful process for the business that can be led and directed by IT: As stewards of our technology and systems, we are in direct management of these links in the chain that connects every team in the business—every individual in the business—to our customers.

With this connection, every second we can remove from the chain of systems and technologies is a second we can improve the speed with which we serve our markets and our customers. Never underestimate the importance of removing but a single second from the speed of a workflow or a business process. A second might not seem like a lot, but seconds quickly become minutes, and minutes quickly become hours, and then suddenly we have delivered a significant improvement in speed.

This is a key cultural mindset—every
second matters. Fight for every second,
and we get to big time savings, big speed
improvement one second at a time.

If we only look for those big time savings, hour or days, they are very hard to find; we will quickly lose our energy and conviction, and it's unlikely we will ever meet our goals. But if we embrace the idea of saving every second, anything is possible. This mindset gives us encouragement because seconds are easier to find, and we are much more likely to keep going. Then, over time we begin to see larger time savings, giving us some validation of the hard work and more energy and a commitment to keep fighting for those seconds.

It is only possible to measure progress if we know the current baseline speed: in other words a measurement of all current business processes and tasks and exactly how much time is required on average to complete each. We look at this process at the beginning of the chapter and create the baseline so we can be clear about the current state of speed. With this we can then begin to quantify all speed improvements in every large and small business process across IT.

Many opportunities are created when we send IT searching for speed improvements, including simplification of the business, improved ability to change, along with improved agility, automation, and much more. This full set of improvements should be seen as strategic and core to the future of the business and future success. When we begin to appreciate these activities and how each is related to the other, we can begin to understand just how much value and leverage we can get from these speed improvements and the other activities that naturally go hand in hand with speed.

MEASURE EVERYTHING

To get started in making real and systematic improvements in speed, we need to measure the elapsed time of all IT tasks and business processes—an important activity for many reasons. It brings us a baseline for the improvements we will make in the weeks and months ahead; it brings attention to our speed initiative; and it gives us an accurate measurement where none exists today. We quickly learn that much of the work we do today is not well understood and we certainly don't have a current, accurate measurement of the time it takes to complete this work.

There may be many of these tasks and business processes in place today depending on the size of the business, so the best place to start is with the following:

High-volume tasks

Business processes that are commonly executed

Tasks that are highly manual

Business processes that are considered critical to the business

Business processes that are considered slow by IT or the business

Business processes that directly support customer engagement

If it is not possible to measure all the tasks and business processes completed in IT every day, we should begin with those that meet this profile: They will provide the biggest opportunity for improvement and the biggest potential impact to the business.

This is the work product that IT produces every day for the business and represents what most people in the business see of IT. This is the reality of IT across the organization—the living embodiment of IT. It is a great opportunity for us because for each of these tasks and business processes, there are internal customers and external customers who are using what this work provides, the consumers of this work. When these tasks and business processes are completed more quickly—maybe in the beginning this is just a little faster, but over time this will become a lot faster—our internal employees and customers will begin to notice. This is a big win for IT and a big win for the business.

> **When we referred to measuring these tasks and business processes earlier, we were referring to measuring the elapsed time required to complete a task or business process, down to the minute.**

This measurement must be precise in order to be valuable and give us the baseline we need to track improvement.

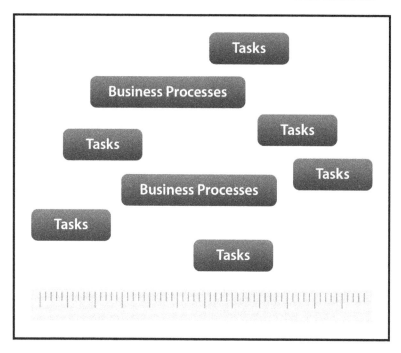

Figure 5.1 Measure Everything in IT

A good way to make this measurement is to take an average over a reasonable amount of time. For example, if a task is performed each day, take the average of the time required to complete the task over the course of a week. Some days might be slower and some days will be faster, so the average gives a good calibration of the typical time required to complete the work. This then becomes a baseline for our improvement. Likewise with a business process that might include a number of tasks. These business processes might take days or even weeks to complete, and that is to be expected. In this case we will need a longer horizon over which to take the average of the elapsed time required to complete the business process. For example, if the business process is executed once or twice per month, then we take a look at a horizon of one quarter, perhaps two quarters, and this will give us a good sample size for the typical time required to complete the business process. In the case of a business process, measuring down to the hour is more appropriate than down to the minute. Remember, we need a precise and pragmatic measurement here in order to track our progress.

Take care to make these measurements of a task or business process before any improvements are made. We want a true current state of the task or business process.

> *Resist the temptation to make any times that are expected to look bad just a little better before we go on record with a measurement. Some very slow times are expected, and this is okay. Make a good measurement and then we can go to work.*

With the elapsed time measurements made of the high-volume and high-visibility tasks and business processes made, this becomes our target list and our baseline. Creating this baseline in itself is an important milestone and should be celebrated. At this point in the process, we should recognize that our opportunity for improvement is very good and that most IT organizations that have made the decision to improve speed and have made these measurements of current elapsed times are highly likely to be successful and to make significant improvements in speed.

Normally it is possible to get some quick improvements to both tasks and business processes through initial changes that are very clear—the proverbial low-hanging fruit that is alive and well in any business. Take these quick improvements off the table and then re-measure what we can call the improvements of Phase I.

It's a good idea to share these improvements with both IT leadership and the business as a good way to market the good work being done and the improvements being made. Celebrate the speed we find in Phase I. This is important in keeping the team confident and energized, because the next round of improvements won't be quite as easy.

But, remember, it all begins with establishing an accurate speed baseline, regardless of what that might be, through accurate measurement of existing IT tasks and business processes.

BENCHMARK OF NOW

With our measurement of current task and business process elapsed times in place, we then begin the work of reducing the time required to complete this work. This process must be thoughtful and systematic, taking care to not overlook any opportunity to increase our speed of completing the work across IT. With this search for time savings launched, the only acceptable benchmark can be now, or the immediate completion of our work. Think in terms of a few seconds or minutes. Anything less than fifteen minutes can be considered now.

Don't make the mistake of assuming this is not possible. On the contrary, we will learn that a surprising amount of daily work across IT can be completed immediately, instantly in many cases. From the very beginning of improving the speed of execution across IT, we must set the standard and expectation that immediate execution is the goal we strive for. Then our teams need to push and explore every possible improvement and simplification to achieve this standard of *now*. We will get a lot of help here with simplification, the elimination of some work altogether, and automation. The combination of these three improvements alone is very powerful and will give most IT organizations a big time savings.

One key to achieving this benchmark of immediate execution is eliminating any initial waiting period that exists prior to taking action on a task or workflow.

Initial delays are common and in many cases account for the majority of the elapsed time for the complete actions. This then becomes the first place we look to reduce the overall elapsed time for the completion of any IT task or workflow—how much time expires between the time we have identified the need for a single task or a business process in IT and the work beginning?

Study this segment of time carefully, and ask questions, including:

What are the causes of the initial delay?

Is there a lack of recognition or resources?

Is it possible to automate the front end of this process to reduce the delay?

Can we provide alerts or any information in order to compress the initial period?

If this is a resource issue, can other flexible resources help this initial stage?

Are there any validation or identity checks that can be automated?

Is there an initial approval required and if so, can it be eliminated?

If approvals can't be eliminated, can they be automated?

Does the team responsible for the work have recommendations on compression?

Can IT provide incentives to help compress the initial waiting time?

Are there any legacy requirements for the process that can be eliminated?

Are there any steps in the task or process that can be eliminated completely?

When we begin the investigation into the compression of any task or business process across IT, it's likely this work has not been done previously at all, and if so, then it has been quite some time. There are often clear and meaningful improvements to be made that can have an immediate impact in bringing us closer to *now*— the immediate execution and completion of the work across IT. I've not seen this process occur in an IT organization that did not yield significant time savings for the majority of tasks and workflows reviewed.

There are just so many opportunities that exist to eliminate, simplify, or automate manual work.

This is a powerful combination, and it is important the work is performed in precisely this order.

We don't want shortcuts or automating work that has not been carefully reviewed and validated. We don't want to automate waste or legacy processes.

Remember, it is important that we reinforce the mindset and goal of completing our work immediately, in less than fifteen minutes, and creating the expectation that if we can't complete our work immediately, there must be a very good case for it taking more time.

This goal enables and empowers our teams to find ways to reach the goal of *now* for many tasks and some business processes, normally a surprising number in the final analysis. But equally important is finding significant time savings for all the other work product that might not be completed to the standard of *now*, but become much faster. All of these time savings are important, and with each savings we are impacting the full organization.

> *Every second saved accelerates the work*
> *of IT and the full business, giving the*
> *business a valuable boost for virtually*
> *everything that occurs every day.*

Taking the good news even further, we will discover that the work done in the pursuit of *now* will bring the teams of IT closer together—both out of necessity and design. This work is best done in cross-functional teams; as we highlight throughout the book, this is a very productive model, a superior way to work every day.

So, we are realizing the dual benefits of increasing our speed, in most cases dramatically, and bringing our teams together to work as one in order to push the cadence and speed of IT and the business.

This unification of IT is true leverage, true value, and a big impact on the performance of the business.

A LITTLE FASTER

When pursuing improvements in speed across IT and across the business, it won't always be possible to find the big leap—those large time savings will exist but won't be common, particularly after our first pass at reviewing all IT tasks and business processes. Of course, we take those big time savings and celebrate them and move on quickly while enjoying the benefits.

But the work continues. And as the work continues to find additional speed improvements, we need to shift our thinking.

> **The mindset must be to find anything that allows us to execute just a little faster. This will be how we travel the remaining journey of improving our speed—getting just a little faster, in small steps.**

With these small steps we can accomplish our big goal of *now* as the original and first target, and then get as close to *now* as possible with every task and business process.

Every second is important. These seconds grow quickly, more quickly than we might realize, and become minutes; the minutes become hours, and the hours become days. This is how we build a faster IT and a faster business.

The numbers are important, and we grow to appreciate the cumulative value of seconds and minutes, but there is another big advantage in this approach—the psychology of taking small steps toward reaching a big goal. This helps us to stay energized, to build confidence that we can ultimately meet our goals. People can see the possibility of finding small time savings and of making a task or business process just a little faster. Can we find just a few seconds to save here? This is the question, and our view will be that this is very much within our reach.

Focusing on finding just a few seconds or minutes will let us keep moving forward.

Another approach that helps is having a new team, always a cross-functional team of course, review a set of tasks or business processes they have not reviewed previously. In this model our teams cycle through the daily work of IT looking for any and all time savings. What one team might not see, another will. And so it goes, small steps forward.

> *Expect that several iterations of this process will be required to reach our goals, but with this iterative approach, we can make amazing things happen.*

It bears repeating that the future landscape of IT and business will be speed-obsessed, and as such, every second truly matters. Mere seconds and minutes become the margin of victory and the margin of loss—the winning of new clients and the loss of clients.

> *Customers will naturally seek the fastest delivery of a product or service. This will become the new high ground of any market.*

This is the battleground of the future, the speed of our systems and the speed of information flow pushing the business forward and across thresholds of speed that we thought were not possible before.

This opportunity should be repeated to our teams—so much is at stake here. The very ability to win new customers, the fundamental capacity to outpace our competitors, will rely on these time savings we can create in IT.

The business is counting on us and so we fight for the next few seconds.

THE POWER OF SIMPLE

There is something wonderful, powerful, and timeless about simplicity. This is an important step on our journey, and it sets the stage for much that IT will accomplish in the future. There is so much more to simplicity than we might appreciate.

A quick reminder of just some of the advantages of simplicity:

Simple scales well

Simple is reliable

Simple is repeatable

Simple enables speed

Simple saves money

Simple can be replicated

Simple is easy to learn and easy to train

Simple can be readily automated

Simple eliminates waste

Simple improves transparency

Simple is robust

And this is just the beginning as we begin to appreciate just how much good there is in simplification. It is important to recognize that simplicity is a form of maturity, a form of elegance.

> **Simple should never be confused with simplistic, being limited, or creating any form of compromise.**

The evolution of simplicity is anything but simplistic—simple is powerful and robust.

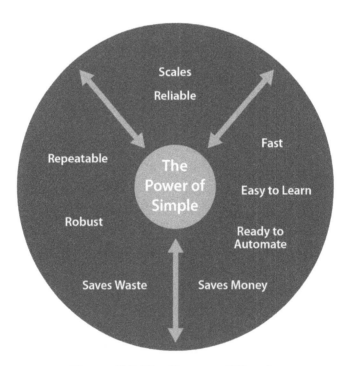

Figure 5.2 The Power of Simple

In terms of our pursuit of speed, simplification is both necessary and valuable. The first important stage in gaining speed in execution across IT is in seeking the elimination of work altogether, and hand in hand with this is a simplification of tasks and business processes. This pays back to us immediately and will improve the quality of our work while saving precious time. In some cases these immediate time savings can be great.

But any simplification goes beyond these immediate advantages and prepares us for more. By simplifying our tasks and business processes, we gain speed with even the continued manual execution of work, and at the same time we are preparing the organization for automation. This important future step is only possible with tasks and business processes that have been cleansed of waste and simplified where possible.

The process of simplification is so valuable, it can't simply be a casual endeavor. Yes, we need to take the clear and obvious simplifications where we can. But then we need to run through the inspection again and push harder, dig deeper, questioning everything. In almost every case there will be additional elements and additional layers of simplification that are possible. Each step that can be simplified, each approval that can be simplified or removed, every single work activity must pass this inspection and bring a higher level of simplicity.

This is a healthy, valuable, and vital exercise for IT, and no part of IT is any more or less important. We need to look at everything and every opportunity to simplify our work.

At the same time we recognize that simplification of our work will inevitably result in a simplification of our systems. This brings an additional set of benefits.

Referring back to our earlier list, we then reap the benefits of cost, reliability, speed, scalability, and much more. All these things are valuable individually and follow from our commitment to simplification.

Simplification holds a place in a very disciplined and structured approach to bring speed to IT. With it then follows the benefits of bringing IT processes together and of eliminating queues, integrations, handoffs, or any other form of disconnected and segmented work. This traditional model is blocking us from achieving the speed we are capable of and the automation that directly enables this speed.

These things go hand in hand. By simplifying we create a singularity across IT that is a natural complement to simplified work and simplified systems.

AUTOMATION

The work done across IT on simplification and the elimination of waste bring significant benefits of their own, but there is much more at work here. We have laid the foundation for one of the most strategic and impactful shifts in IT for the next ten years. The next decade will see a push to the automation of a majority of the tasks and business processes performed across IT every day and every week.

It is certainly true that some of the work performed in IT will not be automated; this work can include unusual business processes that are not performed commonly, escalations, and special strategic initiatives. But the bread-and-butter work of IT is an excellent candidate for automation. It's work that is well understood, and the time has come to take this effort and leverage the powerful resources and tools of automation.

It is easy to get excited about automation, which brings with it a number of impactful benefits, including:

Scalability

Speed

Reliability

Offloading of our people

Leverages humanity

Shifts people to more strategic work

Agility

Consistency of performance

Improved support for 24/7 operations

Improved offering of self-service

What we have before us today is a combination of increased pressures from the business on IT to focus more on initiatives, including speed and scalability, while at the same time having vastly improved automation tools at our disposal. The timing is great because we need these tools more than ever, and in the recent past, the tools were simply not up to the task. But things have changed.

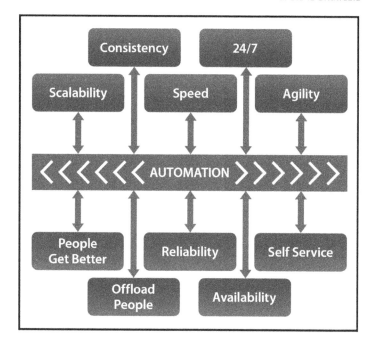

Figure 5.3 The Leverage of Automation

Automation tools today can model our people's decision-making with regard to simple tasks, more complex tasks, and multi-step business processes. Automation tools can also model the decision-making associated with business rules and ensure these rules, once configured with the oversight of our people experts, are executed and enforced correctly over and over again without fail. This is another benefit of automation—perfect consistency of performance along with the additional value of scalability.

> *Automation does not make mistakes,*
> *get tired, or have a bad day.*

It is important that we engage our people experts in capturing this knowledge in the models of automation so we are getting the very best of insights and organizational wisdom captured in the automation models. We can then leverage this knowledge as automation is executed again and again every day. Think of this as hundreds, thousands, and millions of decisions made correctly and tirelessly every day—a wonderful thing that automation brings us.

As the business grows and succeeds, the automation is ready to take on a growing number of tasks and requests. Automation scales naturally, and when designed properly can scale with virtually no limits. This becomes a part of the shift from IT being a tactical element of the organization to being a strategic element of the business.

> *Yet another powerful thing is possible with automation: the ability to shift our people from repetitive and tactical work to more strategic work, including innovation.*

This is an assist we need from automation, as it has historically been difficult if not virtually impossible to find more time in our day so our people have time to think, have time for strategic work, have time to focus on innovation. Automation can make this happen.

So how much of our IT work should be automated? We will discuss this point in more detail later in the book, but our benchmark is to reach 90 percent automation in IT in the next five years. True, this is an ambitious number but one that is achievable. We explore this rich topic in more detail in the chapter entitled "The 90/90 Rule."

Based on my work with IT organizations over the past fifteen years, I would estimate the level of automation today in the average IT organization to be at about 20 percent. So what we have ahead of us is a significant increase in the degree of automation, but this is something the business desperately needs from IT whether it recognizes the need or not.

Going back to our list of automation benefits at the beginning of this section, we can be reminded of the impact automation can have on speed, scalability, agility, leveraging our people, around-the-clock operations, self-service growth, and much more.

> *This begins to look like a what-we-need-most-in-the-business list.*

Surely this profile is about much more than IT and certainly very much about transforming IT and then transforming the business. Automation is one element on a very short list of strategic resources that can make this a reality. As with so many of our other transformational elements and shifts across IT, the success of automation will also bring IT together and almost inevitably then bring the business together. These things go hand in hand as we make these changes in IT which create our singularity of purpose and unity of motion.

ADAPTABILITY

Speed is about much more than linear, blind speed moving straight ahead. With thoughtfully designed speed, we get the additional benefit of the ability to make quick course corrections as changes occur in the business. We can certainly call this agility, but I prefer the term *adaptability*, as it is more descriptive of what we are seeking here.

> **Adaptability is about quickly and precisely making adjustments to the systems and solutions of IT in order to address changes in the business and marketplace. The elements of speed and precision are equally important here.**

The precision of changes is critical—quickly making changes that don't bring us a new solution that is a good fit for the business does not do us a lot of good. But quickly adapting to changes in the business with a precise fit for these changes is a very powerful thing for sure. We know changes in the business will occur; it's only a matter of time. If anything, these changes are coming more quickly than ever, and the stakes are higher than ever.

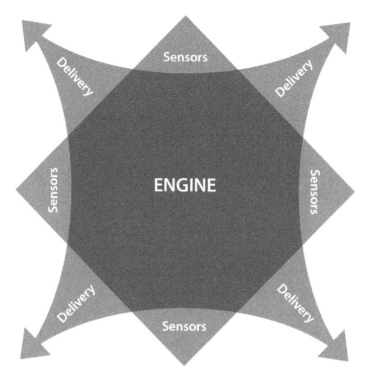

Figure 5.4 The Powers of Adaptability

This is a combination of the remarkable changes in the market, changes in the expectations of customers, and the accelerating changes we are seeing in technology. All of these factors are colliding to put more pressure than ever on business, and given the linkage between technology and the business, the connection between the business and IT is inescapable.

This brings us back to speed. The ability to create new and precise solutions for new business requirements, but done slowly, is a problem for everybody in IT, in the business, and ultimately for our customers.

Adaptability has three important elements:

The front end, or sensors that enable IT to identify changes in the business

The middle, or the engine that defines necessary changes to IT and our systems

The final leg, or the deployment and delivery of new solutions to the business

In order to create true adaptability in IT, we must mind each of these three elements. If any of the three are missing, we simply won't be able to consistently execute on our ability to be adaptable on behalf of the business. The good news is that each of these three elements can be a simple design, and each of them likely exists in some form today as well as being a natural benefit to IT for many other reasons.

The front end of sensors are created through connections to customers first and foremost, then connections to the business in the form of connections to key business owners, and then an external view with the marketplace. All of these support our adaptability but are also important in building a better understanding of our customers and what requirements are emerging in the business. This is not only valuable in helping with our adaptability but helps with our push across IT to be more proactive, to be more strategic, to move closer to our customers, and to drive innovation on behalf of the business.

This wonderful cycle is virtually unlimited in the good it provides to IT and the business and only comes to life through the sensors that we carefully put into place.

Once these sensors are up and running, they are very productive in feeding information into IT on a constant and real-time basis. The information can then be a catalyst and provide early detection of changing business conditions or new business requirements or a new growing need on behalf of our customers. This adaptability can be in the form of a predictive action—based on the information we have, we anticipate a requirement to emerge, and IT makes the decision to take proactive action driven by this anticipation. The second primary form of our adaptability is a quick and early action based on real and timely information. This reaction can be so quick with the right sensors in place that we create a blurring of the line between proactive and reactive.

> *When the reaction of IT is fast enough and based on quality information, reaction begins to look a lot like proactive action.*

This is another important benefit of the sensors we have created internally with the business and externally with our customers and the market.

First, we should commit to getting this full set of sensors into place, and then we can define how we best leverage the information over time. Create the sensors, and then we have created the opportunity to reshape how IT works every day. And this is the fun part. With these sensors feeding information into IT, we can then define the adaptability processes that take action based on the sensors' output. These adaptability actions are closely linked to innovation and the strategic realignment of IT. So we are enjoying the leverage these sensors create: a very high degree of reusability for the rich information flowing into IT.

CHAPTER 6

THE CUSTOMER OBSESSION

"Obsession" is a powerful and dynamic word, and the meaning here is perfectly appropriate.

The essence of obsession is a thought or idea that preoccupies and dominates our thoughts and actions every day. This can be nothing other than the customer for the IT of today and of the future.

No other single thought can bring IT together, unify IT, like the customer can.

The customer is a never-ending source of
clarity, understanding, and inspiration.

Of course we need the clarity and understanding, but the most important element of all could be the inspiration, which helps us to appreciate that the work we do every day is helping real people in real organizations. This is a vital connection because sometimes we can feel detached or distant from the very real and hardworking people who are our customers.

I can think of no more valuable or necessary activity in IT today than speaking directly with a customer, joining a customer conference call, or conducting a face-to-face on-site meeting to see their offices and operations and hear firsthand about their business today and what they see for the future.

This is how I recommend approaching a customer meeting—spend a lot more time listening than talking, and ask simple questions. By simply listening, we find that the customer will tell us everything we need to know. The biggest single mistake made in business today is not listening enough, not learning to be great at listening.

This listening and the relationship and trust it creates is the very best of the customer relationship and a priceless source of value for both IT and the customer. This very simple model, a direct and ongoing engagement with the customer, is likely the single greatest force that will drive the transformation of IT over the next ten years, unify IT, and then drive the alignment and unification of IT and the business.

Sound like a lot? Well, it certainly is, and only the customer is capable of driving such widespread and impactful change. And given the changing needs of IT and an increasingly complex market, the clarity a customer can provide is needed in our organization more than ever.

Yes, the customer has always been there, and in some cases IT organizations have appreciated the customer connection and have committed resources and time to developing this relationship and the priceless information it can bring us.

But this customer engagement and focus has not been common; it has not been a widely accepted model for how IT must work every day. Not at the level we are discussing here.

This is the change that must happen now, to reshape the future of IT and to unify IT and the business. As we will explore throughout this chapter, there are many different channels and models for how we create and then nurture the customer engagement, fueled by our healthy customer obsession. No two IT organizations are the same, so there is no single template for how we engage with our customers. So, we will explore some examples of how we move IT closer to the customer in ways that are easy to mobilize, easy to sustain, not disruptive to the organization, and done with some good common sense.

This engagement with the customer then pays back to us in so many ways that are natural and without requiring lots of effort or brute force. There is a wonderful momentum that gets created here and carries us forward with very little effort. It is not uncommon today for there to be some ambiguity or lack of focus in the requirements that are delivered to IT on behalf of the customer. Normally, these requirements have been collected and documented by people outside IT and then delivered to teams within IT when necessary. These requirements have in some cases been interpreted and documented two or three times before the final form reaches IT.

The result is the IT organization being one, two, or three levels removed from the source of these requirements, the customer. This model is common today and no fault of any organization.

But like so many other things today, this model is no longer acceptable, and a big change is in order.

This change will do many things to the benefit of IT and the organization, including bringing a much-needed clarity with regard to what clients need from the business and a model that is faster and more transparent, communicative, agile, and conducive to innovation. This change is not intended to imply that a passion for the customer was lacking in IT previously, as that is certainly not the case. What we do need to recognize is that by being some number of levels and people removed from the customer, IT was fundamentally challenged in achieving the level of engagement required with our customers that would result in a deeper level of understanding of customer needs and, with this, a fundamental mastery of priorities and the details of the requirements that will drive our development and delivery of both internal systems that allow the business to support our customers and the systems that touch customer directly.

For some, this direct engagement with customers across IT will seem crazy and problematic.

> *For others, we will understand that this is not only desirable but absolutely critical. It spawns a powerful mechanism if we are to truly transform IT and fundamentally change how we think and act every day while at the same time creating a new model for how IT partners with the business.*

Look closely and I believe you will see there is no other way to elevate and unify the IT organization of the next ten years, thereby creating an organization that is equipped for the next twenty-five years.

FIRST AND LAST

A natural cycle occurs when any IT organization identifies the need for a solution or system and then works toward the final delivery to this need. This cycle can take many different forms, and it does today, but we now begin to understand that there can be only one "first" in this cycle, and that is the customer. And there can be only one acceptable "last" in this cycle, which brings us back to the customer.

It is no coincidence that the first element and the last element of any process are the two most influential in the process.

Yes, the customer has been present in some cases in this cycle of definition and fulfillment, but the role the customer plays in most cases was not the focus of our efforts.

As the primary catalyst for IT and the business,
there is no better place for the customer
than here. This is our natural beginning.

The customer can provide real and clear descriptions of a new service or system or possibly a new technology that is required to better meet their needs. In the past IT has sometimes received these definitions after they were originally received by another organization. The information is then interpreted and passed through several steps and transitions until it reaches the IT organization. As with most things today, there are good reasons for this flow of information, but this process does not provide the necessary focus on the customer or the necessary understanding and clarity that IT must have around customer requirements. A depth of understanding is only possible with a firsthand view and with a dialogue that expands and clarifies any requirement that represents so much more than what can be captured in a document.

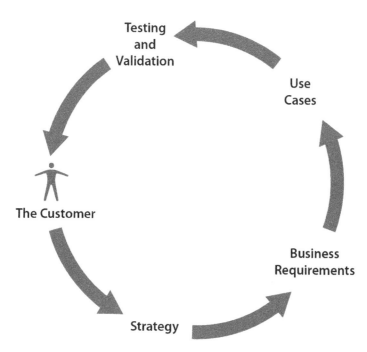

Figure 6.1 The Customer Is First and Last

So, a change is needed, and now more than ever, IT must have the vivid understanding of customer needs, how those needs are changing, and the in-depth insight that is only possible with a direct and open engagement and dialogue with our customers. There is simply no substitute for this model, and it is not possible to further delay making this change in our processes.

> *Extending this wonderful cycle further, while*
> *the customer is the first step in the process*
> *and the very best trigger for action across*
> *IT, the customer must also be the last as the*
> *best and ultimate validation of a solution.*

Sometimes we can lose our way in the final execution of delivering new solutions, updating existing solutions and anything that allows us to serve our customers. As with the beginning of the customer cycle where IT must be closely engaged, the completion of the solution cycle is only possible with the same customer closeness and the engagement of IT.

This brings us full circle and creates a process that is continually renewed and validated by the customer. We will find that customers are all too happy to be engaged in this process and will immediately add value to any effort. I often hear people hesitate in contacting a customer to request some form of communication, feedback, or discussion as they are concerned about asking a customer for their time and being perceived as an inconvenience or worse yet a burden.

Nothing could be further from the truth.

> *My experience has been that customers*
> *are eager to become more involved with*
> *the organizations that are providing*
> *solutions to their business in any form.*

It is the rare exception that a customer would not welcome the opportunity to communicate and work more closely with anybody in the business who values their views and insights, and this is certainly the case with the IT organization. Not the norm certainly, but customers have a natural desire to get close to the "technical people" in the organization, and we will find them to be willing and enthusiastic partners.

It will become increasingly clear that this customer model of first and last is the only model that is timeless and will naturally steer our actions every day to the best possible conclusion—a happy and loyal customer. A successful customer. A customer who appreciates the value our organization can deliver. A customer who recognizes a strategic partner over just another vendor.

Put another way, we look to the customer to initiate the process to deliver a new or updated solution or system and then to have the final say in the success of the same solution or system. Of course, the journey from start to finish should also engage the customer in order to avoid any misunderstandings or confusion in the final stages. Think of customer engagement as constant and transparent. With this goal in mind, we are far more likely to be successful. What exactly this model should be will vary from organization to organization depending on many factors, including industry, size, delivery timeline, budget, and resource availability.

A good way to craft the right model for your organization is to speak with the customers who will be participating in the process. Discuss your goals for their involvement, their goals for participating, and you will quickly converge around a model that works for everybody.

Customers have great ideas, and we only need to be willing to hear them.

Then, with this common understanding, we can get to work and accelerate toward what is likely to be a successful result.

DIRECT ENGAGEMENT

Once we fully understand the value and unique insight a customer can bring to the processes of IT, we then move quickly to create an engagement model that will provide the framework for how the work with our customers can move forward.

This process should include the following fundamentals:

Direct customer engagement

Frequent communications

Complete transparency

Respect for the customer's time

Opportunity for the customer to network with other customers

Careful management of the customer's expectations

Flexibility in how the customer participates in our process

Documentation of key customer feedback

Early preview of work product

Real-world test cases to validate customer solutions or systems

There are likely other elements as well, but this is a good start. It is important to remember that customer participation is valuable to us, absolutely critical to our future success, and as such it should be managed and respected accordingly.

A clarification is needed here. I am not suggesting that IT strike out on its own to create this customer engagement model. That would make no sense and would be disruptive to the business.

Figure 6.2 Direct Customer Engagement

We want to create this engagement with customers by leveraging the existing relationships we have across our Sales, Marketing, Account Management, Technical Support and Services organizations. By leveraging any of the customer-facing organizations any way we can. In most cases we will have existing relationships with these customers, and we want to leverage those relationships while expanding the partnership even further.

The engagement of IT can come in many forms, including:

Joining regularly scheduled conference calls

Participating in customer training events

Joining a customer on-site meeting

Participating in customer appreciation or other social events

Attending customer conferences

Helping with customer escalations and helping any way we can

Joining a planned customer visit to your corporate offices

There are many great opportunities to be part of the discussion and to join in the process going forward. Remember, this is about further extending the IT understanding of customer needs in order to improve the systems and solutions that indirectly support our customers and those that might be used directly by these same customers.

> *This is not about anybody failing to do their job well or trying to fix something that is broken— this is simply about us getting better, about our business improving and evolving, and IT helping to drive the partnership forward.*

The colleagues of IT in these customer-facing organizations will normally be happy to have IT join in, particularly when we can bring specific knowledge and expertise to the process. This is part of the value IT can bring and what the customer will naturally appreciate and recognize.

Once our IT people have established a relationship with the customer, it gets a bit easier. We can request additional calls, clarifications, information, and the like. This is the fun part—having a natural and ongoing dialogue with the customer—a dialogue that is good for everybody. The customer will come back to us with questions too, so this will certainly not be a one-sided discussion.

This open dialogue then creates the opportunity for a virtually unlimited number of possibilities in how we take the relationship and partnership forward. Brainstorming sessions, exchanges of ideas, early previews of possible solutions, prototyping, and much more that both support the customer engagement and enrich our commitment to innovation. There is so much that becomes possible when we put the customer at the center of our processes.

Any IT process that was run internally focused with little or no customer involvement previously will be immediately transformed when the customer voice is added.

COMMUNICATION & TRANSPARENCY

There are partnerships and then there are partnerships. A true partnership is built with honesty, integrity, and commitment. From the very beginning, the engagement of IT with the customer will be modeled around a true partnership. Nothing less will do, and we should expect and demand nothing less of ourselves.

The dedication of IT to a true partnership with the customer is very much in line with how we work across our own business, and it all originates with our focus on the customer. Really, the model of internal work should be designed after how we work with our customers, and a key element of this partnership is open communication and transparency. This fundamental principle is what builds trust and delivers on our commitment every day.

Great communications are not complicated and, if anything, should be simple and natural. A frequent and informative communication model with customers works well because it is simple, easy to live with, and practical. Simpler is better and more often makes things better still. This makes communications less burdensome for IT to deliver over time and to be consistent in delivering to this model every day.

*Large, complex, and formal communications
tools, like reports, long conference calls,
and long debriefs, are increasingly
challenging and they just don't work.*

This communications model takes time and precious resources and can be expensive and inflexible. It is far better to have a short chat or send a short email or even a short message when updates make sense. Think in terms of how we work with our colleagues across the business. Think in terms of how we communicate with those we feel we have a close working relationship with. These communications find a natural pattern and in most cases are more frequent and more informal.

We are often in touch and share information openly, and so the risk of outdated information, confusion, or a long silence all but goes away. This model is a good one and more and more how we get business done.

*Fast and simple is a good model for many
things in the future of IT as we are discovering,
and communication is no exception.*

This is a good place to start, but at the same time we need to recognize that every customer will have preferences, and we need to discover what works best for them.

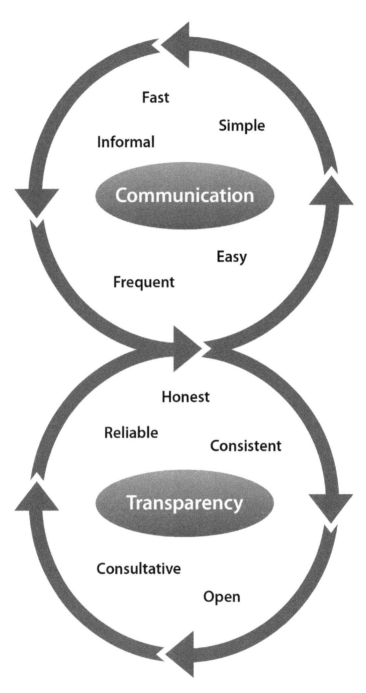

Figure 6.3 The New Communications Model

It might be that weekly updates include a ten- to fifteen-minute call providing the necessary information to track progress on projects and initiatives where a customer is engaged currently. Then at other times when activity is high, this schedule might be expanded to include a couple of calls per week and a supplementary email describing key milestones.

Video calls can be another useful tool if some sharing of visual information makes sense, including software demonstrations or screening of prototypes. We can also use video call technology to have whiteboard discussions for more sharing of ideas. It can be anything really and there are no right or wrong answers here. Communication tools will continue to improve and give us options for how we work together without the need to sit in the same room. There are times, however, when face-to-face makes a lot of sense. It's a personal touch that will never leave us completely.

This is all about what works for your IT organization and the customers you are building a partnership with. It's an easy discussion to have, and customers will be very clear on what they prefer and how you can build an effective communications mechanism. Listen to what they share, and from this we can build the right model.

> *Transparency is an important element*
> *in our communications. Open sharing of*
> *all information is a good goal to have.*

In virtually every case we should share with our customer as we would share with our colleagues in the business.

This is good news and bad news alike. Customers will appreciate the quick sharing of any challenges or setbacks, and although there will be some natural disappointment, this will quickly go away and we will find the customer focused on working with us to meet the challenge. And in most cases the customer's assistance will be valuable. It will be faster and easier to find solutions with assistance from our customer than without their support.

There is another important consideration to the sharing of bad news with customers that goes beyond getting their help in finding a solution to any challenge. The open sharing of bad news will build trust and strengthen the partnership. It is only natural that we hesitate to share bad news; after all, this is not easy. But when we do, the customer will instantly recognize this important gesture and will appreciate the honesty. A small thing perhaps, but very important nonetheless.

This is an important reality in our focus on the customer, in building a strong and important partnership, and in bringing IT together and closer to the customer.

There is simply no path to customer success
without good communications and transparency.

USE CASES

It is important to take our communications and daily work with customers beyond the high-level discussion of goals, business needs, roadmaps, and the like. This is certainly important but there is another level of detail that brings us a more in-depth understanding of customer requirements.

Specific examples of how a customer will use a solution delivered by IT—we will call them use cases here—can help bring customer requirements to life.

> *These use cases provide a vivid illustration*
> *of exactly how a solution or system or tool*
> *can help a customer in their daily work.*

Sometimes the written word on requirements does not quite provide the detailed understanding we need. There is a level of ambiguity here that is hard to overcome—just a natural risk in relying on written requirements exclusively.

Customer use cases are a great source of information and a living reference for IT and the full business. They can help bring insight and understanding into the daily work of the customer like few other things can.

This is the reality of how our customers use our solutions. They bring clarity to the full development process and the life cycle of a system.

There is more good news—we will find that customers are eager and happy to provide these use cases, and they'll recognize the value and assistance they bring to the partnership. While it can often be a challenge to write up and document detailed customer requirements, use cases are more natural and quicker to capture. Use cases can be shown in video recording or live as a person or team is working, or we can use an IT business analyst or liaison (more on this later) to observe or sit with the customer to capture the use case. These can also be done in a whiteboard session, with some simple language and a few diagrams to fully capture the flow and information around the use case.

The key here is that the use case is a very natural and efficient vehicle to capture the customer need. It is not an easy discussion to have when we begin with a question along the lines of "What are your key business requirements?"

> *It is far more productive to simply ask the customer about the work they do every day and to show us a few examples of their key tasks and deliverables.*

Because this is the fabric of the customer's business, the work that is performed every day, it is right there in front of us. No need to create something new, document requirements, or create something that might or might not be useful. It is also difficult to ask a customer to step away from their daily work to create this documentation or description.

Customers enjoy showing what they do and how they get their job done, so it does not take much convincing for them to share. Even better, they appreciate our interest and recognize this is yet another way to strengthen and deepen the partnership. I have been fortunate to be part of many such sessions and can't recall a single time a customer pushed back on sharing, nor a single time when this sharing occurred that the IT team did not learn a lot from the session. These exchanges are invariably productive and enlightening.

Just a few use cases are all we need to get started. A combination of simple language and a visual aid is a good start, but when this is not possible, drop the language and focus on diagrams or a video as the primary reference. We can then ask for more information or discuss clarifications with the customer later.

In some cases IT will be improving an existing system, and in others IT will be replacing an outdated or inadequate system or a manual process. Each of these situations can benefit from the sharing of the use case. Remember, this is about how the customer gets their job done today, and the extension of this discussion is how we improve their work, allow them to take a meaningful step forward, and perform better than ever.

> *While engaged in this discussion, it's important to start with today and create a solid foundation of understanding there, but then look at the future. A horizon of twelve to twenty-four months is reasonable.*

What new requirements are coming? What changes do we foresee in the business? What new business initiatives are being launched next year? Is the business anticipating possible mergers or acquisitions? M&A activity is common in many industries, and this activity has an immediate and significant impact on IT. This is a good scenario to discuss with the client. Is growth expected? Significant new hiring? Just a few simple questions to get the discussion flowing, and it will take a natural course.

In all exchanges with a customer, it is very
important to remember to listen. We can learn
so much if only we are committed to listening.

Some have called listening an endangered skill, and it's a good point. We need to listen far more than we talk in any customer meeting. I will make this point repeatedly because it is a case of a small thing we can change today and one that pays back to us in so many ways in the future.

Use cases then become a great reference both to jump-start our delivery cycle but also when the need arises to validate and test our systems and solutions. There is no better testing resource than customer use cases. This is, after all, exactly how our systems and solutions will be used every day by real people in a real business. QA professionals are very good at creating test cases and scenarios on behalf of our customers, but make no mistake—there is no substitute for the real thing. Use cases directly from the customer are as good as it gets.

We can't go too far astray with a good set of use cases and illustrations from a customer.

COMMUNITY

The relationship between the business and the customer is important, even vital. With IT joining and extending this relationship, both the business and IT will get better, and the customer will benefit from both the extended relationship and what is likely to be an improved product. A more targeted and valuable solution is likely to result from the enhanced partnership.

But there is another relationship here that needs to be created, really a network of relationships. These are the interactions and communications and sharing of information between customers. This is very important to most customers as they recognize the sharing can result in important learning and potential time savings when implementing best practices and business processes that other customers have completed.

> *There is an immediate interest and appreciation in making these introductions between and encouraging the interactions of customers. Customers enjoy sharing with the people of IT and will be equally eager to share with other customers.*

Don't think for a minute that as a facilitator we need to provide any meaningful oversight here. It's just not necessary. All that is required is a simple introduction and then the customers will take the discussion forward and agree on the best way to work together. If anything, we don't want to get in the way. Customers are very good about sorting this out and are naturally respectful of each other's time.

Customers can bring some valuable real-world experience to the relationship along with lessons learned, what worked well, and common mistakes to avoid. This can bring great insight to a discussion with other customers. It is then often true that both customers will contribute something to the exchange, and often both customers have experiences and insights to share that help the other. We all understand this is a journey, and many other organizations are on the same journey, albeit at a different stage. So it is possible that another organization has completed a stage of the journey a different customer is about to embark on. This insight is tremendously valuable when it can be shared.

> *Extending the circle further, the sharing between customers goes beyond what occurs with any two customers—a community is formed that consists of many customers, and the sharing grows and grows.*

It is possible, for example, for a customer team to offer some experience, some best practice insight, or some process design to the full community and not just to a single other customer. Yes, the two-party sharing is part of the community, but we can also encourage customer-to-community sharing.

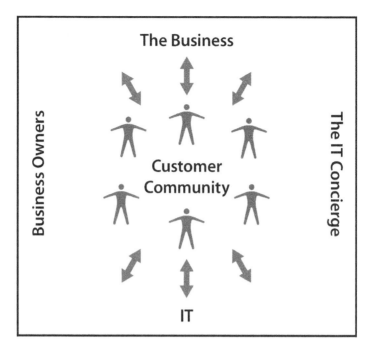

Figure 6.4 The Customer Community

Each case of sharing and communicating between any member of the community and the rest of the community builds the bond further and motivates other customers to share. With each case of contribution to the community, the bond of the community is stronger and the pull to contribute something on the part of every customer grows.

This is a wonderful model, a powerful model, and one that grows without boundaries. Sharing can include tools or technologies that have been developed by one member of the community and then shared for the common good. This can also include business process design, best practices applied to a business model, strategies that worked well, new innovations, and more. With this broader scope of sharing, others share in kind and the scope and value grow.

As a business and as an IT organization, we can form and encourage this community. One key here is not simply waiting for the sales or marketing organizations to create and expand this community. If the customer community is in place today, IT can get involved and bring additional options and content to the users. It is good to focus on content and technology that customers will find valuable, content that is not readily available from other sources.

IT might be perceived as an unlikely contributor to the community, but that should not discourage us.

We might even get some resistance in the beginning. But the community values expertise, knowledge, technology, and content, and IT can bring all of this to the cause.

In many ways this is the ultimate value in the work we do with our customers. We increasingly value knowledge, experience, domain expertise, and advanced skills of any kind. Sharing of this knowledge will be greatly valued by customers of every type. Taking this a step further, the community will only survive and succeed if we are able to contribute meaningful and valuable resources, and so IT can add something to the process. This could include discussions and previews of new systems and solutions, creative and innovative approaches to real business problems, showcases of new and unique customer uses of products and systems, new types of use cases, technology training as a unique community offering, reviews of product roadmaps, and so much more.

It only takes a little time and resource to get a community started, and then the community grows quickly, and we have helped to create something wonderful.

Don't underestimate the boost IT can
provide to this growth and nurturing. We
need more of this sense of community in
every segment of every market today.

Finally, a sense of community will help to bring IT together, to unite IT in all we do, and this extends further into the business. The role of IT in this community can help to bring the much-needed glue to the unity we are creating for IT as the catalyst and then the business. This can bring the community closer to everything we do, and then in turn bring the business closer to the community, which is valuable for all involved and a shining light we need more of today.

INCENTIVES & RECOGNITION

People respond to and appreciate recognition in any form. Everybody is busy today, and there is so much pressure on the business, along with a dramatic quickening of the cadence of IT and the business. Sometimes we forget to take the time to recognize the good work done by our people.

Recognition only takes a minute and does not carry a cost, so this is where we can begin. It's fully under our control and something we can do every day. Recognition can be for any good thing done during the day; we should make it a priority, and then a natural part of our routine. Managers can be good role models and set the example for recognition. There is no such thing as too much recognition. Good things happen every day, and although we can't recognize every one, some of these should be called out and shared with teammates and management. This is a lot of fun and helps to create a healthy culture. People see this happening and want to be part of it in either offering the recognition or being on the other side of it and being recognized for doing well.

Among all the things we can do to be recognized
on any given day, there is nothing better
than doing good work with a customer.

This stands above all else. So, when praise and recognition are being given, it won't always be for work directly with a customer, and that is okay. But when the recognition is related to a customer, we make a little bigger fuss. People will notice and they will remember. This is a fantastic way to set the tone—set a powerful example in what we do every day.

> *Another element of recognition and a great enhancer to our culture is to deflect praise. Most good results in IT and in the business are created through the efforts of more than one person.*

As any individual receiving praise, always take a moment to turn the light of recognition onto others, taking a good thing and making it into something even better and bigger. Never miss the opportunity to recognize others, to share the great work that others have done, and to never be outdone in the recognition that comes your way. If anything, when you receive praise for a good deed, double the praise to others. It is always there—it could be praise for a manager for selecting a person for the assignment, for having confidence in a person to put them onto a key project, or for teammates who were instrumental in getting a good result.

There are so many good stories to be told when IT has success. This is important and, even more, it is fun. There are always heroes behind the scenes when good things happen in the business and, even more importantly, when a customer success happens.

> *Recognizing teammates builds a healthier culture, builds respect across teammates and across teams, and makes our people trust one another.*

The next success is more likely because our people are focused on all the right things and know their efforts will be rewarded. This is a wonderful culture to be part of—a culture that renews itself and is healthy in the daily thoughts and actions it takes. This is a lifestyle.

Although we should never underestimate recognition alone, we further focus on and support the right results with customers by creating incentives and compensation plan structures that monetarily reward our people for delivering results with our customers. We have likely all witnessed the power of a comp plan—few things will get the attention of our good people in IT like compensation and bonuses attached to the right plans, the right priorities, the right daily work, the right activities, and the right results. There must always be an element of results for our incentives, as this underscores the importance of real results that are tied to the business. Another dimension to incentives and comp plans is that we must ensure this does not stand alone. While it clearly motives our teams, and people are naturally driven by the fundamental needs of a paycheck and the opportunity to earn even more, the value of simple recognition remains.

> ### There is tremendous leverage in recognition and pay working together.

When we do both, great results are likely to follow. This should be the plan: Making a shift in our culture and our daily work to increase our focus on the customer but to then back that up with an increased focus on recognizing people and teams when they do a good service for a customer or create a good result. It's a beginning we can create quickly because it is fully under our control and something we can start tomorrow. This is the first leg. Then, when the next cycle of reviews and merit increases comes, we want to take the opportunity to put incentives in place where possible, tied to deliverables and metrics that are directly customer-related. This can be anything because every business is different. Sometimes it's easier to get these bonuses approved than to get salary increases approved, but either one works well. Both are best when that can be done. But regardless of the form this takes, we want to begin a shift of compensation from the standard structure we have today in IT to one that is more focused on customer-related performance.

It bears saying again in closing that both recognition and mone-tary reward further support and accelerate our obsession with the customer. This improves the daily work and quality of life of our people, which in turn improves employee satisfaction, employee tenure, morale, teamwork, and changes our culture.

Of course, it all helps bring IT and the business closer together.

> *This customer model and all of its natural dimensions helps to create the singularity that is our future in IT and in the business.*

This is the single greatest force to create One IT.

THE SINGULARITY OF IT

The normal motion of IT has us focused on many goals and deliverables every day that are almost always driven by function or organizational teams, and we are very much focused on these tactical objectives to the exclusion of all else. There are exceptions and some exceptional organizations, but make no mistake—this is the norm. These teams and the talented and dedicated people that make up the team are hardworking and capable people. A tactical focus on a number of function-specific objectives is not intended to be a criticism but rather a simple description of how IT works today. These functional elements can also be called silos, as they often are, and the tactical objectives are normally driven by a daily or weekly cadence of what can be delivered during these windows.

This model is what it is, but does not move us closer to the singularity and unity we must have for the future of IT. We can get better at completing these tasks and the work product they create through better people, better technology, and better processes, and each of these is certainly within our reach. But while this might bring us some incremental improvements, it does not create the strategic shift that will separate leading IT organizations in the future from all others. For this to be possible, these organizations that stand alone will be successful in shifting from the traditional tactical lifestyle to a strategic focus—one that goes hand in hand with a singularity of purpose across IT and brings all of our teams in line with a number of trans-IT priorities. This shift requires a different level of focus and a new cultural alignment that affects everything we do.

This new focus can only be the customer.
The powerful and unique force that
can bring the singularity of focus to
all of IT can only be the customer.

The customer(s) we serve are something we all share across IT, the true origin of all our efforts and all the systems, all the tools and technologies we utilize every day.

The previous elements of this chapter include some of the specifics changes and actions we can take to increase our focus on the customer, and all of these make a difference. It all begins with something very simple—recognizing the special place the customer holds in the IT organization and in our circle of business, and then making a commitment beginning with IT leadership and extending through every team and every individual across IT to move our daily attention to the customer and channel our passion and energy to this same customer.

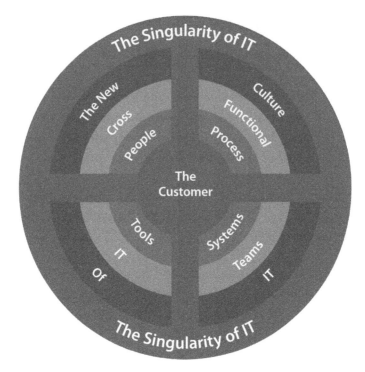

Figure 6.5 The Singularity of IT

This is the beginning, a fundamental shift of our mindset and attention. It is the only possible beginning.

This wonderful cycle then begins to change virtually everything, and as the powerful cycle began with a simple thought, it ends with an equally powerful result—a unified IT brought together through this singular focus that was our beginning. Focusing on the customer unites all our teams in IT because it creates a new priority that occupies the highest level in our daily planning and daily work. This does not imply that the many priorities and deliverables we have today go away. They certainly don't. But what does happen is that we now have a clear context that reaches across every organization in IT and brings a new level of clarity, including PMO, Datacenter, Security, Compliance, Service Desk, Endpoints, Servers, and more.

The local focus and priorities that have driven our daily work, very much focused on the function, are now re-qualified within the customer-first model. When there might have been some disconnected activity or even confusion before, we can now better qualify the use of our time and resources every day across IT. A focus on the customer now creates a fundamental set of questions that help us improve our focus, clarify our priorities, and sharpen our investment. These questions include:

> *How does this effort benefit our customers?*
>
> *Do we have a good understanding of customer requirements?*
>
> *Have we established metrics to validate the expected result?*
>
> *What is the level of risk with this investment?*
>
> *Can we get customer feedback through the process?*
>
> *Do we have a good understanding of the investment itself and the delivery timeline?*

Your organization will have many more good questions that allow us to self-monitor and self-govern our IT investments to maximize the value to our customers. Some of this is not new, but what is likely new is framing the evaluation and selection of these investments in terms of the customer. This will create a shift throughout the process, although some of the fundamentals won't change because there is a consistent element to the IT projects of the past and the projects of the future.

Focusing on the customer from the beginning of any systems or solutions or technology project across IT will have benefits beyond the project itself.

*This creates a powerful and common
thread that binds all our work together.*

Consistency and singularity are created, which is the only future of IT, and a model and momentum are built that will influence and then change the business. The customer provides the purpose, clarity, and singularity we need every day in IT, and this singularity naturally spreads to everything we do in the business.

An energizing force is created here that once again only the customer can provide, because this is our single source of truth and is the benefit of transforming IT into the organization it has strived to be but in most cases could not achieve—an organization that is strategically focused and proactive in mobilizing our resources to better serve the current and future needs of the customer.

*With this simple model and joined with the
needs and success of our customer, there are no
limits to the value IT can deliver in the future.*

CHAPTER 7

BUSINESS PROCESS DESIGN

In order to unify IT and the business, a critical element of our daily execution must be cleansed and redesigned—our business processes. It is natural and therefore common that business processes have been structured over time to reflect the organizational structure of largely independent silos. This creates a number of challenges that must be overcome and recognized as no longer acceptable.

Some of these challenges include:

Segmented business processes along organizational structure

A high number of integrations or queues

Delays designed into the process

A high degree of manual work

Unnecessary work tasks and approvals

Poor visibility across multiple and related processes

Low level of automation

Processes designed with little to no consideration of speed of completion

Specialized tasks with few if any consumers

A high degree of complexity

Little or no consideration of scalability

Integrations that are problematic to modify or upgrade

Reliance on legacy tools and technologies

Obsolete deliverables

These challenges were not created in a blitz of poor design but rather slowly, over many years and likely many transitions of people and teams. Processes evolve as business needs change, and changes are then made quickly and cheaply to meet the immediate needs of the business with little or no thoughtful design for the future. This is not a limitation of our good people but is due to time pressures, lack of resources, and lack of advanced tools to support these same business processes. We simply made the changes needed at the time as quickly as possible and then moved forward.

This natural evolution, step by step, has occurred in IT organizations globally for the past thirty years. Some organizations have begun to make the necessary changes, and certainly some good work has been done over the past five to ten years, but these organizations are the exception, not the norm.

Today, we are fortunate to have a better understanding of a Strategic IT, more experienced staff, vastly improved tools, dramatically more powerful technology, and the recognition of the vital role technology and IT play in the organization. You might be thinking this recognition has not reached your organization, but that, too, is changing. All of these considerations and the powerful forces of global markets are colliding and creating a fundamentally different IT and business.

There are many implications of these forces of change, including how IT executes its work every day, which brings us to the backbone of execution across IT—our business processes and business rules. This is the structure and pattern IT follows every day.

> *Given the convergence of all these factors and the implications for IT, the time is right to carefully review all the business processes of IT. Every element of every process must be reviewed, evaluated, debated, and carefully vetted.*

This work is long overdue, and it is likely this new business process foundation we create will operate for the next ten years and beyond, so we need to get it right. It is likely this is the age, if not longer, of many of the business processes in place today—a reminder of the longevity of the business processes we create.

Yet another consideration in the redesign of our business processes is the increased use of automation and AI in the next five to ten years. This creates another important driver in our careful updating and improvement of all business processes and business rules in that many of these will be captured by automation and intelligent technology. When that occurs, they need to reflect our current and best thinking.

> *It is unacceptable to automate any business process that contains obsolete decision making, approvals, or tasks. This is a waste of time and resource and can result in slowing down the daily work of IT, or worse yet, making the wrong decisions or executing work that is unnecessary.*

This raises the stakes even further and brings more attention to the need to improve and cleanse all the workflows and business processes across IT. This chapter will take a look at a number of principles and activities that will help us to get there.

CRITICAL REVIEW

The responsibility to review the business processes, business rules, and workflows of IT falls on IT itself. The people of IT know these things best and are best qualified to conduct this review in a way that looks deeply and carefully at every task and every minute of our time commitment to daily work. This is a review of everything that drives the operations of IT every day.

> *There is an important principle behind this review—it is fundamentally necessary that IT embraces the idea of conducting this review of our business processes, and that IT is proactive in then conducting this review proactively and within IT.*

There is so much at stake and so many implications to this review, we can't wait to be directed to conduct this work, and we should not blindly trust an outside organization to come in and conduct this review for us. There are many organizations that provide this service, but I'm convinced this is not the time and the place. An outside consultant or an agency, while no doubt qualified and with good experience, does not know the business the way we do and does not know or understand the current state of IT and all its nuances the way we do. This is a time to leverage our most knowledgeable and most talented thinkers in IT to drive this review. It won't be easy, but with this organic work, we can mobilize quickly, leverage our own people for the review, and fully own the results and next steps.

> *We are identifying our own problems*
> *and developing solutions, all of which we*
> *can fully own and take accountability for.*
> *This is a vital element to our review.*

IT driving IT forward and wholly defining a new generation of business process.

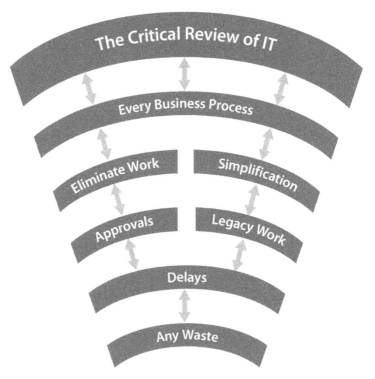

Figure 7.1 Critical Review of IT by IT

If there is a strong desire or even mandate to leverage outside consultants, as driven by executive leadership, or the need to leverage a specific expertise, for example, another option for IT is to conduct the first review iteration internally. This will normally yield significant results and allow IT to address some of the big issues straight away and get these solutions in place. The review can be done quickly with cross-functional teams and demonstrate progress quickly. It's a great opportunity to leverage our experts who know the current business process, technologies, and systems of IT best. This then is connected to business requirements, and the combination yields our new and improved business process.

Remember, the scope of this review is every business process in IT that is performed on a regular basis, as improving these processes will give us an immediate return. If it is necessary to further prioritize, look at the top tier of the high-volume business processes and then look at strategic business and mission critical processes. These workflows directly impact the business, enable revenue, or affect customers.

Many of these business processes are executed frequently, sometimes many times per day, so any improvements will provide this value back to the business immediately.

The top improvements we are looking for are:

Elimination of tasks or approvals

Simplification wherever possible

Retirement of a full business process—this is critical

Automation of highly manual work

Elimination of any manual approvals

Elimination of any obsolete deliverables in any form

Simplification or elimination of any legacy business processes

In most IT organizations, many of these improvements are possible when we take the time to conduct the review with these goals in mind.

It is helpful to have a cross-functional team of our experienced IT staff conduct the review because they might identify improvements or ask questions that had not been brought to light before. For example, a security business process designed and operated by the security organization should be reviewed by experts from other organizations, including the server team, the service desk team, and the compliance team. Likewise, the security organization should be a reviewer on the business processes for these organizations, and so a matrix of review is constructed: a careful and in-depth review where everything is questioned and anything that is not clear is discussed and debated. Any elements of the business processes that survive will have the benefit of this thorough vetting, and we can be confident we now have a stronger and more efficient model for the business processes going forward.

With this we have a clean model on which to begin or continue our efforts at automation, leveraging AI, and the use of other strategic and intelligent technologies. This is only possible and a good use of our resources if this critical review, this cross-functional review with our most experienced and skilled people, has been completed.

Organizations that leap directly to employing these strategic technologies without conducting this internal review will discover that we are automating waste, inefficiencies, and unnecessary work. This is a terrible waste of time and a terrible waste of our precious resources. Then it is necessary to backtrack when we discover the business processes were not healthy or ready for automation, AI, and more. This is a big setback for the business. So the review should happen as soon as possible, and then we can proceed with the important automation and AI initiatives.

These strategic technologies will play an important role in the future of IT, and we can't afford to do anything less than maximizing their value.

Remember, this review of all business processes is for IT, by IT, and through IT. This sets the tone for so much more in the future, and the connections to a unified IT are inescapable.

THE VALUE OF SPEED

A few themes will dominate our thinking as we approach the review and refinement of the business processes across IT, and one of these is speed. It's important to understand the "why" of this business process review and to connect our improvements to outcomes that will improve the performance of IT. In many cases this improvement will be significant and in a few cases strategic. The impact of speed to IT and to the business should not be underestimated. The role of speed grows and becomes a strategic asset to the business in terms of how we serve existing customers and win new customers.

This is the very lifeblood of the organization and our future.

As global markets produce a remarkable array of products in virtually every market segment, products become more commoditized, and consumers are left to evaluate the value of any product or service in new, broader terms. Other things begin to matter much more.

These new priorities will include quality,
which has a timeless appeal and will always
have a place in the market. And speed rises.

We begin to take note of the speed with which a product or service is delivered to us and in a manner that meets our fundamental requirements. This speed expectation is growing today due to powerful mobile devices, social media, online purchasing, and so much more. Information is increasingly everywhere, and always at our fingertips when we need it. This is the impatient and distracted mindset of today's customer. With this, we are left to increasingly appreciate how speed can be a fundamental game changer. In a business that leverages technology and systems to serve customers as most businesses do today, the ability to drive improved speed is very much about IT.

> **The speed, or lack thereof, created
> in IT is the throttle for the speed at
> which the business will run.**

This is both a big responsibility for the good people of IT and at the same time an exciting opportunity—an opportunity we must embrace, because today so much is possible. Virtually anything is within reach with a good strategy, talented and dedicated people, and passion. So as we work through our business process review, it helps to have a yardstick with which to measure existing processes and potential improvements. We need to look for potential speed improvements, as every possible elapsed time improvement is important.

Think of this as squeezing every second from each task and from each business process. As I have mentioned elsewhere in the book, never underestimate the importance of a second. Taken in isolation we might write off a second as not making a difference. But it does, it makes a big difference. First, the mindset of *every second counts* will affect how we see everything and our commitment to be thoughtful and rigorous in all our reviews. If we are focused on finding every second of savings, then we will. Secondly, as we begin to remove seconds and minutes from our daily work and business processes, we realize that the seconds add up quickly. Soon we have hours, and then hours become days, and we have arrived at significant time savings. We got there one small step at a time.

Speed has a cousin in simplicity, as
simple things tend to be faster, more
efficient, and more scalable.

We will look at simplicity in a following section, but it is good to remember that as we crawl through every task and every business process in IT, we are always on the watch for an opportunity to simplify and to increase our speed. This is strategic and this is powerful—a big boost to IT and to the full business.

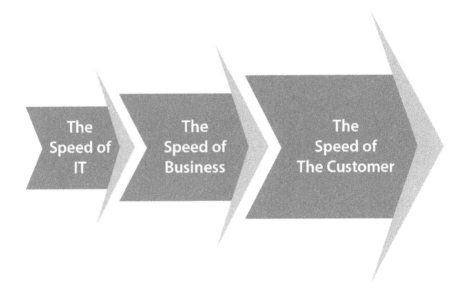

Figure 7.2 The Value of Speed

In some cases, the current speed improvement will make the next improvement possible when it was not previously. Every speed improvement clears the way for further leaps forward, and each improvement, each step of accelerating the work we do every day in IT, has a wide circle of influences across the business. As our improved speed gathers, people in IT will begin to notice that what took a day previously is now done in an hour. What took a week before now takes only a few hours. What took half a day before is now done in twenty minutes. People will notice. People will recognize this extra time we have now received back is a priceless opportunity to work and think differently. For so many years, we did not have the time to think. What a wonderful and powerful thing that freedom can be.

As this work is completed more quickly in IT, the impact and influence of speed quickly spread to the business. Then each of the compressed business processes in IT begins to clear the way for work being completed more quickly in the business.

> *This chain of dependencies exists in every organization, and as our systems execute more quickly and our tasks and business processes are completed in a fraction of the time, the pace of the business quickens in virtually every way.*

Another remarkable thing happens as this speed builds in the business. We can now bring this speed to our customers.

The products and services an organization delivers to its customers, whatever that might be, can now be delivered more quickly, because the powerful chain of actions and systems that enable this delivery, that enable customer fulfillment, are now moving so much faster, we can pass the very best of speed onto the customer. This changes everything.

Now, customers begin to notice a new cadence in the business and naturally recognize the value this brings, cultivating customer loyalty and customer appreciation, and improving the competitive position of the organization in the market.

This powerful and boundless chain of value was created by the speed improvements made in IT. We need to constantly remind our teams in IT of the impact these refinements in speed will have on the business and of these powerful connections to our customers. Some of our teams will not understand or appreciate these linkages, and so we need to help them see the impact.

This understanding of the customer linkage then helps build our commitment and focus on continuing with the improvements and brings us back to the search for every precious second.

SIMPLE

Simple is a wonderful and powerful concept, in virtually any context, and it certainly has an important place in the unification of IT.

Simple is elegant.

Simple is refined.

Simple tends to be naturally fast.

Simple is timeless.

Simple is easy to understand.

Simple lends itself to reliability.

Simple is easy to learn.

Simple is inherently scalable.

Simple is naturally efficient.

This is only the beginning of the wonderful attributes of simplicity, and so it makes the strategy of *simple* easier to appreciate.

As we embark upon this journey of reviewing and improving the business processes of IT, simplicity is an important goal to keep. For every task, business rule, and business process we review, simplifying the work and streamlining the process will pay big dividends. If we reflect on the strategic goals of this business process review, it becomes clear they are very much in line with the goals of IT, and this in itself says a lot. Our tasks and in particular our business processes are the daily heartbeat of IT. The execution of these workflows bring life to the organization and deliver a service and create work products that allow the organization to function and to be productive. The goal of *simple* then enhances every business process; the process itself is improved and at the same time prepares IT for the important work that lies ahead. This includes automation, improved velocity for IT, and the use of intelligent technology. All of these important initiatives are disabled by complexity. Existing complexity can paralyze IT and the teams or people who are working to deliver what is required across IT every day.

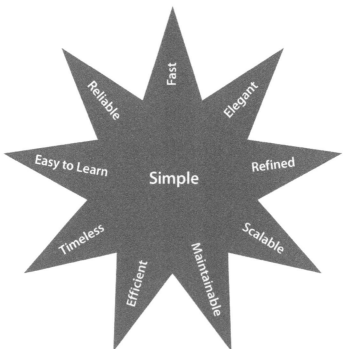

Figure 7.3 The Power of Simplicity

I address complexity in other chapters of the book, as it requires some attention, but we should recognize now that every case of complexity should be carefully examined. The removal of complexity is an assist in meeting our goals of what can ultimately be great simplicity. Where we find complexity in any form—business rules or a process that is difficult to understand and execute consistently—we must make every effort to convert this complexity into something that is simple and at the same time accomplishes what is required. A good way to describe this is turning complexity upside down. Our goal is not to just reduce the complexity, but rather to convert what is currently complex into something very different by turning complexity upside down and converting a unit of work or a stream of work into something simple yet powerful.

> *The opportunity to make this important*
> *conversion from complex to simple is*
> *everywhere and a wonderful source of*
> *energy and velocity for all of IT.*

Remember, there are so many linkages—countless linkages between the work and systems of IT and the business—that any improvement made virtually anywhere across IT will be a boost to the business.

With regard to the goal of *simple*, a few questions we should ask as we inspect any task or business process would include:

> *How can we make this work more simple?*

> *Is there any unnecessary work being executed?*

> *Is it possible to eliminate any steps in a multi-step process?*

> *Is any segment of the work difficult to understand or difficult to execute consistently?*

Has any element of the work proven to be unreliable?

Is it possible to eliminate any dependency on specialized skills or tools?

Is it possible to eliminate any element of work that is problematic to upgrade?

Is there an element of the work for which the cost can be reduced?

Is any segment of the work difficult to automate and how can this be addressed?

Are there segments of the process that can be completed in less time?

What we learn is that the characteristics of *simple* are very much complementary to reducing cost, improving speed, improving reliability, and preparing for the important initiative of automation.

> ***Lest you question the benefits of simple,***
> ***we are reminded of just how much value***
> ***this brings us, today and in the future.***

NATURAL BEGINNING TO NATURAL END

With every business process across IT, there is a fundamental structure that must be understood. This understanding helps to guide our design of improved business processes and aligns a business process—the work and tools that support the business—with the true business requirement that must be fulfilled.

In order to create this alignment, it is necessary to look beyond the current structure of the business process or workflow and find and then recognize that the current model of the business process might not match up directly with what the natural beginning and end of the real business need truly is. The evolution of the business process is often misaligned with the natural flow of work in order to utilize technology or tools or to recognize organizational structures along with the expertise of our people.

> *These organizational and technology limitations sometimes result in a business process being fragmented or separated into pieces that are more aligned with the limits of a technology or the structure of an organization.*

This is an artificial yet very common structure, and while it is understandable to a degree, it must be overcome as we perform the business process design. Misalignments slow us down and create complexity, cost, and additional work.

> *There always exists a natural beginning,*
> *or trigger, for the business process.*

Work is initiated based on a need, a circumstance, or a request. The work required to meet this need then commences and is executed until it reaches some conclusion. What IT needs to identify is this business trigger, and then trace the work sequence until it comes to a full end.

This is the *fulfillment* of the original need or request.

The full sequence of tasks then becomes the true and only definition of the business process. It should be fully natural and uninterrupted. This then aligns the work we do, including any technology or tools we utilize in order to complete the business process, with the business itself. Fully in synch with the business requirement. There should be no gaps, delays, or detours in getting this completed.

> *Unnatural barriers slow us down and*
> *create a headwind for the business that*
> *is of our own creation and, as we come*
> *to realize, fully under our control.*

When we recognize that many of these business processes are completed repeatedly, in some cases hundreds or thousands of times per year, it is easy to appreciate that having any segmentation or gaps of these business processes creates a costly overhead and tax that is a terrible burden on IT.

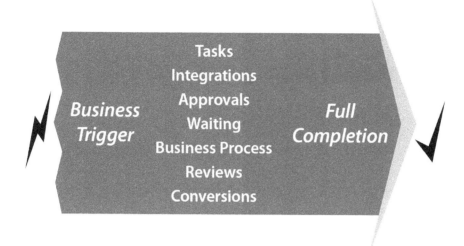

Figure 7.4 The Model of Natural Beginning to Natural End

This exists in every IT organization today to one degree or another.

> *The mission of IT is to find these natural triggers*
> *and natural completions to each business*
> *process and to then realign our work and tools*
> *to mirror the natural flow of the business.*

Herein lies something tremendously powerful.

Imagine the boost we provide the business by removing all the noise and clutter and extra work that is currently blocking our path in completing this work in the most natural and streamlined manner.

A few examples of this overhead in the business processes of today:

Integrations between systems

Waiting times

Handoffs between teams

Unnecessary manual approvals

Data conversions and translations

These examples are typical of what we are looking for and very much in need of the meticulous inspection of IT. Every living case of these examples should be carefully reviewed and validated and eliminated, improved or simplified. Each of these improvements then moves us closer to our natural and most uninhibited flow of work.

Not unlike a garden hose that has been twisted, we are simply trying to create a free-flowing business supported by streamlined and natural business processes.

> **The natural flow of work not only brings our work, tools, and technologies in harmony with the business, but will also naturally increase our speed, reduce costs, and reduce the risk of service interruption.**

All of these things are poison to the business, and the cleansing is best driven by the good people of IT. Now is the time, and IT is the organization to drive this rejuvenating and empowering change across the business.

AUTOMATION

Automation has the ability to transform our execution of business processes and as such the daily rhythm of IT like few other things can.

The time for a true focus on automation has come, made possible by a few converging factors that have accelerated the real value automation is capable of delivering to the organization.

These factors include:

> *Automation tools have improved dramatically in the past five years.*

> *Automation naturally supports our focus on serving the customer.*

> *Automation is uniquely capable of advancing our focus on speed.*

> *AI will naturally follow and complement our investment in automation.*

> *The demand for 24X7 operations is directly enabled by automation.*

Automation can free our people to focus on a Strategic IT.

The drive to a proactive IT is only possible with automation.

Thoughtful automation naturally creates scalability.

A high level of consistent execution is enabled with automation.

With this simple summary, it is easy to see how automation can be a strategic force in the future of IT.

Yes, we will see automation appear repeatedly throughout the book in several contexts because it is simply unavoidable—automation is one of the pillars of the transformation and unification of IT.

> **Only a select few things occupy this group of strategic influencers, with two being a focus on customer and a new culture for IT. I enjoy discussing these things, and they are certainly central to our discussion.**

We are in the midst of creating a relentless search for leverage across IT, and automation is capable of creating this. It's one of only a few things, including AI perhaps, that can create true leverage across IT over the next decade. When we do find these opportunities for leverage, it is important to double-down our investments in these areas in order to accelerate our progress and help shift IT from a tactical lifestyle to one that is strategic.

> **The evolution of IT will tend to follow the path of our investments, and if we simply invest in the things that make us a little better, the things that are obvious, if you will, we continue to evolve slowly and keep the current fabric of IT intact.**

But if we seek and find the investments that create leverage and then focus on these investments, we create a new path to a proactive and strategic IT. Automation can help to get us there and should be one of the top two to three investment areas for IT over the next five years. This merits a review of your current IT investment priorities.

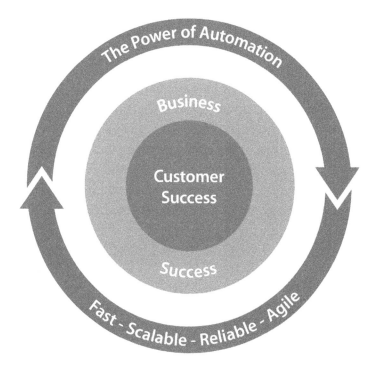

Figure 7.5 The Wonder of Automation

Ask your organization if these investments are tactical or strategic. Do they create leverage for the IT organization and for the business? This process never stops, and it helps to sharpen our strategy and our focus, leading us methodically through the journey that lies ahead.

This is another example, in the context of automation, of what will naturally unify IT and then unify the business. We are simply building a model that is focused on customer success, speed, and agility, and this both addresses the current and future needs of the business while at the same time slowly but surely brings the teams of IT together and united around the common cause of these strategic business initiatives and business needs. With this focus, our teams will find a way. The good people of IT only need to have a refreshed set of goals and objectives, and the forces of good begin to work and create the powerful pull to bring our people together.

As we review business processes and begin to systematically implement automation tools along with improved applications and then inevitably intelligent technology, we focus on these results and lose sight of any traditional structures or boundaries that at the time might have seemed important and even natural. But now, focused on business requirements and with the shining light of the customer, all our teams are pulled together, step by step, closer and closer, until all of IT is fully united—with our eyes on the prize of the customer and the success of the business, which quickly brings us back to the success of the customer.

> *With the focus on success and on real results,*
> *we are able to build lasting change and a new*
> *unified model for IT and for the business.*

Not magic, just hard work, with our relentless passion in IT on the right things. Streamlined and faster business processes buoyed by automation are just one thread, albeit an important one, that helps to carry us there.

COMPLEXITY IS POISON

Throughout the themes we develop in the book, we repeatedly visit a core set of powerful ideas and strategies that will help to drive IT forward through our transformation and toward a unified IT and business. While it is important and fun to discuss these wonderful things that propel IT into the future, it is no less important to discuss the risks that can keep us from reaching our goals, from realizing the exciting future of IT.

> **We must understand and identify the things**
> **that steal our time, create risk, and sap**
> **our energy. This is complexity in action.**

One of these risks, one of the truly dangerous things that stand in our way on the journey to the future of IT, is complexity. As the section title indicates, it is not much of a stretch to call complexity a poison—a powerful poison that can exist everywhere across IT and certainly exists in virtually every IT organization today. With awareness comes an improved focus and determination, and in this case we're raising the awareness of IT to the dangerous properties and implications of complexity living within IT.

Complexity can take many forms and shapes, but is ultimately about tasks or processes that exceed in scope what is necessary to achieve the desired outcome. Another form of complexity is tasks or processes designed for requirements of the past that no longer hold true, and as such, even business processes that were right-sized in the past are often now out of alignment with current requirements.

When we refer to being out of alignment in the context of complexity, it is in reference to any work that fits the following simple profile:

Unnecessary work

Overly intricate processes

Any work that is difficult to understand

Tasks that are difficult to complete with the desired result

Processes that are difficult to perform training on

Systems that are not able to be upgraded

Systems that require specialized (and expensive) skills to maintain

Processes that can't readily be explained to others

Systems that require a high level of upkeep

Processes that are slow to complete

Systems that are difficult to change

Systems that are unable to scale

Although these examples have some differences, they share the common characteristic of creating risk and cost in the business. Both of these things are bad, exactly the opposite of what we are trying to create for the future of IT.

Risk is unacceptable for many reasons, including the additional challenge of making it more difficult for IT to move quickly, and risk creates a distraction that takes us away from more strategic work. What we find is that managing risk continually pulls us away from the strategic agenda that should be our full focus. This simply is not possible when we are surrounded with risk that demands our constant attention.

> *The good news is that we now have a review of all business processes on the new agenda for IT, and this is the perfect opportunity to inspect for complexity and address it immediately.*

Ideally, the process or system that is clearly holding complexity can be eliminated or retired entirely. We will discover this is possible in some cases, perhaps legacy systems with no clear support for current IT and business initiatives or limited support for current systems that are clearly on the decline. This trajectory should always be noted when inspecting systems or processes—is the fit for this item with the future of IT growing stronger or weaker? If the trajectory is negative, the system or process is a good candidate to be retired. Taking this a step further, it is likely these examples with a negative trajectory will also meet our criteria for complexity. It is a natural relationship.

At the same time, those systems that display the attributes of *simple* are likely to show a positive trajectory and are increasingly valuable to the business. These are the systems and processes on which we should double-down.

If it is not possible to eliminate the process or system entirely, then we need to focus on a significant simplification. This will transform the system or business process from something that is creating risk and cost and slowing us down into a system that supports increased speed in the business, reduced cost, increased leverage, and improved scalability. These are the natural qualities of simplicity that are all but impossible with complexity. But if we are able to carefully inspect and then update and simplify a currently complex system or process, we have made a wise investment in the future of IT, and what was complex before has been realigned into something very different and very good.

One more note on this process—some complex systems or processes that we try to save, that we try to simplify, will be discovered to hold other problems, and simplification won't be possible without a great deal of time and cost. This is not common but it does happen.

> *In these cases, where we discover the*
> *process or system just can't be simplified*
> *and changed to meet our new profile, it*
> *is best to get a clean start and replace*
> *the system or create a new process.*

In the end, this will cost less money and take less time, and we will get a better result. Be sure to recognize when this case is in front of you and don't simply continue to pour more time and resource into something that is fundamentally ill-equipped for the future of IT.

Our business process review brings us the perfect and timely opportunity to find every case of complexity and then simplify if the system or process can successfully be realigned, and when it cannot then quickly shift into building a new, cleaner, and more agile replacement.

CHAPTER 8

IT BUSINESS MANAGEMENT

A new role will emerge across IT in the years ahead as we navigate the transformation and unification of IT. This new role is inevitable as it closely complements the evolving strategy and execution of IT. For the purposes of this discussion, I will call this role IT Business Management as it captures the unique place this role will take in the organization. The ultimate title in your organization might be different, but the mission of the role and its makeup will likely be very similar.

The purpose of the IT Business Management role encompasses the following:

A mix of technology expertise and business acumen

A good communicator

A liaison across IT and with the business

Works directly with key business owners

Engages directly with customers

Discusses and develops IT strategy with the CIO and VPs of IT

Communicates and enriches IT strategy to and with the IT organization

Is a key driver in the innovation efforts of IT

Owns key IT deliverables and IT budgets

Is active in the market as an advocate of IT

A nontraditional IT mix of skills but with strong technology experience

Similar to the traditional role of product manager in marketing/development

Considered to be a key leadership role in IT

Supports both inbound and outbound activities

Helps to unify the many teams of IT

Represents IT in key business planning sessions

This is just the beginning of the exciting role this position occupies in the business and in IT.

Note that this position is equally comfortable driving a technology or systems discussion as a discussion on business requirements and market needs. As this is not a common combination of skills, filling this role will not be easy.

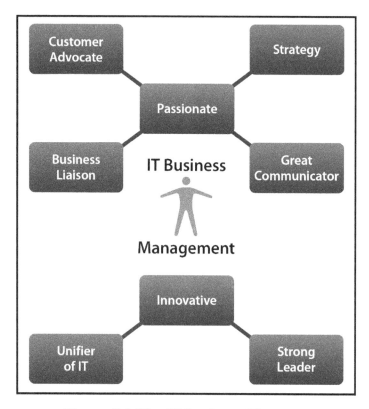

Figure 8.1 The IT Business Manager

But this is to be expected, and as this role will have a high degree of visibility and a strategic and diverse set of responsibilities, these individuals will be exceptional performers with a very diverse set of skills. An individual we are prepared to invest in, now and in the future.

In some cases we will look outside the organization for this hire, by using a backfill position, for example, but redefining the role. Another possibility is promoting a talented existing staff member in IT who has demonstrated the ability to deliver results, has earned the respect of their teammates and IT leadership, and possesses this unique combination of skills. It is also possible that as IT becomes a more desirable organization to be a part of, this role can be filled by a transfer or promotion from another department outside IT.

> *All scenarios are good for different reasons.*
> *It is important to bring new skills and*
> *new ideas, a fresh view, into IT as it has a*
> *positive impact on the culture and on the*
> *capabilities of IT. At the same time, it's also*
> *good to promote and develop from within.*

This creates a much-needed career path within IT and will help retain our most talented people and increase the options for growth within IT. Many IT organizations are struggling with retention and with visible and exciting career path options. Unfortunately, this can lead to our best and most talented people leaving—precisely the people we need to retain to help drive the transformation of IT.

We must recognize that this role brings us a multitude of benefits, including the impact the role itself will have on IT and on the business every day.

IT Business Management is precisely capable of nurturing our partnership with the business, unifying IT, and creating the working model that will ultimately unify the business.

It will quickly become natural to add more of these roles across IT and to task them with driving key IT initiatives, facilitating the innovation programs across IT, partnering with and aligning the daily work of IT with the business, and then creating and managing our customer connections.

> *The good people of IT will recognize this is*
> *fundamentally good and want to be part of it.*

NEW SKILLS

New skills are a priority in the future of IT, beginning with an awareness that IT must add these skills to the organization and then develop a plan to deliver on this awareness. These skills can be developed in our existing people and targeted in new hires. It is unlikely we can reach our goal of adding these new skills with just one approach or the other.

A collection of expanded skills continues to drive the transformation of IT and enable our organization to deliver on the strategies that are forming now. A strategy is the beginning, but it must be supported and brought to life by people and teams who can deliver the daily work that brings the strategy to life.

A few examples of the new skills in IT include:

Communications

Creative and design

Customer-facing

Systems and tools requirements

Budgeting and financial management

IT Service Portfolio management

Business case development

Cloud and related operations

AI and intelligent technology

Automation design and deployment

This is not a complete list, but it's a good start. Note the mix of skills related to strategic technology, including AI and automation as well as new skills focused on running IT more like a business in the beginning and then more like a strategic business.

There should not be any confusion here about the technology elements in the context of IT Business Management, as this raises an important point.

> **The IT Business Management role itself includes many of these skills and will also be tasked with driving the nurturing of these skills in IT today as well as bringing new people and new skills into IT in the future.**

These new people can be transfers from the business as IT becomes a more desirable organization to join (yes, it will happen) as well as new employees from outside the company with the right mix of skills.

Figure 8.2 The New Skills of IT

Why would this responsibility of nurturing new skills fall to IT Business Management? Because our IT business managers will be responsible for a mix of many things, all of which make IT and the business stronger, and this is only one example. The boundaries for this role are largely removed because the charter reaches from end to end across IT and then naturally extends into the business. The IT business managers will recognize the value of a more diverse culture, a broader set of skills, and what these improvements will bring to IT and the business. This is very much in line with the mindset of driving a strategy and then all the actions necessary to transform IT and to influence and then unify the business. We must empower the IT business managers to think strategically every day about the success of the business and the success of our customers.

Strategy and focus are the right place to start, and then we work our way back into IT.

*We will discuss this point further later in
the book—the concept of inside-out thinking
versus outside-in thinking across IT.*

A very big difference exists between the two. Inside-out thinking has been the traditional model of IT and has focused on the tactical operations of IT every day, with limited connections to the business and very little if any direct engagement with customers. This is a simple statement of our past and is in clear contrast with the new mindset of outside-in thinking, which creates a beginning in the market and with customers, and then creates processes that work from this origin back into IT. The beginning sets our context and goals for all our actions.

*Put another way, this changes our
grounding from one of technology and
systems and tactical operations to one of
market awareness, customer engagement,
clear strategy, and business results.*

It's a cultural shift along with the shift in how we work every day, and it demands a new set of skills and new roles to emerge across IT.

This recognition then brings us back to IT Business Management, which is but one example, although certainly an important example, of how this new model comes to life across IT and then makes it possible to drive the business alignment and unity that is our future.

BUSINESS CASES

Business cases are a healthy practice that encourages and drives a more complete and more business-focused approach to IT investments. This creates many good results, including:

Business cases might very well be in use in IT today, but this is just the beginning. Financial management for ITSM, for example, is growing in usage but is often limited to the service management practice. We are recommending the standard use of business cases for all major new IT initiatives and investments, accompanied by a cross-functional review with a cross-functional team makeup. This creates a number of new and healthy behaviors, including a more complete risk and benefit assessment, a much-needed sense of accountability to deliver the expected results, and improved communications around expectations with IT leadership and the operations teams of IT.

Most IT professionals today would agree that we are working to run IT more like a complete business from top to bottom, and this is simply another step forward.

It is also important to recognize that we need a role to drive this process, and it is a natural for IT business management or its equivalent. This small team of talented people can help change the culture of IT and validate the value of this important role.

This process creates a wonderful and healthy set of discussions and due-diligence practices across IT as teams prepare to form and then bring to review the business case for a new project, initiative, or investment of any kind.

The cross-functional review process is important because we want to drive a strong discussion, a spirited debate where needed, and a thoughtful and detailed review of the business case.

> **It should be known across IT that these reviews are not easy and require careful preparation.**

Naturally we begin to focus our investments on the stronger cases, those with the best risk-to-benefit ratio, with those teams that are the best prepared and with the best plan for success. There should be a level of healthy competition for the resources of IT. These resources are precious, and our investments of resource should ultimately go where they will have the biggest impact and to a team that is fully accountable and prepared to drive IT and the business.

This is a naturally powerful and transformative process.

For example, we are training our people to plan better, to prepare better, to be more complete in considering the benefits and risks of an investment, to weigh one potential investment against another, and to prepare a business case where the business elements are as important as the technology elements and maybe even more so.

All of this is creating a process that will naturally shift our thinking from a mindset that is dominated by technology, tools, and systems today to one that recognizes business considerations as equal to the elements related to technology.

The business case discipline drives these behaviors from day one.

When we begin to require business cases for new phases of exist-ing investments or net new investments, our people take notice immediately. They will get the point very quickly, especially when required to bring a business case to a review with their peers. Remember, the peer part of this review is important because we want the benefit of the cross-functional review and different per-spectives in the room for the benefit of vetting the business case itself. But we also want other key people in the room in order to witness the process itself, to reinforce the right priorities along with what *not* to do in a business case review. People, especially our best people, will pick this up quickly, and the quality of the business cases will improve dramatically in a short period of time. This is exactly what we want to drive—better business cases will translate to better investments and better outcomes. This extends even further into improved communications across the organiza-tion as well as improved accountability.

You are likely noting a pattern here:
building good business practices
and a shift in culture across IT.

This is precisely one of the outcomes we are attempting to drive and one that is much needed in IT—all facilitated through this pro-cess of business case review and the IT business managers.

PEER REVIEWS

The previous discussion on business cases touched on peer reviews, which in itself is an important process, so let's take a closer look. There is a great deal of good in conducting discussions and planning with key people across the organization. It improves the quality of our planning process, as we are getting the benefit of the experience and insights of our most experienced and talented people, but it also builds a sense of team and a stronger culture.

Our colleagues are able to help us all get better, to plan more effectively, and to then execute more effectively. There is a strong desire in all of us to do our very best work for our teammates. They are counting on us, and we know IT is counting on us. We discover that we can do things for our teammates that we might not normally feel driven to do for ourselves. There is another dynamic here, and that is compelling role modeling that happens amongst peers. Our people quickly take note of the very best work being done by our teammates, and we are naturally drawn to perform at this same level. But if these ideas, strategies, and plans are not shared broadly, they can't have the influence that is so important to building a strong culture.

Visibility and sharing help us in so many ways; they are completely organic to the organization and fully under our control.

With this realization, we just need to create the right forum and opportunity for sharing and reviews to take place.

A good way to start is by implementing the requirement for business cases in support of all new IT investments over a reasonable cost threshold. We then assign a small team to create the business case and name a leader to this cross-functional team. The team is then given a reasonable yet aggressive schedule to create the business case and to then bring the business case to a peer review. These reviews should be done on a regular schedule—monthly is about right—and a few business cases will be on the agenda. Each review is given a time slot on the agenda, and we have a group presentation that includes those teams with a business case on the agenda and a few other key people with a good mix of experience and key roles in the organization. This is an awesome forum to be part of and one that will yield great results for the organization.

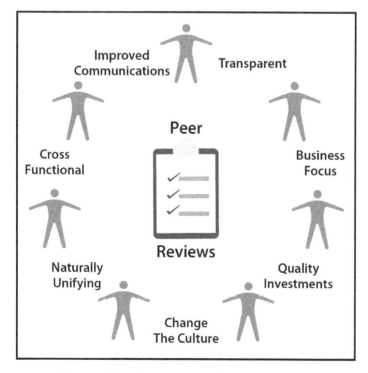

Figure 8.3 The Motion of Peer Reviews

An executive sponsor should be present at the reviews, but the majority of the discussion and debate will be driven by the peer group. People will appreciate being part of this and will ask great questions and help to flesh out and advance the business cases. This then builds a higher level of visibility and sharing, and we create a broader understanding of new projects in the IT roadmap, the directions we are taking with investments, and the underlying strategy driving our investments—creating a strong sense of buy-in for the transformation of IT and across all the teams of IT.

This helps to break down any silo-oriented nature of previous investments and helps us focus on the broader IT strategy, activity, and project mix.

We are using this forum to grow and encourage business owners who share the responsibility and leadership of the organization going forward.

When we discover an activity that directly supports several of our strategies, it is something we need to invest in. This is true leverage and very different than a typical activity that supports just one of our goals or strategies.

Peer reviews are an example of the former and a great example of a simple forum we can create quickly, one that is fully under our control and directly supports the following things that are important to the singularity and unification of IT.

Peer reviews:

Improve communications across the IT organization

Reinforce a focus on the business elements of IT

Demonstrate the characteristics of a sound business case

Enable cross-functional planning and execution across IT

Improve the quality of IT investments

Model best practices for defining risks and benefits for IT investments

Encourage open discussion and debate for IT investments

Bring a cross-functional review to key IT initiatives

Drive a shift in the culture of IT to one that is business-oriented

Create accountability for the teams that win approved investments

Encourage improved transparency for IT budgets

It is easy to see why the combination of business cases and peer reviews drives so much positive improvement across IT. These simple additions to the daily work of IT will improve so much of what we do and help to shape the culture of a unified IT.

PROACTIVE ENGAGEMENT

Proactively engaging with the business and with IT drives big results and, just as important, a big change in *perception*. The perception of how IT works and plans every day will improve dramatically with our engagement model shifting from reactive to proactive.

> **The little things matter. This is a case of getting
> just one step ahead of the daily rhythm of IT
> and of the business versus allowing our teams
> to stay in step with what is normal for IT.**

We can make this one-step-ahead model work with just a bit of commitment and planning. For this to be possible, IT Business Management must create both an active projects list and an initiative roadmap of the projects and investments expected to happen in the next twelve to twenty-four months. This list will change over time, but that is okay—what we need is a working list of what is expected to launch in IT in the future and then to help mobilize these initiatives and drive the next steps in planning and execution for these investments.

A few things to keep in mind:

> *IT Business Management should take ownership of creating
> the roadmap.*

Start with strategic initiatives and then add tactical projects if possible.

Be ready to drive new discussions and planning—this won't be natural to start.

Create a dialogue with IT leadership to shape the roadmap.

Openly communicate and share the initiative roadmap when available.

The initial scope should be IT but can then be expanded to the business.

Have the mindset of getting ahead of IT and the business.

Understand and accept there will be resistance to this new activity.

Welcome participation from the operations team across IT.

Design this process to be cross-functional from the beginning.

Drive and own the process from within IT but welcome the business to join.

Constantly ask about new investments and initiatives.

It is key to identify new projects and investments early, then drive them forward.

Communicate often with the CIO and VP IT.

Welcome feedback and comments from all teams

The tone of this roadmap effort should be open with frequent communications and cross-functional participation. It should be another platform for IT Business Management to drive good communications across IT, to shift our focus to more strategic activities, and to encourage and reinforce proactive work as a natural day-to-day model.

Remember, this is not the only track of proactive engagement, but it's a good example and a good activity that represents a platform that both helps IT and the business while at the same time reinforcing the proactive work that should occur every day across IT. We need to think in terms of everything we do both large and small that will unify IT and will also then be extended to unify the business. It should be rare that we create a new process or new program within IT that would then not directly benefit the business.

What is good for IT and One IT must then be good for the business and One Business.

We should not wait for the business and our colleagues that are key business owners to take these actions but see this as our responsibility in IT and we can be the agents of change and the leaders that IT and the business desperately needs. Don't wait, we should make this happen.

IT and the business are now inextricably linked into the future and much of what the business needs will rise from within IT.

Make no mistake—the organization might not have an active awareness of the need for the leadership of IT with this proactive engagement being only one example of this leadership but the need is there and it will only grow.

Desperately is a strong word, but it captures the reality of what is there inside the business and will only get stronger. Much stronger in fact.

We as IT professionals have this tremendous opportunity in front of us to reshape the future of IT, which brings the organization a stronger IT for the future of the business. A stronger business will then begin to take shape as the technology of IT becomes more strategic to the business and critical to the future success of the business.

BUSINESS AGILITY

Most would now agree that improved business agility is important to business survival and, more importantly, to business success. In a market with increased global competition, shorter product life cycles, our pervasive dependence on mobility, social media, ubiquitous information across our professional and personal lives, and an increasingly impatient and demanding customer, agility is critical.

For those businesses that will emerge as the new market leaders over the next decade, agility is much more than something we would like to have. It is a fundamental element of the business model.

There are specific actions that must be taken to help create and then to drive business agility, and like many things that are important to the future of IT, there is often no explicit ownership of this strategy in IT today.

> **Yes, this strategic charter of agility within and beyond IT is another great fit for IT Business Management.**

Don't get too hung up on what we are calling this role. You can call it anything that makes sense in your organization, recognizing this is a new role that combines technology expertise with business understanding and great communications skills. This is a unique combination, but these skills do exist in some talented people, and this kind of person and leader is the right person to take the charter of agility forward.

Agility can naturally begin within IT as our technology and tools and systems are closely linked with our ability to be agile. While this is a good beginning and a natural place for us to start as an IT organization, all of this initial work should be done with an eye toward business agility. We should always ask, "How does this action enhance our IT agility and our business agility?" There might be actions we take to improve IT agility—for example, critical systems issues that should be addressed quickly and are more tactical in nature—that won't readily apply to the business. This is just the reality of the tradeoffs we might need to make in order to keep the business running.

> *But the preferred strategy should always be to make agility improvements that can be leveraged for both IT and for the business.*

One example of an agility improvement is enhancing the scalability of key business systems. This could include CRM, for example, or the ERP system. What are the implications of doubling the number of users for these systems? Are we able to open an office in a new country with the associated currency, tax, and language issues? How quickly can we enable this to occur today, and what changes can we make in our systems to support this action being compressed into a fraction of the time? These are very real challenges that happen every day in IT organizations and can either assist the business in accelerating forward or slow the business down. The key here is the fundamental ability of your IT organization to quickly and effectively address shifts in the market, shifts in the business, or new customer demands.

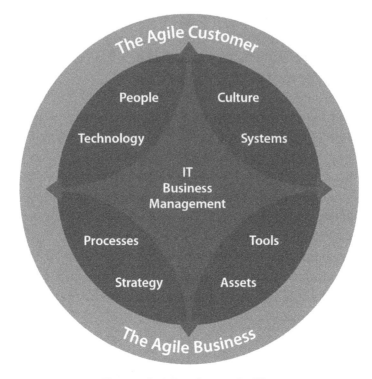

Figure 8.4 Business Agility

Note that we are using scalability here as but one example of improved agility for IT and the business, and so it is very much in support of the broader idea of agility. In this context, don't confuse the methodology of *agile* with our discussion on business agility. The former is something very specific, while the latter is a broader descriptive use of agility to mean many things we can do to improve the ability of a business to change and adapt to changing market conditions and new customer requirements.

Most IT organizations today would agree with the goal of improving IT agility and the broader goal of improving business agility. This is very likely on the roadmap for the CIO and VP IT. But at the same time it is a matter of the current ownership of that activity and a team chartered with driving this forward, creating a plan, and then leading the implementation of the plan. This is a great fit for IT Business Management as an activity that is strategic in nature, should work across all the teams of IT, and takes a strong commitment to communication and balancing the many priorities of IT while coordinating a broader effort with the business and key business owners.

> *It's not easy, but this is precisely the type of high-value initiative we should expect IT Business Management to own and drive.*

This is where this new role can have an immediate and visible impact and bring to life this important effort where it would likely lie dormant far into the future. A unique set of skills are required, and as these skills are not commonly available in IT today, it can serve as a very real and high-impact example of why we need the role of IT Business Management and where they can contribute quickly and have a real impact on IT and on the business. It could even be used as a proof point that bears watching and will bring some much-needed attention and validation to the rapidly expanding role of IT and the new talent this organization is attracting and mobilizing. This will surely get noticed and noticed quickly—another living example of the shift from reactive to proactive across IT and the increased focus on driving strategic IT initiatives for the greater good of the business.

Seems like a lot, but this is very achievable, courtesy of IT Business Management. Better yet, this is only the beginning.

CHAPTER 9

ELIMINATION OF WASTE

The organization of IT has grown and matured over the past thirty years. Much has changed in the world around us, and the dependency of today's business on technology and data has grown dramatically. As IT has moved forward and the nature of IT has changed to keep pace with the remarkable changes in the market and the global marketplace, there has been some accumulation of legacy systems, legacy tools, and legacy data: solutions created out of need at a given time and then taken forward over the years. In many cases, these systems have resulted in a potential waste of time and resources today.

Evolution and accumulation are simply natural and could be said of virtually any organization with a thirty-year history, but IT is somewhat unique in that there exists under our management a diverse collection of tools, technologies, and information. These things have a broad and growing scope for many organizations, and it is likely there has never been a focused review of every element herein to determine what makes sense today.

It is true these are very broad categories but a sample of the diverse portfolio IT must manage. Given the nature of this diversity, there is perhaps an even greater risk of outdated business processes, technologies, systems, tools, tasks, and data.

> *Note this includes the work that occurs*
> *around these tools and systems. This is just*
> *as important, perhaps even more in need of*
> *review than the systems and tools themselves.*

Each of these elements individually represents a number of historical requirements that are significant, but taken together the scope
is large, even enormous. As such, it is critical that we perform a
comprehensive, exhaustive, honest, and critical review of everything we have in IT. These broad categories address much of it but
are certainly not a complete list. But if we simply focus on business
processes, tasks, systems, and technologies, we have immediately
crafted a large scope that brings with it a great deal of what we
manage and the work that is conducted every day within IT.

> *This is a big effort, so where do we start? It*
> *helps to start with the business processes*
> *and tasks that are performed most*
> *often because they represent the biggest*
> *potential for time and resource savings.*

These can be simple processes or tasks or they can be complex
business processes with many steps. Either is okay. Identify the
work that is done most often, the business processes we are called
on in IT to execute most often, and begin here for our review and
careful evaluation of potential waste. This work is not simple or
easy but offers a huge potential value for the organization.

Create a working list of these targeted business processes and
tasks and then assign an owner to each and form a small cross-
functional team to conduct the review. Remember, we are looking

at absolutely everything in the process in order to identify work that can be eliminated, time that can be saved, and any simplification that is possible. It helps to give the team a targeted timeline within which to have the review completed and to then bring the recommendations back to a panel that includes the other operating teams conducting similar work. This sharing of information between teams is important and will help to improve the process and increase the speed at which we can complete this important work.

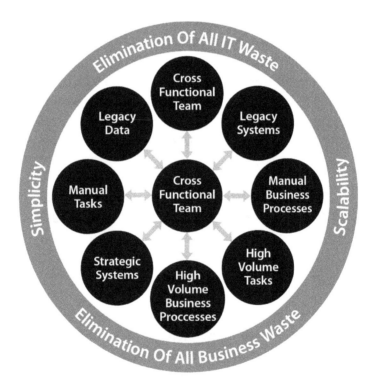

Figure 9.1 The Elimination of All Waste

Here is another case where we want to deploy a cross-functional team to conduct the work. It should not be a team formed within the same function, for example, a team from the security organization to review security business processes and tasks. This is a natural inclination, but it won't give us the complete and objective review that is necessary.

> *A cross-functional team will see this differently*
> *and bring a mix of perspectives and expertise*
> *to the review process and as such will be able*
> *to identify elements of potential savings and*
> *waste not possible with a single-function team.*

Our cross-functional team will also ask questions and probe into areas that would potentially go untouched with a single-function team. We need to create an important mindset and tone in order for the process to be successful.

Beyond the high-volume tasks and business processes, the next area we want to investigate involves what we would deem the strategic or high-visibility tasks and business processes. These might not be executed in high volumes, but they are widely regarded as the key work and high-impact work done across IT. These business processes and tasks often have strong visibility with the CFO, COO, or CEO. This is a natural and important extension to our list of investigation and review items.

> *Conduct the review of the high-volume*
> *business processes and tasks first so we*
> *have a chance to sharpen the process and*
> *apply some improvements and lessons*
> *learned for the process before moving on*
> *to the strategic business process list.*

These enhancements will help yield even more value and impact from the ongoing review.

Note that the business process and task review, with an eye for waste at all times, will naturally be connected to technologies, tools, and systems. It is important to take on a review of these systems as a necessary extension of the review. There is potentially great savings with these systems and in particular with legacy systems that are expensive or older. The best option is always the elimination of work or retirement of a legacy or specialized technology or system that no longer makes sense. It is very likely these systems have never been carefully reviewed or questioned, so now is the time for this critical vetting to take place.

No exceptions—every tool, every application, every system should be reviewed. Where the system in question can't be retired completely—and this is sometimes the case due to practical considerations, including the lead time required to execute such an action or to source a replacement system—we turn our attention to simplification and streamlining. Simplification alone offers big potential time and cost savings, in particular for the older systems, which in many cases have been operating in IT for ten to twenty years.

> *View this not as work that is undesirable*
> *or to be avoided (yes, this does happen) but*
> *rather a great opportunity to bring speed*
> *and value to the business. Always emphasize*
> *the magnitude of the opportunity.*

The more business processes and tasks operating and connected to technology and systems the better, as this brings us a more compelling upside. This work can be tedious in the beginning, but as we begin to see real savings in terms of both time and resource, our teams will receive encouragement and energy, and the momentum will build.

People will want to be part of this, and more and more ideas will come, driving further savings.

CLEANSING OF IT

The process by which we eliminate waste across IT should be thought of as a much-needed cleansing, which is not a bad thing. It is healthy and responsible. It is easier to understand this when we come back to the thirty- to forty-year history of IT in many organizations and this work has never been conducted in earnest. This calls to attention the support and focus we need for this review to be successful and quickly can lead us to conclude that it is in line with us being good stewards of the business and can offer big potential improvements and savings.

This cleansing is on two paths—both the review of our work in the form of business processes and tasks, as well as the technologies and systems of IT. Both of these elements need to be reviewed and questioned carefully and both offer big advancements. Remember, savings are not just about money and resources. Yes, these are important, but in the new measures of IT performance, time and speed are perhaps the most important of all. The good news is that this dimension of speed can be improved greatly in many organizations.

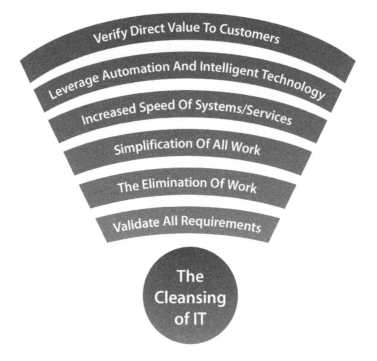

Figure 9.2 Our Cleansing of IT

For most IT organizations, this cleansing will bring us a speed improvement with the performance of our business processes and tasks of greater than 50 percent. For some organizations that are able to perform several iterations of this review—the recommended approach—it is possible to achieve up to a 90 percent reduction in the time required to execute the targeted business processes. As always, every organization is different and results will vary significantly from business to business, but these numbers are achievable and for some teams can be beat.

The process of cleansing IT is not magic. It is hard work and careful review of all the work that is performed every day, the technologies and systems we utilize to conduct this work, and the validation of all of this in the context of current customer and business requirements.

We clarify business and customer requirements because we also need to question any internal or IT-driven requirements. With regard to the questions we ask ourselves regarding internal requirements for the work performed by IT staff:

Is this requirement valid today?

Why exactly are we performing this work?

How does this internal requirement directly support our customers?

Can we eliminate this work altogether?

If not, can this work be simplified?

How can we complete this work more quickly?

What assumptions have we made about the deliverables?

Are all the deliverables absolutely necessary?

Can we identify the consumers of all the deliverables created?

Have we verified the work product with those people directly?

Is it possible to automate any of this work?

Are there any handoffs or waiting that can be eliminated?

Any manual approvals that can be eliminated?

Are there alternative approvals to prevent waiting on a primary approver?

This is tedious work that will take some time, but in virtually every business process or task inspected, we will be able to make improvements. Sometimes big, sometimes small, but even the small improvements add up and should not be underestimated.

The biggest possible return we can get on this review is the elimination of a business process or task completely. This always brings good savings and frees up the valuable time of our people. We will discover that some business processes were created to support a legacy business requirement that no longer exists or no longer makes sense. When we find these, it is a very important step forward for the business and is good in every respect. It saves people time, money, resource, and helps us to go faster.

When business processes or tasks can't be eliminated entirely, we then look at how they can be simplified or combined. Look for tasks that can be combined and achieve the needed results a little more efficiently, or business processes that can be reduced in scope. Again, this saves time and resource and improves our speed.

> *Every small improvement is making the business just a bit leaner, a bit more agile, and a bit faster. This is the essence of the future of IT.*

If we are not having some spirited debates through this review, then we are not looking closely or critically enough.

The cross-functional review teams should be questioning everything. And we need to be convinced the work being performed is truly needed and valuable. If that is not clear, we need to dig deeper and keep asking questions. We want to have the discussions and debates because we can't get the real improvements without them.

It's yet another reminder that we need our strongest thinkers in the cross-functional review teams, as this will bring us the best ideas and the toughest questions, and in the end we will know that we have squeezed every possible improvement out of our daily work and our systems. We will discuss the technologies and systems more in the following sections.

LEGACY SYSTEMS

Most organizations have some number of legacy systems. These can be older commercial systems or in-house developed systems that made sense at a given time for a given set of requirements. For the purposes of this discussion, we will define a legacy system as one that has been operating for ten or more years. Because technology has changed so much, the global marketplace has advanced, and the evolution of technology has accelerated, these legacy systems need to be evaluated in the context of the organization today. Equally important is looking at the current trajectory of the business and what demands will be placed on IT in the next ten years. We simply can't make investments that make sense today; we must make investments that are agile and scalable and will bring value back to the organization for the next decade and beyond.

As a track within our elimination of waste across IT, these systems must receive the same thoughtful and careful review, and each legacy system naturally represents a significant opportunity for savings and speed due to their very nature of being a legacy.

It's not that these legacy systems were poorly designed, managed, or operated, but so much has changed in the past ten-plus years, it would be very difficult to deploy a system then that could possibly meet the many new demands of the organization today. We might find that some of these systems have held up remarkably well, but we will also find some that have simply not been able to adapt to the current needs of IT and of the organization.

When reviewing legacy systems it is good to start where the biggest opportunities for improvement can be found: the most complex and costly systems. These might be systems with a large scope of functions, or they could be systems that require a number of admins and consultants to support and keep running. This could be either an in-house developed system or a commercial system, and in either case we are looking for the ability to retire the system altogether, as this always brings the best results, assuming the organization does not lose required capabilities. If retirement is not possible, the next objective is to greatly simplify the scope of the system to refocus it on the key requirements of today, recognizing that some expansion of systems over time is natural and some of the expansion in scope will not be necessary in the organization today. The following things are examples of questions to be asked and areas to be investigated:

Is the full system required by the business today?

Can other less costly systems replace the outputs of the system under review?

Are we able to verify each output/function of the system as required?   Is the system such that it can be upgraded as needed?

Is the system such that it is able to be enhanced quickly?

Does the organization have a less costly replacement available?

In the case of an in-house system, is there a superior and comparable commercial system available?

Are the users of the system happy with its performance?

Is IT able to verify the need for the capabilities/outputs of the system?

Do we understand the true total cost of ownership (TCO)?

With a true TCO defined, is this acceptable?

Does the system deliver the required benefits?

If retirement or replacement is not possible, how can the system be simplified?

Has the system been able to keep pace with the changing business?

Is the system generally regarded to be Agile?

Does this system have the ability to serve the organization well for the next ten years?

Does the system have the ability to scale as the organization grows?

Does the system have the ability to take on new requirements as the organization changes?

Does the system deliver acceptable speed of performance?

Is the system able to provide for a needed level of automation?

This is not intended to be a complete list but rather one to help get your review and investigation started. Your teams will no doubt have many more good questions, and once this process is begun and with the goal of a careful and complete review of the system, your good people are likely to get to the right answers.

> *With this, the organization can then plan for*
> *next steps and provide systems that are fit*
> *for the next ten years—a good and practical*
> *horizon to plan for—and systems that are agile,*
> *upgradable, and fast. This must be our blueprint.*

The same general approach and these same questions can be applied to both legacy commercial systems and in-house developed systems. Both are candidates for replacement, improvement, and simplification. Both should be subjected to the same careful review, with an understanding that the upside is very big for the organizations, and IT must assemble a portfolio of strong and capable systems for the future.

This is another case of fit for the new IT and for a unified IT and a unified business.

UPGRADABILITY

Upgradability is an often overlooked attribute in the systems of IT but a very important one. Systems that are difficult to upgrade, sometimes impossible to upgrade, represent a big risk and a big cost to the organization. In virtually every case, these systems also bring with them a growing amount of waste due to problems in upgrading. These things go hand in hand. With so much changing in the marketplace and with technology, it is important that our systems of IT are upgradable with little to no impact to the staff of IT.

This might seem to be common sense, but it is remarkable just how many systems are not designed to be upgraded or have been managed in such a way that they become difficult to upgrade. Both of these considerations should be understood so that IT places a priority on acquiring commercial systems that are strong with regard to upgradability and that we manage our systems in such a way that over time we don't compromise the ability of the system to be upgraded.

What does that mean exactly? It means that systems should be managed from day one in such a way that protects our ability to upgrade the systems over time. This includes a few things, most notably keeping up with system updates and maintenance releases.

It also includes avoiding any temptation, even driven by what is perceived to be an important current requirement, to modify, extend, or customize the system in such a way that it will potentially block a future upgrade.

This happens all the time. The IT organization might not realize the longer-term implications of customizing a commercial tool or software application. It is common and understandable to have a current business requirement surface, even one that is considered important to the business, and IT then modifies or customizes a commercial application to meet the immediate need with all the right intentions, without understanding it could later disable an upgrade or a series of upgrades. For many IT organizations this sets them on a path to live with a growing limitation and a growing problem in that the system will grow increasingly outdated, increasingly expensive, and less relevant and less valuable to the business.

It's a powerful cycle that is difficult to break and it exists in countless organizations: a commercial system that has diverged from the standard commercial path and has become increasingly difficult and expensive to maintain and non-agile. This is further exacerbated by the increasing pace of change in the business just when we find ourselves with a system or a number of systems that can't take advantage of the R&D efforts of the software vendor (software applications are a great example of this problem) and the many bug fixes and enhancements.

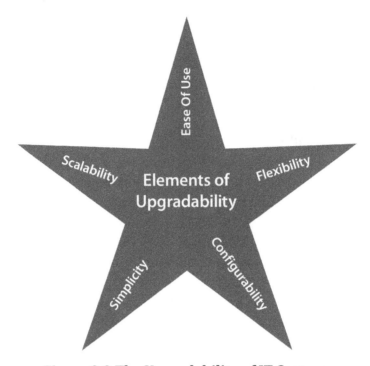

Figure 9.3 The Upgradability of IT Systems

Software applications show many of these characteristics, so we will look at this case more closely. Most IT organizations rely upon a portfolio of software applications to operate every day. This is no small matter and for most IT departments, the number of applications can exceed fifty. Some organizations have over one hundred unique software applications deployed. Each of these applications is sold and supported by software vendors who also dedicate R&D resources to improving these applications over time.

> *The ability of an IT organization to minimize the risk of legacy systems becoming a liability in the future begins with the original selection of the application.*

The flexibility of a software solution to take on new requirements

and to change over time should be a priority, as this is closely related to the path IT will take with this product in the years ahead
when it becomes necessary to make changes to the application
as driven by changes in the business. These changes in the business will bring new business requirements, which in turn will
translate into the need to update/modify/configure/extend the
software application(s) that directly supports the appropriate
business function.

It is common to have software applications in the IT portfolio that
are not flexible and not well-suited to making these changes. They
create little option but to customize or extend the system in such
a way that can compromise the ability to stay on the commercial
upgrade path and take advantage of new product enhancements,
patches, issues fixes, and other updates. What this does is create a slow growth of cost and a widening gap of system capabilities. Most software vendors, and all of the best vendors, have a
product roadmap that includes innovation and software improvements that greatly benefit clients.

It is beyond the scope of this book to explore this point in great
detail, as fun and interesting as that would be, but a real key here
that deserves mention is to elevate the importance of flexibility
and configurability in the selection of new software applications.

Not always a priority, this characteristic of software systems is
vital and has everything to do with the value and daily leverage
of the solution over the next ten years. There is a growing trend
in IT organizations to keep software solutions in place for longer periods of time to improve the return on these large investments, to bring more stability to daily operations, and to save the
organization precious time and resources. Evaluating, selecting,
and implementing software applications is time-consuming and
expensive.

The software systems that are highly flexible, configurable, and

scalable are likely to bring the most value over time and to provide a longer term of usefulness and business fit.

> *This high degree of upgradability then*
> *reduces our legacy systems' risk and cost*
> *and provides a core set of applications*
> *with long, useful lifetimes, likely several*
> *times that of traditional systems.*

This will become one of the key criteria in the selection of new software solutions for IT. Systems that are highly configurable, scalable,
and upgradable bring a higher level of value to IT and the broader
organization.

This awareness will then in turn reduce the risk of costly legacy
systems and extend the life cycle.

SCALABILITY

As IT professionals we should have a mindset of anticipating success, growth, and change, enabling us to get ahead of these issues and to be ready when change in whatever form it takes comes to IT. For those organizations not prepared for growth, when that time comes and we must scale the systems of IT, there is a high risk that problems will occur, and this impacts our ability to move forward... sometimes in small ways, often in very big ways.

IT should see this as an opportunity, and one that brings us back to some of our core strategy elements of working more strategically, more proactively, and to drive innovation across the business. There are a few simple questions we can ask ourselves that will set us on the path of being prepared for the changes that might come in the business and the numerous elements of growth that directly impact the systems of IT, including:

> *What is our overall grade for the scalability in IT today?*

> *What are the limitations of our critical systems (email, Internet, phone, ERP, payroll, CRM, order quoting and processing, for example)? This is where we begin.*

> *For mission critical systems, what is required to improve scalability to an acceptable level?*

In the event of rapid growth, through a merger or acquisition, for example, what limitations do our critical systems have today?

What is required to eliminate any hard limits on user counts and transaction volumes in our systems today?

What systems would fail if we increased usage or transactions by a factor of 2X, 5X, or 10X?

If we have anticipated failures at these scale thresholds, what does it take to remove the limitations?

Does IT have home-grown systems or legacy systems that are considered critical but with poor scalability?

Does IT have a backup or failover capability today for critical systems?

These simple questions will rapidly expand into an important evaluation of how IT can scale today and better prepare for the future. It is certainly normal for IT organizations today not to be in a high state of readiness for scalability. This is okay.

> **The key is to drive these scalability reviews now, under our own initiative, to create a plan to improve scalability for the future and to get ahead of any changes in the business that would drive increased scale. Worth saying again—it's critical we get ahead of this issue before it cripples the business.**

It is likely we can find some quick and effective improvements to be implemented in the short term. Take these quick wins because every scalability improvement will better prepare us for the future. Other improvements will take more time and more resources, and this is to be expected as well.

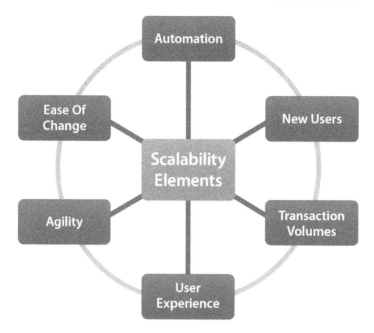

Figure 9.4 The Elements of Scalability

It might be necessary to have a two- to three-year roadmap for the scalability of IT and implemented in multiple phases during this time. This roadmap can take us from Poor today, which is very common, to Good or Excellent at the completion of the roadmap. This is a strategic investment for the business and very much within our reach.

> *We are touching on a simple and important relationship here—systems that are not able to scale effectively are creating waste for the future.*

These systems become the legacy systems of the future and will ultimately be rebuilt, redesigned, or completely replaced. Even some modest planning now for scalability can help to reduce this risk and ensure we have systems that can adapt to a changing and growing organization and continue to provide value.

Agility or the ability to accommodate changes in the business quickly and effectively along with scalability are two of the primary system characteristics that determine the useful life cycle of systems in general and in particular for software applications. As the business becomes more focused on increasing the useful life cycle of software applications from the current five to seven years to something more like ten to twelve years, agility and scalability have a great deal of influence over our ability to keep software applications useful further into the future.

Attempting to add scalability into systems that are in place and operating is difficult at best and expensive, so it is normally the case that systems have scalability designed in or they don't and making a fundamental change to this model is very challenging.

There are no secrets here, scalability is about some basic planning and focus at the beginning of the solution selection or build life cycle. With this focus on scalability as a key attribute of the system we are then drawn to enhance the characteristics of the system in the area of scalability and to ensure that scalability is a priority throughout the process of deploying a new system or working through an enhancement cycle for an existing system.

> *True scalability will normally come along*
> *with some other desirable attributes*
> *including a simpler user experience and*
> *a greater focus on the configurability of*
> *system automation and business rules.*

This combination will become increasingly important to organizations selecting new solutions in the future and will help create the longer system life cycle we discussed that will begin to exceed ten years for the best systems.

SPECIAL REQUIREMENTS

We will define special requirements as unique business work or systems that serve a small subset of the organization. This could include requirements associated with a single or small group of clients, requirements tied to operations in non-domestic countries, special documents or deliverables created at some point in the past, and unique work or business processes in support of legal contracts with partners or vendors.

All of these requirements and the work and systems that support them were created with good reasons at some point in the past. But market conditions change and the business changes, and it is possible, even likely, that some number of these requirements no longer make sense. This is a great opportunity given that these requirements can be significant and can result in systems that are in part or fully dedicated to these unique requirements in addition to tasks and business processes that support these same requirements. Special requirements in the business can be very complex due to their nature and can create a significant amount of work. By their very nature these requirements can create a high level of cost and complexity.

*With this in mind, it is important to review
these special requirements carefully, knowing
big savings can be found and large amounts
of waste can be identified and eliminated.*

It makes sense to mobilize a small team dedicated to these requirements because they might take some time to find, and it's best to have a team focused solely on this. In some cases it will be easier to trace the major business processes in IT back to the origin because we are doing this review of all tasks and business processes anyway as part of the broader review of IT in the search of waste. When we find the origin, or catalyst requirements, we can then qualify it and identify if this requirement is valid today or if the need has changed or gone away completely. We then look at the fit of the requirement with standard business needs or with a special business requirement.

It is always best, and a bit exciting too, to discover that the original requirement is no longer valid and the work or system can be stopped. In most cases, this is a big time and resource savings that we can realize immediately. It is surprising how often this is possible simply because people will continue to perform the same work week after week and month after month until something big changes or we look at this differently, which is exactly what we are doing.

*IT is calling a timeout and verifying the work
is absolutely necessary and the systems IT
is operating are supporting a current and
necessary business requirement versus
a special requirement from our past.*

If the requirements do prove to be necessary and current, then we take the opportunity now that we have started to determine if the business processes, tasks, or systems can be simplified. Full elimination of work or a system is great, but simplifying this same work or systems is very good and can eliminate waste on its own. Then, remember that we are likely reviewing many business processes and systems, hundreds or even thousands of these are possible, and some savings found in most of them can add up to very big improvements, big cost savings, and big advances in speed.

TECHNOLOGY AGILITY

Yes, agility appears yet again in our discussion, and it is hard not to love this strategy.

Agility is wonderfully powerful and has a place and some context in many of our discussions. Agility is fundamental and timeless. Agility is very much in the DNA of our future IT and a big advantage of a unified IT.

> **Agility is a natural force that shapes our technology, shapes our culture, and helps to unify IT. Even better, agility is of strategic value to the business and helps to change the perception of IT across the organization.**

A fully unified IT will bring us a quantum leap forward in terms of agility. This agility comes naturally with the unification of IT and does not require big new projects.

Agility should not be an abstract concept but rather a business asset that becomes increasingly necessary to support what are normally disruptive shifts in the business, including:

A merger or acquisition

A new audit requirement

New governance or compliance requirements

Opening a new division or operating unit

There are a few fundamental concepts associated with agility, and these concepts should frame our investments in enhancing existing technology and for the selection of new commercial systems. We want to keep this simple, including:

Begin by making agility a critical priority for all technology.

Evaluate all technology against a yardstick of agility.

Prioritize agility above standard features and functions.

Execute test cases against new technology to validate agility.

Evaluate new technology with scenarios that simulate changes in the business.

Prioritize existing technology enhancements that improve agility.

Agility won't happen without a focus on making investments that improve agility. The IT organization has a natural focus historically on capabilities, features, and product requirements related to specific functions. This has always been our priority, but now there are a few things that demand a shift in this thinking. It must be a short list or we risk diluting the focus that is so important as we navigate through the next decade of the transformation and unification of IT.

The short list of our new technology priorities looks something like this:

Scalability

Agility

Speed

User Experience

This set of critical attributes will shape our technology investments over the next decade.

Most IT professionals would agree these things are important, but the point we are making here is different—it is now necessary to prioritize these things above all else. What was important previously now becomes critical, now becomes more important than the continued race for more features and functions. This is especially true for the many software applications that support the operations of the IT organization and the business every day.

> *Agility holds so much value for the business because it directly supports business strategy. It is not just a technology thing. There is much more at work here.*

For example, we know the pace of change in business is growing, but what are we doing in IT to address this and to be proactive? What are we doing in IT to bring some strategic impact to the business? These are questions we always need to keep in mind, questions that will shape the changes in IT over the next decade. In the interest of working more proactively with the business, this is a great opportunity to make this happen.

We know that change is a constant in the market today, and it is only a matter of time before changes will come in our business, so the strategy of agility is a great opportunity for IT to move forward and to better prepare the technologies and systems of IT for the next major opportunity that comes to the business.

It is a fact that when change does come to the business, it will come with little warning and it will require us to move quickly. IT must make a fundamental choice, it is a clear contrast:

> *Do we wait for change to come, not knowing what it might be, and then react as quickly as possible when it does come?*

> *Do we take actions now and assign resources to initiatives that will better prepare IT and the business for the next big change, the next big shift?*

The traditional model for IT in most organizations has been the first option, because we focused on the operational needs of IT, which fully occupied our resources and thoughts. It is not easy to carve resources out of the daily work of IT to focus on a new priority that is not pressing us today, not a perceived high priority for IT.

> **But this is what we must do to drive improved agility, because an easier and more convenient opportunity will never come, and we just can't wait.**

Create the focus now, assign a team to drive this activity and drive a new mindset in IT that understands the impact to the business of working more proactively, working more strategically, to ensure IT is ready the next time agility is needed.

CHAPTER 10

THE IT CONCIERGE

The IT Concierge is a fantastic and rejuvenating concept for the future of IT and reflects the spirit we are building across our energized organization.

The IT Concierge represents so much more than what might be visible from the role itself. This is the embodiment of a new IT, a shift in how we work across IT as teammates, and how we will work with the business.

We can define a concierge as:

> *An employee with the role of assisting others in whatever they might require, and in improving the performance of their daily work...*

Perfectly stated. Extending this to IT might be a very different idea and something some might question—what place could a concierge possibly have in the world of IT? Okay, that is fair because we do need to recognize this a sharp departure from the traditional role of IT.

But in many respects it makes perfect sense in terms of what the role will do for the organization and the timing of this role appearing on the landscape of IT. This is a role of helping others to do their job better every day, a role that encourages teamwork and good communications, which is all very much in line with bringing value to the people of IT and then to the business. The expertise in IT today can help in so many ways if we just make it available at the right time and to the right people. This does happen sometimes today, but it is not systemic and it is not the sole focus of any one job. The timing is right for the IT Concierge in that it creates some focus on an outreach to the people of IT and in bringing the powerful knowledge and resources of IT to them. And this is just the beginning, as this model will begin in IT but then get extended to the business. Both are important, but the IT Concierge working with people across the business and with key business owners, proactively, is a powerful formula for learning and for success.

The IT Concierge becomes an ambassador to the business and is looking to better understand how each team across the business performs their jobs today, and what the new requirements will be on their role in the future.

> *This all begins with a better understanding*
> *of how our teams work and what our*
> *teams deliver today across the business.*
> *A better understanding across IT makes*
> *many powerful improvements possible.*

With this understanding the IT Concierge will work with each individual and each team to better leverage the resources and knowledge of IT to do their job better every day, to have a bigger impact on the business today, and to then have a positive impact on our customers—effectively making all our people better so we can better serve our customers.

The IT Concierge does not wait for problems to occur or wait for people to be faced with a big challenge that needs immediate attention. This might be unavoidable at times, but this role is more focused on contacting people *before* they have an urgent need or critical problem. The IT Concierge will work to contact all the teams of IT and of the full organization to start a dialogue and discuss how IT can help now and in the future.

This is very much a proactive and forward-looking engagement.

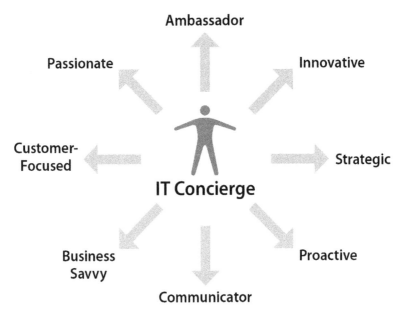

Figure 10.1 The IT Concierge

This discussion begins along the lines of—We are excited to offer a new IT service to the organization called the IT Concierge and we are here to help you do your job better every day... The significant resources of IT stand behind this role and have created the role to help ensure every person in the organization has open access to the powerful technologies and systems of IT. We are here to help. Nothing is too small and nothing is too big. In fact, it helps to talk about the small stuff too because that helps IT to better understand and because small stuff sometimes turns into big stuff later. The key is an open and ongoing dialogue about how IT can help propel people in their daily work to get their work done a little faster, a little better, and to have a bigger impact on the business and on our customers.

> *The IT Concierge can enable a remarkable chain of value—the resources and services of IT helping people to work better every day—which then translates into a better product or service delivered to our customers.*

It is a virtual certainty that if we assist our people in doing their job better every day, we are creating a happier and more empowered workforce, which in turn will carry this positive momentum all the way to our customers.

Never underestimate the power of a single person or a single role. The IT Concierge can bring this new model to life.

In the beginning the IT Concierge won't be understood because this is not a traditional role. There will be questions and some who are skeptical, but that is okay. This is to be expected because many people are not comfortable with change. But this will all change quickly as our small team of IT Concierges go to work, and they will soon earn supporters as both IT and the business see what these talented people are capable of. This shift will bring more support, and people will begin to wonder why we waited so long to put this new role into place.

This mindset shift from doubting to excitement is only natural for changes that bring great results, and this is exactly what the IT Concierge will bring us: a big impact very quickly, and a new way of working collaboratively and spanning the business.

TRUSTED ADVISOR

Trust is built one small step at a time, and through hard work.

The IT Concierge will directly and indirectly create new relationships and partnerships across IT and throughout the business. These circles of influences will know no limits and will have a powerful impact on our culture. Because cultural change is so important to the new and unified IT and the unified business, we pay attention to those things that can serve as catalysts for this change. Cultural change doesn't just happen; we can't mandate cultural change. What we can do is make small and thoughtful changes that will reinforce the new thinking and new actions that then begin to reshape the culture bit by bit.

The IT Concierge is a great example. This role is all about the following simple things:

Helping people

Fostering teamwork

Proactive outreach

Aligning IT and the business

Great communications

Results focus

Partnership

Customer engagement

This is a formula for both the role and for elements in our changing culture. The IT Concierge makes a lot of sense because the IT organization today offers services to the organization, and service delivery is a natural part of the charter of IT, IT Service Management, and far back into history with the traditional Help Desk.

New IT service models today include Service Catalog and Self-Service, which are powerful, much-needed models that have proven to be very effective. But these models are focused on automation, and the IT Concierge is very different—a personal and human element that complements these delivered through automation.

This human touch is a much-needed complement to that of automation and the growing influence of AI. We should not make the mistake of assuming the human element in our daily work fades away. Far from it.

> ***We need this human element more
> than ever, the human touch, the unique
> human engagement and insight.***

As we will discuss later in the book, automation and AI will only grow and continue to improve. One often overlooked part of this evolution is the up-valuing it provides for humanity. The offloading of high-volume tasks, well-defined tasks, and other work that fits the profile of automation and AI will enable us to focus our people on the important work that people are so well suited for.

Which brings us back to the IT Concierge.

This role is a unique combination of business understanding, good communication skills, and technology expertise. These skills are not common in a single person, but that is to be expected, and in the beginning this is a small team, so we are only looking for a few people. This role might be a new hire, depending on the staffing and budget circumstances of the organization.

Figure 10.2 Trusted Advisor

The role might also be filled by a promotion within IT or a transfer from another organization in the business. Remember, this role is along the lines of a strong consultant, a product manager, a technical support manager, a customer success manager, or a business analyst. Every organization is a little different and titles vary widely, but these are a few common titles.

Whether we fill the role internally or go outside for a hire, it's important to find these core skills of business, communications, and technical in equal portions. It's equally important that we have the right person or a small, strong team because we need to ensure we are delivering a big impact from the beginning.

> *When we add even a single talented person to the IT organization, it makes a big difference. These individuals change how everybody around them thinks and works.*

This new role will also raise expectations immediately for what we expect of ourselves across IT, and what the business should and can expect from IT. This is ultimately a good thing, and exactly what we want. This shift in perception helps to move IT to the strategic organization we know it will become, and a proactive partner to the business. Working closely with IT and with the business will build trust, and the recognition of the IT Concierge will expand. This then naturally leads to the high recognition of Trusted Advisor, recognition that comes with time and with this role having an impact on the business.

When this recognition begins to occur, the initial model of the IT Concierge reaching out to people across IT and to our key business owners will begin to shift to a model of scheduling appointments with the IT Concierge as their time becomes more in demand.

This, too, is a good thing and to be expected.

It will likely lead to adding a few more people to the team, and so the influence of the IT Concierge continues to grow, and they become more involved in the daily work of IT and of the business.

When we reach the milestone of ten years from now and look back on the unification of IT and the business, the IT Concierge is one of the roles that we can point to as driving this change.

COMMUNICATION

Strong communications skills are a key part of the IT Concierge role. This is not a typical and widespread skillset for the IT staff of today, which is to be expected because it has not been a priority in the traditional IT model that favored domain expertise and technical experience over all else. But make no mistake, we do have great communication skills in some of our IT staff, and the IT Concierge role can be potentially filled by moving the right individuals into this role if possible. The roles we can look at include Customer Success Managers, technical support leads, or senior staff on the service desk. It is always preferable to promote from within and in particular into a role like this one, which will have a unique and exciting job description and a high level of visibility in the organization. The IT Concierge will quickly earn the reputation of being among our rising stars in IT and a significant contributor to the business.

All of this assumes strong communications skills as a key element of this role being successful. From these skills will come high-quality communications and an increasingly natural part of how we work every day across IT. Seems like a small thing perhaps, but it will make a big difference in both the content of these communications assisting our people in doing their job better and having access to the right information and in changing the culture.

Our people will quickly see the value of improved and more frequent communications, and this will move others to participate and join this circle of communicating. It is an awakening that many people will want to be part of and contribute as they understand it has helped them perform their daily work.

Some people in every part of the organization will be surprised, as "good communications" is not a typical description of the IT organization today. This is understandable and largely true, but let's take this on as an opportunity—an opportunity to contribute and to have an impact in a manner that is not expected.

The scope of how the IT Concierge works and influences will grow quickly. It might begin within IT as we build a model for the connections of our people and mobilizing cross-functional teams to support key initiatives. The IT Concierge can help to facilitate the formation and makeup of these teams and in some cases can be a member of some of these same teams. The initial connections of the Concierge will be outreach and contacting key people and key teams across IT; the role won't have a history, won't be understood, and so we are contacting people to explain why we have created the role and how the Concierge can help. Word will spread quickly, and after some initial period of education, the demand for support from the IT Concierge will grow. The need for outreach will be reduced but not eliminated entirely because we have many organizations to contact and to establish new relationships with.

We will discover that many organizations across the business have never worked directly with IT beyond the occasional call to the Help Desk. This is to be expected and, yes, this is an opportunity to be embraced. A chance for IT to make a difference.

As the scope of the IT Concierge grows, communication will always be a priority. Good and frequent communications will improve the work of IT and begin to bring our teams closer together. In the beginning, the focus will be IT, but the Concierge will have an even bigger impact on the business. The collaboration of teams can be encouraged and supported once begun by the IT Concierge, who will have good visibility of the top initiatives of IT and then of the business. This will happen naturally as the Concierge in the beginning is helping with problems and issues, then extending to consulting and advisement support.

> *There will naturally be a connection between these consulting and discussion sessions conducted by the IT Concierge and new or soon-to-be-launched projects and initiatives in the business.*

Effectively, the IT Concierge becomes a valuable resource to the business in discussing and planning how the resources of IT can best be leveraged as we launch new initiatives, both tactical and strategic, both internal and customer facing. As the success of these consulting sessions grows, the business and the key business owners will increasingly turn to the IT Concierge team as a valuable resource in the business. With this model the Concierge becomes the new face of IT to the business, further reinforcing the requirement to have a mix of business, communications, and technical skills in this role. This is a high-impact role both because of this unique mix of skills and the passionate, talented people to be placed in the roles.

Communications is always vital to the role and becomes a vehicle for the visibility of these business initiatives and customer initiatives across IT. In many cases, the people of IT who have had limited to no visibility of business initiatives in the past will now have a new view of this activity through the updates of the IT Concierge. This can be a very productive mechanism for IT, as the Concierge is our real-time and transparent connection to the business. Important information is then brought back to the major teams of IT, including Service Desk, Security, Asset Management, Servers, Endpoints, Data Center, Compliance, the PMO, and much more.

> *This creates even further value born of these communications by allowing the primary IT teams to be more proactive in supporting these new initiatives—which would otherwise not be visible until much later and often only when there are problems.*

Any remnants of reactive behavior then further perpetuate the perception of IT being a reactive organization. But help is on the way, and the IT Concierge will help change this model through frequent communications that enable IT to first be informed, and to then act proactively as our Concierge team is providing updates and sharing key information.

This is a powerful cycle of visibility and transparency that will continue to grow.

INNOVATION

A focus on innovation is a natural for the IT Concierge as a further catalyst for the growing focus of all of IT on this important strategic investment—in many ways central to the future success of virtually every organization. In the beginning the IT Concierge can be a facilitator and bring the right information back into the IT organization, originating with customers and key business owners. Over time, this role will grow beyond facilitator to sponsorship, enablement, and even the contribution of strategic ideas and content. The IT Concierge will in the beginning ensure the right people are mobilized across the business to fuel innovation and that the right people are at the table when the key discussions occur.

> *Very soon, and as a natural evolution of the IT Concierge role, the IT Concierge will take a place at the table and contribute key ideas, concepts, and recommendations.*

In many ways, innovation is about ideas and brainstorming—raw concepts and ideas, a select few of which will later become the very idea that makes a breakthrough in innovation possible. These all started as crazy ideas. The IT Concierge will understand the importance of both innovation and this dialogue, a cultural shift really. Better still, the IT Concierge is in a unique position to create the focus on this important topic and to then drive and encourage the necessary forums and discussions; the IT Concierge is an ambassador between the technology experts of IT and the key business owners across the organization. As such, this bridge between IT and the business can spawn these discussions and push them forward. Then as we progress with new innovation processes, the Concierge can also leverage the communications channels they have created to share this information with the broader organization while at the same time looking for future contributors.

> *Think of the IT Concierge as a talent scout for the business—always looking for great thinkers and talented experts who can bring knowledge and great ideas to the innovation process.*

Creative new solutions to real business problems are likely to come from these very people, and they will appreciate joining the process because they will naturally understand it is critical to our future and will have the highest level of visibility across the organization.

Innovation always starts with asking questions and raising ideas. From this humble beginning ideas begin to blossom, and we can then evaluate and test ideas until a few rise to the top and earn more focus and investment. The complete process will be close to the heart of the CIO, CTO, and CEO, and these are examples of organizations and senior leadership the IT Concierge will communicate and coordinate efforts with across the business.

The IT Concierge is a unique ambassador whose role could also be clarified as:

Communicator

Advocate

Coach

Expert

Innovator

This is a good summary and captures the essence of the role well. These things must be kept in balance because each complements the others and in turn allows the other activities to be successful. But with the skills we have in this role and the multidimensional feedback the IT Concierge will receive every day, these talented people will be well equipped to maintain this balance.

> ***Another important quality that will be embodied in the Concierge is passion. Never underestimate the value of passion. Passion is charismatic, and passion is contagious.***

Because the IT Concierge will be working with so many teams both within IT and across the business, they will have a big influence on our people and our culture. In recognizing this, the Concierge will play an important role in reshaping our culture. And with the wonderful and compelling impact passion can have, the IT Concierge must display this strong quality in everything they do as a way to seed the organization with this transformational tonic. Our people will be drawn to this passion, and good people know something good when they see it and feel it. This then begins to change the IT organization from within and can then role model how we think and how we act as a business to all the organization and to the key business owners. Just as the IT Concierge and IT Business Management will drive the reshaping of the new IT, these same leaders will have a prominent influence over the complete business.

Yes, this leadership coming from IT seems unlikely, and many would say this will never happen, but it will happen and just when the business needs leadership more than ever. There is simply no better form of leadership today than organic innovation that is tied to real customer needs—the heartbeat of the business.

PERSONALIZED SERVICE

"Personal" would not be a term most people would use to describe the IT of the past. In many ways, IT has been wired to be impersonal due to a focus on process, structure, efficiencies, and savings. These primary metrics leave little room for IT to focus on and to deliver personalized services. But due to a new market climate, changing customer expectations, and the needs of the business to change how we service these customers, IT must become more personal so the business is then able to become more personal. Meaning more tailored and more targeted services and products for our customers.

The business simply can't make this happen without the support and, even better yet, the leadership of IT.

The ability to deliver more personalized service to the IT organization and to the business is a natural fit for the IT Concierge.

This is very much in line with working more closely with individuals and teams, bringing a better understanding of how IT can enable our people to do their jobs better. It allows IT to refine the model of service delivery to make each service more targeted, focused, and personal. More personal service begins with better communications, which leads to a better understanding of the business requirements of each team. The partnership of IT with the business comes to life in many ways, and one is certainly the IT Concierge and the dialogues that are created across a few teams in the beginning and then extend to other teams over time. As we achieve some success and begin to deliver more personalized service solutions, every team in the business will join this model.

> *Word travels fast. When something is working, the business and people will want to leverage this unique resource.*

It goes even further. The IT Concierge will be a strong leader with strong organization skills beyond the communication skill we mentioned previously, so when this person gets involved in an initiative, it is likely to go well. Our teammates will have a good experience that makes it easy and natural to call on the IT Concierge the next time we need help with a new service, need a more personalized service, or need to brainstorm on how we meet a new challenge in the business.

The increasing connection between IT and both the IT Concierge and the IT Business Manager will help more personalized service to grow and blossom.

> *This is an important cycle. Personalized service does not just happen; it must be driven by engagement and understanding and constant communications.*

The better we understand the needs of our employees and the customer, the more effective IT can be in delivering more personal service, including:

Understanding preferences

Understanding the history of service

Updated contact information

The preferred way to communicate

More frequent and informal communications

Improved transparency

Brainstorming on how to improve services

Creative new services

Feedback on user experiences

This profile begins to shape how improved personal service becomes real. It comes from the ground up, through a relationship and teamwork that make the understanding natural. It expands through communication and feedback.

> **More personalized service does not take as much work as what we might assume. It is just a matter of listening first and foremost, and then a little thoughtful planning.**

Personalized service makes a big difference, but it begins with a desire to make IT more personal. This can spring from the IT Concierge if it does not exist today across IT, and we can use this role as a much-needed catalyst to create a focus on being more personal. Even better, the IT Concierge is in a position to directly enable and drive this change. The Concierge is working directly with users, business owners, and even customers and with this direct engagement will have firsthand knowledge on how exactly we can improve existing services and what new services could be valuable to those people we are delivering services to.

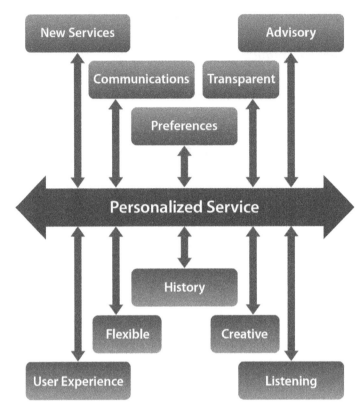

Figure 10.3 Personalized Service

The circles of service delivery are different for every organization—whether it's employees only or a mix of employees and external customers. All of the above can benefit from more personal service, referring back to the checklist above. This is simple stuff but at the same time very impactful and valuable to the people we serve.

This is a good time for a reminder that the IT Concierge is a key leader in the organization, both in the IT organization and across the business: a key leader who can directly improve the quality of service and the ongoing evolution of more personalized service, which then creates cultural change. And with cultural change, anything becomes possible.

It is important to recognize that this cultural change, from the ground up, can begin in IT and then spread throughout the business. This is but one example of the singularity we can bring to IT and then the singularity of IT coming together with the business—the essence of our future.

MARKET AMBASSADOR

The unification of IT and the coming together with the business will include a shift over time from what is very much an inside-out organization today to one that is outside in. To be clear, the "inside" of inside out is technology and IT, and the "outside" of outside in is the customer and the broader markets we serve as a business. This can be any vertical in any country in the world—every organization is delivering a product or service to a customer somewhere.

The daily work of IT is fundamentally focused on technology and then moving this technology outward through a delivery and deployment cycle to arrive at a user or customer—the chain fundamentally originating and focused on technology. This is the inside-out model.

The inside-out model is in contrast with the daily work of IT being fundamentally focused on the customer and then moving inward to technology and determining how technology and tools can be leveraged to address real customer needs—the chain fundamentally originating and focused on the customer and on markets. This is the outside-in model.

Traditional IT has been very much an inside-out model as evidenced by the daily work, daily focus, and roles and skills of the organization and how they are oriented. The good news is that more and more of the IT organization is beginning to understand this must change and that the single greatest source of truth and clarity is in fact the customer.

> *While the transformation is not yet complete,*
> *we should all recognize that IT will transform*
> *to very much an outside-in organization over*
> *the next decade. This powerful force of change is*
> *now unstoppable and is absolutely necessary.*

As this change happens, we desperately need direct engagement with customers and the market to bring the valuable communications and feedback that bring clarity to the outside sources. This goes beyond the customer and will include the marketplace recognizing that business is increasingly on a global market landscape and our strategy needs to be shaped by the customer first, but then influenced by other factors, including market trends, competitive pressures, new market shifts, and much more. This market understanding requires a view into the market and a number of market-facing activities.

> *A combination of market insights and*
> *customer engagement can be provided*
> *uniquely by the IT Concierge as their activity*
> *and scope extend into the marketplace.*

Participating in market forums, key tradeshows, training events, relationships with market influencers, press interactions, and much more creates a broader understanding of the marketplace and lends a nice balance to the current customer group. We always begin with the customer of course, but then focus on the "outside" of outside in.

Not that any of this is unnatural for the Concierge—to the contrary, this is very much in line with our charter and very comfortable for the role. The connection to the marketplace is necessary to create real understanding and real depth.

> *The IT Concierge can then bring this information back to the IT organization and the broader business and serve as another Lighthouse in the business for the evolution of our strategy and insights into our Innovation initiatives.*

This unique perspective is in short supply in most organizations and certainly within IT. The IT Concierge then naturally grows as a recognized leader, which further supports their charter, and the impact they can have on the business grows and grows.

Having valuable insight into the market and the influence the IT Concierge begins to have in the business further advances the partnership between IT and the broader organization, changes the perception of IT, and brings IT staff into a new set of activities and discussions where IT has traditionally not been present.

Every organization has a few superstars with a unique set of skills and a level of talent that allows them to have a bigger impact on the organization than most. These people are the future of every business and make the success of the business possible. We all know who these people are. But if we look back, how many of these superstars of the past have been in the IT organization? Very few? None? That would be the response of most people, especially the business owners outside IT. It's not easy to hear, but often true—the reality of where we have been and the journey we have traveled.

> *I'm suggesting that the roles of IT Business Management and the IT Concierge will join the ranks of the business superstars of the future.*

The people who fill these roles become not just leaders within IT, but rather recognized leaders of the broader business—the few "go-to" people in the organization who can get things done and bring a unique level of talent and knowledge to the strategic initiatives of the business. The people we call on to lead, to drive strategy, to bring innovations to the business, and to reshape the perception of IT.

I'm confident this will happen, and this change has already begun. You might not see it, but it is there.

This will make the IT organization a place people want to work, which in turn will allow us to attract and retain a new, more diverse and younger workforce, further accelerating the transformation of IT and all the good that comes along with. Truly exciting days are ahead for the wonderful people of IT as we get some help in our journey over the next decade.

CUSTOMER ADVOCATE

No discussion on the future and unification of IT and the business would be complete without a focus on the customer and the related strategies and actions that bring this customer focus to life. It is not enough to simply say the customer is important, or we need to make the customer a priority, or that IT must work more closely with our customers. This is easy and obvious stuff. What is necessary is to create new models, business processes, and roles that bring this customer focus to life and make it real every day. This then creates the authority and accountability to ensure the strategy of customer engagement is put into action and becomes a lifestyle that is natural for all of IT.

In looking more closely at how we bring customer focus and engagement to life, there is no better example than the IT Concierge. It would not be much of a stretch to say this role is perfectly suited to advocate for the customer every day across IT and across the business. The skills makeup, mindset, and charter of the Concierge are all aligned with better serving our customers and bringing value to this relationship...meaning that the top priorities of the IT Concierge are communications, a business focus, and innovation—to name a few—which are each aligned with what our customers need most from a good partner and what forms a strategic relationship. The daily execution of these priorities will elevate the nature of the work we do with our customers and with the business. These needs are very much in synch.

> *As we move the relationship of IT with the*
> *business to one that is more proactive,*
> *strategic, and innovative, we recognize that*
> *this formula for success is a true match for*
> *what we must bring to our customers.*

Even better, we should recognize that each of these elements supports the other. Great communications creates understanding, which then enables IT to be more proactive and strategic. A more strategic focus pulls our attention to innovating and delivering improved and new products and services that create thrilled customers and enable competitive success.

This cycle always brings us back to the customer, who is a natural and necessary element in this powerful cycle. The customer is both the beginning and end—in fact, the only *authentic* beginning and end.

The customer is the only true source of insight and clarity. When we begin to fully understand this, everything becomes simpler and more clear. It really is a remarkably transformational and energizing concept.

> *So, how do we stay true to this primal customer*
> *strategy every day? It must be codified into the*
> *organization and into specific roles that are*
> *in a position to influence and lead others.*

With this structure, customer strategy will become more and more natural and part of what every person in IT believes and acts on every day. Then, it is just what we do and how we work. We just get it.

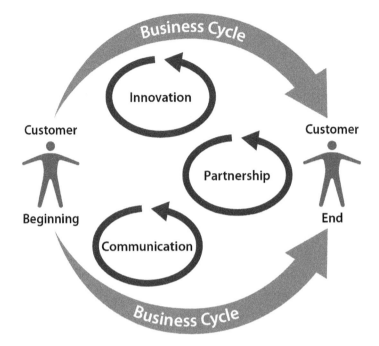

Figure 10.4 Customer Advocacy

The IT Concierge will have customer advocacy at the top of their list of priorities and will work on behalf of the customer every day to ensure that IT has the right focus, is delivering value to our customers, and is acting like the strategic partner we must be. This is shaped by the decisions we make every day and the work that is performed. When we have tough choices to make, the IT Concierge along with senior IT leadership help bring our thoughts back to the customer, and this then ensures the choices we make and the priorities we put in place and then act on will ultimately enable us to deliver what our customers expect and need.

The structure of compensation plans is important and has a big impact on how people work and the priorities they carry every day. As a further extension of the IT Concierge role, some of their compensation will be tied to customer-related metrics and customer success. This is not necessary to create a passion for the customer with the IT Concierge because that will already be in place. It is natural to the people in the role.

> *A customer-focused incentive enables the IT Concierge to share in the success of customers and to be recognized as customer success grows and becomes more evident. This sets a new standard and a new expectation of the best possible type.*

As such, it only makes sense that we position the role of Concierge to share in customer success because it then creates happier workers in IT, including the Concierge; it improves employee retention, improves quality of life, and will attract talented employees from across IT and across the business to the IT Concierge role. This is a desirable cycle and one we want to thoughtfully create due to the good it brings the organization and the customer.

Although we have used the IT Concierge as a prime example of compensation tied to the customer and customer success, this particular incentive will become more widespread across IT. Not traditionally an organization that leveraged bonus plans and financial incentives, IT will make this increasingly common and use this compensation to bring attention to the key elements of strategic performance that we want to drive in the future. Compensation is an effective way to make this happen. If we want to change behavior quickly, a comp plan is a great way to drive the right behavior. A couple of examples of what we want to connect bonuses to would be customer success and innovation. Customer success metrics are not hard to find and are normally readily available.

Compensation and recognition strengthen the customer advocacy cycle and further advance the role of the IT Concierge as a valuable role in every respect—one that will fulfill the need for key contributors in IT and people who can have a big impact on the customer.

> **The IT Concierge will be a passionate megaphone for the customer across IT every day, one who represents the needs of the customer and can bring this perspective into every conversation and every meeting.**

This is exactly what we need to further sharpen our culture.

CHAPTER 11

THE POWER OF EASY

"Easy" is a revelation when we experience it.

Just a few examples of why it is easy to love easy:

> *Easy saves time.*
>
> *Easy builds loyalty.*
>
> *Easy naturally brings people back.*
>
> *Easy is convenient.*
>
> *Easy makes people happy.*
>
> *Easy reduces or eliminates training.*
>
> *Easy is intuitive.*
>
> *Eusy saves money.*
>
> *Easy is fast.*
>
> *Easy creates flexibility.*

Easy makes people look good.

Easy is unifying.

Easy naturally eliminates waste.

Easy simplifies our lifestyle.

Easy boosts user satisfaction.

There is much more to *easy* than meets the eye.

> **Easy does take thoughtful design and careful planning. Easy must be a design goal of technology and systems from the very beginning. It is not easy to bring easy into existing systems.**

It is much more effective to make easy a priority from day one.

Easy is not tactical. Very much to the contrary, we should see easy as a strategic force in the business. Easy very much complements our goal of unifying IT and the business. Look closely and we will find easy working behind the scenes in support of many of the unifying concepts for the future of IT. For example, easy cleanses us of waste, easy is fast, easy save time, and easy improves our ability to do our very best work.

In our ongoing search to find leverage in IT and in the business, easy is a great example of the leverage we need. Throughout the book we will use "leverage" to indicate a force or investment that brings us a magnified return on this investment of effort or money. Leverage is an important and powerful concept, and our search for leverage should continue every day. Then, when we do find an opportunity to create leverage, we seize the opportunity and convert it into the greatest possible result. These discoveries of leverage won't happen every day, so when we do find them, they are precious. We then recognize how important they are, rally around the opportunity, and take the necessary steps to maximize the good this can create.

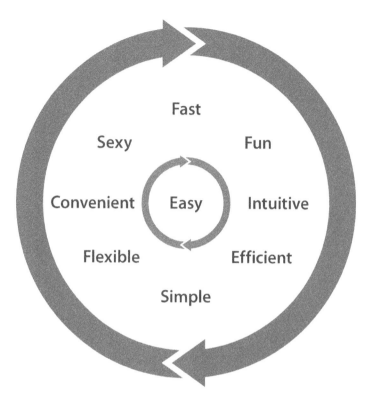

Figure 11.1 The Power of Easy

A wonderful thing about easy is that it can appear in many places. Certainly, across IT and our many systems and technologies, easy is a natural opportunity because so many of our IT tools and technologies today are anything but easy—powerful and robust in many cases, but not easy. This must no longer be acceptable as we pursue technologies and systems that are both powerful and easy to use. Both robust and easy to navigate. Systems capable of handling our most advanced requirements while at the same time providing a comfortable and intuitive user experience.

This is leverage, and this is only the beginning of the power of easy.

VALUE OF TIME

With the increasing pressures placed on business today and, even more importantly, on the people who are the lifeblood of any organization, the value of time has come to the center of what we must appreciate and manage—recognizing that not only do the good people of our organization have an increased sense of the value of time, but it only makes sense that this extends to the people who are our clients.

Customers are increasingly demanding and as such increasingly impatient, and this is closely linked to an awareness of the precious resource of time.

> *A business that can save a customer's time and provide a great product or service experience will generate a significant competitive advantage.*

This growing awareness of the value of time will continue to grow. Time rises to the list of things our customers value most over the next decade, which coincides with our drive to unify IT and the business. These strategies are critical in order to create real time savings and the ongoing optimization of all things related to time. It is simply not possible to optimize time and speed across IT with the current silo-based and fragmented model of IT. Remember, the traditional model of IT was optimized around other factors, and for this, the model worked adequately.

> *But today and into the future, the partners*
> *of time and speed rise to strategic and*
> *should make any short list for our*
> *priorities in IT over the next decade.*

Other short-list IT priority items would likely include scalability and agility, and the same argument can be made—all of this requires a unified IT working together and shedding waste in order to take a quantum leap forward with regard to any of our new priorities. We will visit this inescapable reality repeatedly throughout the book because it is so central to One IT and ultimately One Business.

This is exactly how we must view the strategy to save time within IT, across the business, and on behalf of our customers—there are many layers and dimensions to saving time and increasing the value of time, and an ongoing commitment and focus are required to tap in to these many dimensions. Once we've begun this exploration and are peeling back these layers of IT complexity, we will find many opportunities for improvement.

Figure 11.2 The Value of Time

It seems so simple but yet it is remarkable how many IT organizations have not accepted this change in mindset and, with this change in thinking, begun the exploration and evaluation of everything we do in IT with a new measurement of what is and is not acceptable; what is and is not strategic versus tactical; and what can and cannot be connected to real business outcomes.

This evaluation of everything we do must now include time, precious time. Taking back every single minute we can brings so much value, a big multiple on each minute in fact because time is one of the things that create leverage, including:

Time gives us an opportunity to think.

Time enables a new commitment to innovation.

Saving time improves our quality of life.

Time savings enables our focus to move to the customer.

Time savings in IT can be passed on to the customer.

Time is essential to speed.

Time is perhaps our most precious variable resource.

Customers value time more every day and so must we.

A focus on time will drive real cultural change.

Remember, time is not just time. Time creates value, and time generates strategy and velocity.

> **This is a storm of business strength and force that creates success—first within our organization and then creates value that translates to our customers.**

It is a chain that must be appreciated.

Given the current business dependencies we have on technology and data, we will discover the root of time savings and speed is found in IT. With this, the IT organization discovers another strategy under our control and one that can benefit the full organization, and so we must take on this heightened focus on speed and time savings—the full appreciation of the value of time and how IT can unlock this value for all employees and for customers.

With few if any exceptions, *easy* is a path to time savings. This is a key answer to the question "How." Bring easy to every system of IT and to every customer experience, and the investment will bring us value many times over, and further unite IT and the business by bringing our focus yet again back to the right priorities that span the business. This is the singularity we need to find every day.

A NEW LIFESTYLE

The collision of powerful market forces and new technologies is altering our lifestyle like never before. It seems that these changes occur daily, and there is no indication this pace of change will slow down. If anything it might increase as AI and intelligent technologies take a more prominent place in the daily operations of IT and across the business. I also expect there to be a disruptive mobile technology in the next five years that will change how we work and how we live our personal lives. Think in terms of the love child of the current smartphone, tablet, and laptop, but with a quantum leap forward in the user experience, battery life, and speed of performance.

This type of device would remove any current concerns, inconveniences, and limitations of the current mobile devices we use, and then it becomes natural to use this device for everything we do every day, at home, when traveling, and when working. Not everybody will share my opinion on the dawn of this new device, but it seems inevitable this will occur given the lack of a truly disruptive technology in this market in the past ten years, the remarkable advancement in soft and hard technologies, and the revenue that is now being driven by the mobile device and smartphone markets.

The reference to an improved user experience is an important one: We can't take a quantum leap forward and expect to benefit from a significant disruption of this market without a completely new user experience that complements the hard attributes, including a dramatic increase in battery life and a similar improvement in bandwidth and speed of performance.

We don't yet know what this new user experience will be exactly, but one word we will use to describe it will certainly be "easy," which will mean a few things:

No training required

Quickly accomplish all common tasks

New features are natural and simple

Few steps required to do whatever is required

Attractive and simple interface

Learning interface that saves the user time

Customizable in a simple way

Adapts to the needs of each user

Accommodates a broad range of users and skills

This profile supports our discussion on a new mobile device, but it can apply to the systems and tools of IT equally well. The formula for easy is universal and consistent.

Regardless of the context, easy does create a big shift in lifestyle for the good. This recognizes the continued blurring between our work lives and our personal lives. These things are closely related—the power of technology, the convenience of the tools we use to complete our daily work, and the shifting of our lifestyle.

The lifestyle issue alone is a fascinating one because it is about both our desire to change our lifestyle and our ability to make it happen due to the ability of new technology to support the shift.

These things go together. Desire alone is not enough to change our lifestyle. Yes, it is a start but not enough. Similarly, the ability to change our lifestyle is also not enough. The fundamental desire must be alive in combination with ability and then these things come together to create a model for what a new lifestyle could look like and how it could work day after day. What we are seeing today, for many simple and complex reasons, is possibly the first time our culture has both the desire and ability to make this happen.

It is easier to witness this in action today with a new generation of mobile workforce, a growing number of organizations encouraging working from home offices, and many new companies building a business with small and agile teams that work everywhere and anywhere without the need for a traditional corporate footprint. With some experience occurring with this new workforce and lifestyle model, we have confirmed that when done well, it is possible to live the best of both worlds.

If we are to make this new lifestyle a reality, it must spring from IT; the proper deployment and leveraging of technology and tools is a fundamental enabler to the birth of this model where it does not exist today, and then the acceleration of this new lifestyle. For example, on the work side of this new lifestyle, IT must provide access to company resources, including email and HR systems, in a secure and consistent manner. We simply can't pursue this lifestyle shift if these basics are not in place. Better yet, access is not enough; it must be fast, easy, and convenient while at the same time not compromising on capability. With this simple yet powerful model, anything is possible. We can complete our work when needed, where needed, and how needed. This is completely under the workers' control as it should be in so far as this enables the workforce to take the model forward and in many cases be more productive than we could be working in the traditional model—in an office during normal business hours, sitting at a desk, in the tethered brick-and-mortar corporate office model.

It's important to recognize the ability to work better and not just work differently.

We now know this is possible when the technology and tools and systems are implemented correctly. For example, this flexibility and mobility can enable our workforce to spend more time with customers and in the marketplace and have more flexibility with access and schedules. The other side of this lifestyle is the flexibility this model creates with tending to our family and other interests outside work, which tends to create a happy employee and in turn creates a loyal and motivated employee. This then leads to an employee who better serves our clients, and this is what propels the business forward.

This best-of-both-worlds model makes this possible, elevated, and enriched by the IT organization, and we are able to create better employees and happier customers every day. Amazing.

EMPLOYEE PRODUCTIVITY

A remarkable force can be created when we make the employees of our organization more productive. Improved productivity rolls all the way to our customers in many positive forms—an unstoppable wave that can be created within the organization and, in many cases, rooted in the systems and technologies of IT.

Employees who are more productive are happier and likely to stay in their position longer. In the world of IT this is a very good thing, as we can have longer learning curves than other organizations due to the technology and systems our staff must first become knowledgeable then expert in.

> *Experts can take five or more years to train and to then become fully able to contribute to the many activities for which the organization will call on an expert. In some cases, the development of an expert can take a full ten years.*

Taking this employee productivity and improved retention in the internal context, a single productive employee will then affect all those around them and both directly and indirectly help other employees to become more productive. This circle continues to grow, touching more people every day and every week until we have a dramatically more engaged and productive workforce across the business.

Moving closer to the customer and the market in an external context, a single productive and happy employee can make a big difference with customers. It is simply different and a fundamentally better experience when a customer is working with an employee who enjoys what they are doing, likes working for their company, and is motivated and engaged. This is good for everybody. Then, when this mindset spreads and we have a productive and happy workforce, every customer will know the difference. The root of all this is an IT organization committed to delivering superior technologies, tools, and systems that enable each and every employee to perform their job better and to be more productive every day.

> *It would be hard to identify a single thing that has more potential impact on employee productivity than easy.*

Systems and tools that are easier to use are a simple and powerful formula for our employees getting more done in a day.

We can start with "easier to use" as a good goal, and this would apply to any resource, any system or tool that employees utilize to get their job done every day. Even small steps make a big difference, and small steps is a good place to start. Then we can extend this to "much easier to use" as a criteria users would agree with and can be surveyed on, which creates a growing momentum that can impact every person in the organization. With every person performing their work every day with systems and tools that are much easier to use, we can change the business, and this movement can be born within IT. This is in fact natural for IT because we are the stewards of these very systems, tools, and technologies and in the best position to improve ease of use, and the ease and convenience of getting our job done every day.

Another wonderful thing about easy and the boost it can give to employee productivity is the number of levels that exist within the framework of easy. This is virtually unlimited with boundless opportunities for improvement.

With each step we take in making it easier to leverage the systems and technologies of the business, we are taking a similar step forward with employee productivity. These things are bound together. By investing in easy, we are investing in kind to improve the ability of our people to perform their jobs every day, regardless of their role in the organization, including the CEO, and this touches every person in every capacity. It's a powerful model to think about for a minute and another great example of how IT can lead the business, change the business, and help to propel the business into the future.

As with serving our customers, serving our employees brings so many powerful benefits. The remarkable position IT finds itself in today is perhaps the best position of all organizations to enhance employee productivity and to positively impact customer satisfaction through these same actions. Why? Because today, the roles of technology and tools and systems are so fundamental to how our jobs are performed every day. Technology no longer occupies a few niches in how work is performed. The Internet, ordering systems, email systems, messaging, mobile phones, telephony, and much more make up the backbone of business today, and technology simply surrounds us. It is now not possible to separate how our employees work from the technology we utilize to complete this very work, every minute of every day. This then connects IT as the stewards of this technology to every employee in the organization and brings with it the responsibility and the opportunity for IT to fundamentally change and significantly improve the employee working model and the elevation of productivity. This is no longer indirect and abstract—improved technology and systems with an improved user experience, which should always include easy, convenient, and fast, has a direct and immediate impact on employee productivity.

IT should embrace this responsibility and recognize the potential value it brings us. One small improvement in our systems and tools at a time—this is how we build our future.

CUSTOMER HAPPINESS

Easy naturally creates happy customers. What customer does not appreciate and enjoy an easy experience with a system, tool, or technology? What customer does not enjoy completing a task more quickly and more easily than expected? This is something for all of us in IT to keep in mind—as we make all the technologies and systems across the business easier to use, we are ultimately going to bring this experience to the customer. The lines between "internal" and "external" are blurring at a faster rate, and as such what we do for employees or internal customers will soon benefit our paying clients. This connection is inescapable and should be recognized and appreciated. Even more so, it should be embraced and cultivated.

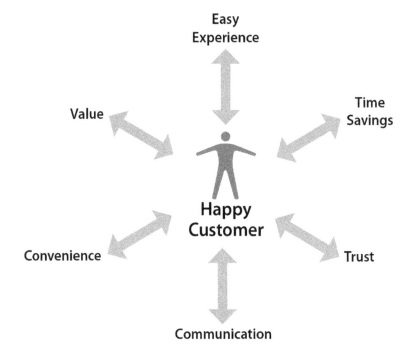

Figure 11.3 The Happy Customer

A happy customer is not just another benefit of easy; it is likely the single biggest value the model of easy can bring us. Where there is a happy customer, success is sure to follow. This is both a natural and critical focus for the people of IT and helps us to support our focus on the customer. The real goal of easy is not just an easier user experience, although that alone is certainly a very good thing. The real goal of easy is to create a chain of value that includes employees and extends all the way to the customer. Easy fundamentally saves time and empowers all the people of our organization to work better and quicker, which enables people in every role to have a positive impact on our customers, regardless of our business and business model.

The universal and unique appeal of easy is that it helps everybody in the business and customer chain, no exceptions.

The timing of a new focus on easy is also important. Easy has always held value, but today perhaps even more so given the current market conditions and the expectations of customers today. Today's market is more global, competitive, and dynamic, which has created a greater emphasis on a broader range of value versus the traditional focus on a product or service alone. Customers expect more, and customers are more discriminating and educated than ever. Small things matter. Things like a great user experience, an ease in getting our work completed, or getting an order or request completed make a difference.

When IT begins the work of making systems and tools and technologies easier to use and focuses on the time it takes to complete common tasks and requests, we should ask ourselves, over and over again throughout the process, how this will help our customers, directly or indirectly. If we are not clear on this point, it might be an investment we should pass on in order to focus on those improvements and investments that will clearly benefit our customers. There is no better test for how we spend our time and resources.

It is not possible to understand the current state of the customer mindset without getting feedback directly from customers.

There is no substitute for customer insight. It is the best information we will ever receive because it's always the truth and nothing but the truth!

We have a history of doing some number of customer surveys in IT, but the need for this information grows as we undertake an upgrade of IT systems and tools to focus more on factors like fast and easy. Surveys are okay, but they are not enough to get us the necessary information to target where we can make our systems easier and to confirm we are getting the right results. On the topic of easy and surveys, we should take some care to ensure we improve the surveys themselves.

The interesting twist here is that surveys are not always easy to complete, which in turn robs us of valuable information that could be captured if the survey experience was comfortable and quick for our customers.

> *So, by making surveys easier we can gather*
> *more information on how to make the*
> *other systems of IT easier to use and more*
> *convenient. Easy brings us more easy!*

There it is again, the wonderful cycle of easy.

We have no more precious asset in the organization today than a happy customer because this is simply our future. A happy customer is more likely to bring us repeat business, will tell others about their good experience as a happy customer, and is likely to stay with the business into the future. In a fiercely competitive market with more options than ever for customers, when we are fortunate enough to win a new customer, we must then take great care and make the necessary investments to keep the customer happy so we then keep the customer.

> *Because technology and the systems of the*
> *business are so integral to operating the*
> *organization every day and in serving our*
> *customers, IT now finds itself in the middle of*
> *this customer engagement and happiness model.*

The teams of IT will certainly receive information from other elements of the organization, including Sales, Marketing, Technical Support, Services, Account Management, and many others, and we welcome this feedback. But as we highlight in other parts of the book, there is no substitute for direct engagement on the part of IT with the customer.

This firsthand customer knowledge is priceless and reduces the risk of losing important information and critical opinions in the translation that happens when customer requirements arrive in IT after some number of interpretations from other organizations. Beyond the direct knowledge and clarity this brings us, working directly with customers will create relationships that are even more important. These relationships bring so many other benefits, it is hard to overstate the importance of this direct contact.

Ultimately, all of us are rallying around the customer and placing them at the center of what we do in IT and all the actions of the business. This is exactly as it should be. "Easy" is just another element in building relationships with thrilled customers, which in turn is the single best path to business success.

CHAPTER 12

STRATEGIC IT

The careful formation of One IT brings with it some remarkable value and an exciting opportunity.

One of these is the emergence of IT as a strategic organization, and possibly the single most strategic organization in the business.

This idea would have been dismissed as crazy talk a few years ago but is now very much within our reach. There is no single thing we can point to that has positioned IT as strategic but rather a number of shifts in the market, a changing customer, and the accelerated evolution of technology.

> *So much of the engine today that drives the business is centered on technology, and this has evolved to the point that business success is directly linked to the ability of the business to leverage technology as a fundamental part of the corporate strategy.*

Not so long ago the world's most valuable companies were traditional businesses like banks, railroads, retail storefronts, and automobile companies. Today, the most valuable companies in the world include Apple, Amazon, and Google. We all have an opinion on what companies will emerge as the most valuable and the potential new model for business over the next decade, but these three very real examples of remarkable value today have achieved this place in the market through strategic management of technology and by creating a unique offering. When most people hear names like Apple and Amazon and Google, they naturally think of some dimension that is technology related. These companies have made technology a natural and seamless part of the corporate strategy. These companies are great at technology and leverage it to deliver a market-leading product or service. This is an important perception and reflects the corporate strategy of these companies.

Certainly most companies won't achieve the level of growth and value these companies have, but the point is an important one— the organizations that experience success in the decade ahead must form a strategy that leverages technology, one that incorporates strategy to better serve customers and create a competitive advantage.

> *There is a version of this insight into*
> *the strategic role of technology in every*
> *organization and with it a challenge for IT.*

We who work in the world of IT must see the business in a new way and see the role of IT as one that is currently shifting from what might have been a tactical organization— perhaps even the most tactical organization in the business—to one that becomes increasingly strategic, and for some, the most strategic organization in the business. This might seem unlikely, but it will happen and for the very organizations that will emerge as the future market leaders. As easy as it is to point at Apple, Amazon, and Google as examples of the world's leading businesses today, most of what will be a new generation of market leader has not yet been identified. This will occur in the next decade as we become familiar with a new group of companies that will become the household names of the future, the new benchmarks of business.

Figure 12.1 The Orbit of Strategic IT

With the new perspective we have today on technology and look-ing at the trajectory of technology today, we must conclude that these new companies will share the ability to put technology in the middle of the corporate strategy and leveraged as a strategic asset. This should not be confused with technology as the strategy, for that can't be the case, and these companies will understand that. Leveraging technology to turbocharge the corporate strategy, to enrich the corporate strategy and make it that much stronger, will come from within, both from R&D and Development and from IT.

We should see R&D and IT as partners in this regard, a new type of technology focused partners with the charter to lift up the business on the wings of data and technology.

There is so much here that is fun to explore and to think about. Innovation is one of the key strategic investments for the next ten years and beyond, and IT is in a unique position to influence and drive this activity—seems like an obvious thing, but surprisingly IT has not been a key part of this activity for most organizations in the past. This lack of IT focus or engagement has contributed to the perception that IT is tactical, reactive, and purely operational. For most organizations, this has been true, but we should see this as an opportunity—a big opportunity to change the perception of IT and much more. To be clear, this is not about changing perceptions. That is not enough, and there is too much at stake here.

We must recognize the unique knowledge and skillset available in IT today, the rapidly changing role of technology in the business, and the timely opportunity for IT to take a new place in the daily motion of the business and to make a new strategic contribution going forward.

This chapter will explore a few elements related to how we make this happen and convert the vision of a new and strategic IT into action.

BUSINESS PARTNERSHIP

Any path to a more strategic IT must include a close partnership with the business. The reasons for this are very simple, including better communication with the business, alignment on corporate strategy, a new engagement with customers, and working with the business and key business owners to drive innovation. All of these activities are closely related and create a new cohesion between the teams of IT and the business. This closeness spans the full organization and is not localized to any single or small group of teams. The full breadth of the business is vital, and this is how IT can gain and then drive technology strategy that is synergistic with the corporate strategy forward.

In the beginning, a couple of key roles in IT discussed previously can be a catalyst to this new business partnership. The people of IT working in IT Business Management and the IT Concierge are skilled and well positioned to accelerate the partnership with the business and IT. The partnership comes to life through the daily work of the people in IT and key business owners across the organization.

We have some work to do here in breaking out of the traditional model that has IT anchored in an operational and tactical role.

In the beginning it won't be easy to move past this tactical role, but we begin to change the model one day at a time and one job well done at a time. People will begin to notice a change and then we build some momentum and the rate of change grows faster. While the shift we need to create a more strategic IT can be jump-started by the talented people in IT Business Management and the IT Concierge team, it will carry over quickly to all the people of IT. This will be natural. We will discover the people of IT are happy to take on this partnership and know this is a good thing for the business and the IT organization.

The formation of a Strategic IT and the growing partnership with the business is driven by a few key elements:

> *Alignment and team-to-team engagement on corporate strategy*
>
> *Formation of new activities around innovation*
>
> *IT staff with ownership of strategy*
>
> *New cross-functional teams consisting of IT staff and business members*
>
> *IT staff working directly with customers*
>
> *The creation of a new IT strategy*
>
> *Communication of the IT strategy across the organization*
>
> *Recruitment of business owners to help drive the new IT strategy*
>
> *Consistent communication of the connection of IT and corporate strategy*

Note that we can and must begin changing the daily work of IT from within, which is fully under our control.

We can't wait for the business to give IT
the charter to become more strategic
because that day will never come.

This new awareness and change must come from IT and drive the transformation of IT from within. It won't be easy because change never is, but we will get a lot of help from people across the business when they begin to see a new IT emerge.

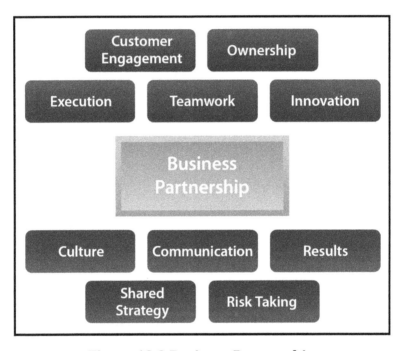

Figure 12.2 Business Partnership

The key to real change and to reposition IT in the business is to drive the real work that must occur every day. Refer to the list above as a start. Once we get started, and the start can be very simple, our people will find offshoots of work that come from the basic set of tasks we use as a baseline. All of this work will revolve around engaging IT with the business on corporate strategy and the developing new IT strategy and complements the corporate strategy.

This new IT strategy is necessary to elevate the corporate strategy through the strategic use of technology in the business. Any corporate strategy today can be made even better by leveraging technology in the right way, at the right time, and in the right place. This is a natural fit, and it becomes possible when we give just a few people in IT the charter to take on this focus. It can certainly be included in the responsibilities of both IT Business Management and the IT Concierge, because these roles will be occupied by people with a diverse skill set, including strong communications skills. These people will also be part of the "new breed" of IT and will have a high profile in the business with a new set of relationships with the key business owners. Although it can start with these people and in particular the communication activities so the business knows about this new focus in IT on strategy, the work will quickly spread to other teams in IT as both IT leadership and the business managers and concierges are actively recruiting other people in IT to join the business partnership and to contribute to the IT strategy activities. This will be an appealing assignment, and the people in IT will be hungry to join in with any strategy activity.

> *We should select some of the up-and-coming stars in IT to join this activity. Talented and passionate people just make good things happen.*

This makes sense for many reasons, including the quality of this work helping to retain our key people and that our most talented people are likely to bring the great ideas we need to shape and sharpen the new IT Strategy. With this strategy in place, even a rough version of this strategy, we must begin to communicate loudly and passionately to bring the business an understanding of the new strategy. Both the understanding and the visibility will further advance the new perception of IT as strategic and as a much-needed leader in the business.

CUSTOMER- & MARKET-FOCUSED

Building One IT must have sources of energy and enlightenment. A source that brings us clarity and magnifies and sorts out priorities. There is no real debate here in that this must be customers and markets.

Note that it is easy to put customers at number one, but the context of the market can be very helpful. Customers and markets complement one another, balance one another. The forces of the market provide a backdrop to the needs of customers and in some cases can give us a vision for the future when the focus of customers can at times be more short term or tactically focused. Tactical needs are important, but a focus on tactical requirements alone does not adequately protect the future of our customers nor provide sufficient vision for investing in their future strategic needs. Conversely, if we are overly fixated on strategic requirements and ignore the practical needs of customers, we create a different problem.

This mix of tactical and strategic requirements, the mix of both market and customer-specific requirements, is important and brings a needed balance to running the IT organization more strategically and creating a stronger partnership with customers and the market.

Regarding the market, IT will develop relationships with market influencers, experts, and consulting organizations. The press, analysts, and consultants with a practice focused on specific markets are good examples. These relationships help to bring a deeper and broader understanding of the market requirements, which in turn enables IT to better serve customers—to bring insights to the customer partnership that don't originate exclusively from the customer themselves. Our customers will appreciate our continued efforts to expand market knowledge and understanding, pull this market understanding into the IT organization, and make it a natural part of the information that flows into the IT organization every day.

This is exactly what can help to transform IT from an inside-out organization to one that is outside in. It's a big shift, and an important shift. The good news is that this is fully under our control and a key thread to the cultural change we must create across IT. The IT organization can take the actions necessary to create these connections to both the market and the customer. We discuss the customer connection at length in Chapter 6, The Customer Obsession. Yes, *obsession* is a strong word, but I chose it carefully because it reflects the sentiment we need to create across IT. This can't be emphasized enough. It is all about shattering the traditional model of IT that keeps the organization somewhat or completely removed from a direct engagement with the customer, and creating a new and direct connection to the customer that is in harmony with and in no way weakens or diminishes the good work done by teams, including technical support, sales, marketing, and account management.

It is always good to start with the customer because they become the center of everything that occurs in the business and in IT. However, this section highlights the natural connection the customer has with the market because the forces of the market can in fact help us better understand the customer. It is best for IT to create a model of connections that does not stop with the customer, but is extended to include the market—both in terms of prominent organizations and individuals as highlighted earlier, but also in building some number of market events into the IT calendar. A major tradeshow, conference, or smaller industry forum is a good experience. Even one or two of these events per year is a good outside-in activity for IT. Once again we are reminded that this is very much unconventional, but that is okay. We are creating change here, and so that just can't follow the normal pattern and expectation for IT.

> *If anything, following the normal and expected patterns and calendar of IT activities should worry us. We can't bring change to the culture of IT if we are doing everything the same way we always have.*

It is necessary to try new things, to think differently, and to take some risks. This is a powerful and healthy thing for IT—a strong medicine that is very much needed. We will address the risk topic in a later section within this chapter but for this current discussion, that of the customer and market focus, there is virtually no risk. If anything, working more actively with customers and in the market is perhaps the lowest risk of any activity we can take on in the IT organization. Think about that for a moment—the customer is our lighthouse for the allocation of time and the broader investments we make every day, so there is only good here.

Creating an IT that is more customer- and market-focused is a matter of daily activity, including the direct work and communications with our customers. These connections are tangible and something we can see every day. This should be encouraged by IT leadership and brought to life by the work that is done every day across IT. But this daily work should be supported by an element of the customer and of the market in the current IT strategy.

Every person in the IT organization should understand and be able to communicate the IT Strategy. And this strategy must include a reference to the customer focus as well as support for the corporate strategy.

This is not the same as the corporate strategy we will find in the corporate overview, on the website, and in tools like the shareholder report. If the IT Strategy does not exist today, that is okay and not uncommon, but it should be created by IT and for IT as a priority in the years ahead. It will take a little time, should be simple and understandable by the average person in IT, and then communicated often and clearly across IT so we all understand what direction we are moving, together.

RISK-TAKING

Risk-taking is a topic that might raise a few eyebrows when taken in any context related to the IT organization because it is so counter to the traditional IT model. The IT organization has grown up with a natural charter to manage and reduce risk. Eliminating risk completely is even better when that is possible. As with many other things in the normal operating model of IT, this aversion to risk was understandable and necessary. It was exactly what IT was called to do, and the IT organization answered the call.

Our view of risk is now changing. This is not intended to imply that risks will be taken where there is not some compelling upside, or that risk will be taken where the consequences can't be contained and could have a significant impact on the business, revenue, or customers.

No, this is about calculated risk—risk in the context of innovation and aggressive advancement of technology and tools. The quantum leaps forward, the big breakthroughs in innovation, and the new creative solutions that leverage technology and tools in the business are not possible without a degree of risk-taking. This becomes another element of the new IT culture, a part of changing the perception of IT.

*We will surprise some people and shock
some others across the business, and that is
nothing less than a good thing...a sign that
we are making progress in our relentless
push for a proactive and strategic IT.*

As part of the risk-taking process we must create a very clear view of the outcome we wish to achieve, a prototype or pilot model in which we can test different models, and a method to limit or eliminate any impact to current operational models if we get a surprising or negative result. It is important that we balance the need to take risks and test creative and new approaches with the need to firewall off technologies and teams and processes from being impacted, regardless of the result. With the necessary protections in place and a good understanding of the outcomes we wish to create, the teams with this charter of testing and pro-totyping new models in IT can then proceed with some fun and exciting experimentation and testing. This is healthy and a great boost to the culture of IT.

It should be clear to all those directly involved in these laboratory activities that we are creating a new IT, an IT organization commit-ted to innovation and to being proactive in bringing creative solu-tions to the business. An IT that is looking to the future needs on behalf of the business and being proactive in testing and develop-ing technology-based solutions to challenges in the business that are years into our future. This will not be easy or natural, but don't confuse that with not being necessary.

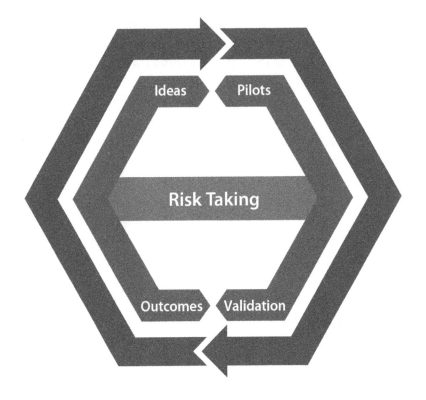

Figure 12.3 Risk-Taking and IT

This is a simple model. The first important step is creating the initiative and then making time for this innovation and risk-taking model. To a degree these things go hand in hand, and an element of risk-taking can enhance the results produced by innovation. Great innovations are not safe and are not contained.

> *Great leaps in innovation are often accompanied*
> *by crazy ideas that are criticized by some*
> *and labeled impossible by others.*

Our teams need to understand that open brainstorming, original ideas, creative thinking, and some risk-taking is important to the process, and the culture is enabling our people to be more aggressive and take some level of calculated risk, which will pay back to IT many times over in the future. This mindset will bring us the opportunity to shape ideas that can change the future of both IT and the business.

Because the stream of brainstorming, creative collaboration, unconventional designs, and risk-taking is all very much unexpected coming from IT and a very unlikely source of this important work, by creating these initiatives in IT, we do more than benefit from the work itself. This is another activity that will change the perception of IT. What we are creating here is exactly what is needed by the business and exactly what is not expected to come from IT.

Risk-taking is the perfect example of a powerful force—a combination of proactive, innovative, strategic, and disruption. Disruption in terms of disrupting ourselves. More on that later. But this powerful force is wonderful in what it can do for the business and how it is all very much not expected of IT.

> *We are going to surprise some people, and*
> *it will be a wonderful thing to behold.*

It will be a wonderful and exciting ride, my friends. Risk-taking is fun, and risk-taking encourages the right people and new people to join the ranks of IT.

An element of risk-taking enables the idea that making mistakes is okay, which is very liberating, empowering, and necessary to IT. When we know it's okay to make mistakes and to learn from those mistakes, it drives our people to be more aggressive and to move faster. All of this is very much related, and it changes the culture of IT, which in turn then drives more of the behavior that we need for our future. Each small piece enables the next piece to fall into place. For example, some degree of risk-taking is necessary for significant leaps in innovation. We simply can't innovate by being careful, by playing it safe, if you will. By being careful and by not taking risks, we are all but assuring that IT will not become a center of innovation that is desperately needed by the business. So we will because we can and then watch remarkable things come forth from IT.

> ***Risk-taking is another transformative***
> ***element that will bring IT together and create***
> ***a powerful pull to unify the business.***

It won't and can't be a single force that creates this unity, but a number of things that all complement one another and both change the culture and create the One IT and One Business that is our single best future. Risk-taking is another of these things that bring us together, united by a strategic purpose.

DISRUPT THE BUSINESS

It can be said that the business will surely be disrupted. This happens in every market and to every organization. Nobody is immune and it is only a matter of time. This time is something we simply can't know nor can we predict.

With this fundamental truth in front of us, it is best to disrupt from within, as it is far better for us to disrupt ourselves and make our future stronger than to wait and to be disrupted by a competitor or a new company that emerges suddenly and changes everything. The process of market and business disruption is natural and happens in every market segment. It is an unstoppable cycle that drives the evolution of markets and businesses. This is both necessary and natural to the evolution of any market domain and is simply a question of "when" and not "if." An inevitable disruption will surely occur, which leaves us to argue about what form it will take and what it means to the market itself.

> *So, what we are suggesting is a very strategic*
> *and proactive strategy—to systematically*
> *and thoughtfully disrupt ourselves.*

We are making a decision not to leave the coming disruption to chance or hope, but rather to make the disruption something we architect into our culture.

Something we create a fertile environment for and encourage.

This then becomes another powerful and energizing thread that runs through IT and throughout the organization. Something that in many ways helps to protect the business and strengthen our future. But this strategy is even more. What this strategy effectively creates is an aggressive acceleration of our innovation activities. We are embracing the idea that disruption is coming and we can't afford to wait, so we in IT will create a set of disruptive forces from within that will enable both IT and the business to take a calculated leap forward. This acceleration and leap will be constructed in order to strengthen the business by anticipating a number of disruptive forces and turning these forces to our advantage.

The model will create a number of disruption scenarios that IT can then put some structure to, and create an operating model around these scenarios. Not all of these scenarios will come to pass, but by working through the exercise, we create a level of readiness, including implementing some number of these scenarios throughout the business which then becomes a new stream of disruption that can run through the breadth of the business, touching many elements of the organization and driving significant changes.

> *Planning for disruption is important in the thinking that occurs, the careful reflection on each of the ideas that come from our brainstorming, and then the modeling of how the business would change and manage each of the disruptive forces.*

This is a healthy, strategic, and powerful process. Something that is another case of very "un-IT-like" thinking and behavior.

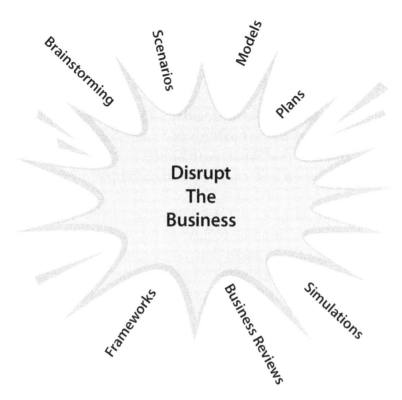

Figure 12.4 IT As Disruptive Force

The disruption planning and modeling process can start in IT and is fully under our control, but after kicking off the process, it will be important to bring together a number of key business owners from across the business. I like the idea of this launching from within IT for many reasons, but as we have discussed throughout the book, every meaningful initiative should be attacked with cross-functional teams—and this is no exception. Launch the initiative in IT, using a cross-functional team of IT skills to help shape the disruption initiative, and then help the strategy and models to take flight by pulling in the business.

This process should not be completely unstructured, so we need to create a simple cadence for disruption influences to carry forward. A quarterly review, for example, could include a set of three to five new ideas to evaluate, and the IT team builds a rough disruption scenario around each model and then presents the scenarios to a team of key business owners.

> *Remember, these scenarios are not simply changes in the business but rather extreme changes that will create significant business disruption, a dramatic business realignment.*

Through this review we can then reduce the number of disruption scenarios and take the group of three to five scenarios down to one or two and then invest some time in creating a simple prototype or model of the scenario which could then be reviewed at an intermediate meeting or the next quarterly review. Over time some number of these scenarios and prototypes will merit the creation of a framework that is sufficiently structured to be implemented in the business to drive change from within and master our own disruption. This implementation, led or facilitated by IT, creates a disruptive force that preempts an exposure we have in the marketplace. It is an important concept to understand and to communicate to senior leadership because there will be a cost and there will be resources required.

This is a healthy and strategic process that ultimately reduces the exposure of the organization and is fully under our control—note that it is a striking contrast to attempting to manage disruption when disruptive forces hit the business without warning and we are left to react and to salvage what we can.

LEVERAGING BEST PRACTICES & FRAMEWORKS

The good people of IT today have a remarkable array of best practices, frameworks, and standards from which to choose in helping the organization to advance our performance in virtually every area. If anything, there are so many of these frameworks and best practices available to us, it can be a bit overwhelming and challenging when trying to make decisions around what is a good fit for your organization and then in what capacity should the selected models be applied. This is very common today and a thought held by many organizations.

My intent here is not to attempt to tell you what framework or best practices approach is right for you—that is just not possible, and there are too many variables to be considered. It is a thoughtful decision to be made methodically and with the participation of a number of your key people and with leadership support.

What I will offer here is a recommended approach, three steps specifically, to help your organization navigate the decision process and make good decisions based on your needs today and the expected needs of your organization over the next five to ten years.

Having spent some time in the past ten years in studying a number of these best practices, including ITIL, DevOps, and Agile, it is clear that each is rich and deep and has much to offer most organizations regardless of size. There are passionate fans of each of these as well as many other frameworks not addressed here, but I have selected these examples because they collectively have the largest following and have achieved the largest application across IT organizations globally. Yes, there are many others, and new frameworks continue to emerge, which is good for the future of IT, but for this discussion and the approach I will propose, this cross-section of the market will serve our purposes.

ITIL, DevOps, and Agile have a very broad appeal and each offers a wonderful collection of diverse elements—there is something valuable here for virtually every organization. For example, ITIL provides a proven and robust process model for IT Service Management with key process structure and process dependencies. DevOps is a unique mix of process, technology, philosophy, and culture that includes a good dose of business common sense, which has helped propel its broad appeal. And Agile provides guidance on how we work more quickly and more iteratively as high-performing teams focused on measurable results and customer engagement. It is easy to see that each of these three example frameworks and methodologies has a strong intersection with the principles of our IT transformation and the unification of IT and our business as One.

As the journey of IT continues, it is likely that these three examples can offer some level of guidance and value to your organization at key junctures of your journey-within-the-journey. But as you consider these decisions, keep the following three-step approach in mind.

First, know your IT Strategy and select elements of ITIL, DevOps, and Agile to support your IT strategy and the strategy of your business. Each of these collections offers a great deal, but they *should* *never be confused with and cannot replace* your governing strategy for IT. This is a common mistake and has caused confusion and a negative impact in some organizations. Some combination of ITIL, DevOps, and Agile can and should play a supporting role, and it can certainly be an important one, in executing against your IT strategy and bringing it to life, but *they are not* **the** *IT strategy.* Know your strategy first and clearly, and then in the context of this strategy, your team can put to work the right combination of these collections to enhance and support the singular strategy that guides our daily decisions and execution. If you are considering ITIL, DevOps, and Agile along with any other of the many frameworks and best practices available today, and it is not clear what the governing IT strategy is, it is critical to take a pause to discuss, debate, socialize, and then craft this strategy before then coming back to how your organization can best deploy these collections to help take your organization forward.

Second, ask yourselves these ten questions as a way to properly set expectations, confirm priorities, make resource assignments, and manage investments. Note that the reference to "investment" in the list below refers to the investment required to take on board the framework/best practice in terms of people and capital investment. In most cases this will be significant.

1. How does this investment directly support and enhance our IT strategy?
2. How does this investment directly support and enhance our business strategy?
3. How will this investment drive value to our customers?
4. Will this investment improve the satisfaction of current customers?
5. What risks are we taking with this investment and its deployment?
6. Do we have an accurate understanding of the costs for this deployment?
7. Do we have any internal experience and expertise with this methodology?

8. Have we identified our people who will be assigned to this initiative?
9. What are the measurable benefits we expect to receive from the investment?
10. Do we have a good definition for what success looks like?

We kept the list to ten questions to get things started, but you will no doubt be able to think of many more questions, and that is good. It's important to be complete and self-critical at this stage. The beginning of the selection process, or the beginning of a new phase of leveraging these frameworks, is the best time to ask these questions and push ourselves for good answers. I reference the beginning of a new phase because it is somewhat common for businesses to do a restart with these methodologies after having experienced poor or mixed results from an initial implementation.

Third, it's not about just one—in many cases a mix, or the right balance of multiple frameworks, will drive the best results. Each of our three examples of ITIL, DevOps, and Agile shares some of the same principles and characteristics but also displays some significant differences. This is ultimately a good thing because we need some broad coverage for what is likely a broad strategy. And so it becomes a matter of understanding the strategy of IT and then selecting the right combination of these frameworks and best practices, and possibly pieces of these and in the right roles, to support and enhance our IT and business strategy. This should occur at the very beginning, and this thinking will then frame the many actions that follow.

Although every business is different, by following these three steps and the many activities that each contains, your team can reduce the risks and challenges experienced by the many organizations that did not meet expectations with their investments in ITIL, DevOps, and Agile over the past twenty-five years and then in turn realize the significant value these frameworks can drive when working in the right role and under the right expectations.

We close this section with a single but very important thought.

The most successful and advanced IT organizations have come to understand that IT is a single wonderful, dynamic, and powerful system. A single system that must be respected and defended against the risks of sub-optimizing the many subsystems of IT.

This focus on the many pieces, elements, or silos of IT is natural and has been common. But now, through the transformational changes occurring in IT and our work to create One IT and One Business, it helps to keep this *appreciation of the system of IT* foremost in our thinking. With this awareness, our decisions and investments and strategies and designs must be to the good of the system of IT, in making this single system of IT stronger. If we are thinking and acting locally in IT, we are making the system of IT weaker.

This strategic principle should be reinforced and discussed frequently by IT leadership and throughout the IT organization as a guiding insight.

CHAPTER 13

IT IS ALWAYS ON

As the business, any business really, becomes more dependent on technology, the inroads of how we live and work every day frequently run back to IT as the center of gravity for so much of what we do. The systems, tools, and data of IT are the fabric of the business and what we use in some combination to complete our work every day. Yes, these systems are becoming far more advanced, flexible, and convenient, but we simply rely on them for virtually all of what we do in IT and in the business every day.

> *There is a fundamental connection between virtually every person in the organization and the technologies and systems of IT that keeps business moving forward and enables the business to deliver its services and products.*

Whether the organization is government, health care, education, retail, manufacturing, services, or any other of the many markets that make up the world of business today, this connection is fundamental. There is very little we can accomplish in our daily work without accessing the phone system, using a mobile phone, accessing email, utilizing an HR system, accessing an ERP system, requesting a service, utilizing a laptop or desktop, or relying on the protection of security tools. All of these things are connected in one way or another to each other and to our people.

> ***This is a marvelous web of people and technology that forms the organization itself; it's a living thing that serves our customers.***

Recognizing what makes this machine go and that it's the very organization itself and with our shared mission of creating happy customers—none of this is possible if IT is not always ready, always able to serve. This is more true today than ever as our systems and technologies have become more indispensable to our daily work and more capable at the same time.

Taking this realization one step further, the people of the organization in every role must have access to the systems and tools of IT at any time. It is increasingly difficult to support standard business hours with the knowledge this concept is quickly dying away. Soon we won't have standard business hours, and this is all driven by today's and the future customer who carries with them a new set of expectations. This standard is built around a simple model:

Personalized service

No waiting

Around-the-clock access to resources

Ability to self-serve

Customizable services and products

Immediate delivery

Flexible engagement model

The profile of the new customer expectations calls to our attention that this is not possible if all the people of the organization have limited access to the resources of IT we have become so dependent on.

The services and assets of IT must be always ready, always capable, and always available.

This calls the people of IT to leverage a number of practices and resources that have evolved and matured in environments like aerospace, emergency services, and military and now stand ready to have a big impact on IT delivering on the Always On model, including:

Automated resiliency

More mature operational processes

Disaster recovery and failover for mission critical systems

Optimized outage response

Robust major incident response

Redundant systems and system components

Real-time communications of risks and service degradations

There is a cost for this certainly, but this must be the standard, and the revenue of opportunity far exceeds any cost. Every organization must start with this goal and then determine how we can best achieve this capability. If there is ever any questioning of this standard, talk to a customer and they will make it clear.

*Put another way, if your organization can't
meet this customer profile, offering the ultimate
flexibility and convenience in how customers
are served, another organization will.*

This is the competitive reality of the market today. Ultimately, we should view it as an opportunity for the strongest businesses to rise. All the others will fade to niche providers or go away entirely, but make no mistake, this is the new reality of our markets over the next ten years. And this new customer profile will be fulfilled faster than what many people in IT want to believe today.

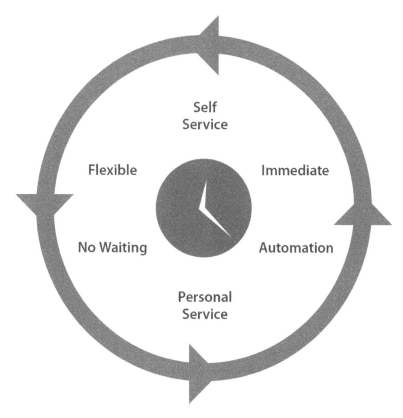

Figure 13.1 IT Is Always On

This strategy of IT Always On has everything to do with One IT.

It is simply not possible for a
fragmented and disjointed IT to make
this transformation to Always On.

It just can't happen and so we can and should rally around the customer as a guiding light in providing the resources of IT to the business and then to the customer around the clock, no exceptions.

IT Always On enables a Business Always On, which then enables a happy and productive customer. This chain is the essence of the successful organization over the next decade.

24X7 IS EXPECTED

The concept of standard business hours is quickly fading away for most businesses. Extended hours are becoming the norm, but increasingly the market is demanding that organizations operate around the clock—driven by the emergence of a new demanding customer. These expectations did not happen overnight. They have been cultivated by a shift in lifestyle as enabled by smartphones and mobile devices that readily provide information to resources and services at any time, and from anywhere.

The backdrop of these expectations is very much a personal experience that evolved through online shopping, online learning and research, social media, email, chat, texting, and much more.

> *What all these influencing models have in common is delivering a personal and satisfying experience to the individual that is highly convenient and always available.*

This model has now become so dominant in how we live, it is unstoppable in terms of the influence it brings to the workplace. I fully expect the models of how we work and how we communicate in business to fall in line with these personal models over the next five to ten years. This force is simply unstoppable given its simplicity and ease of use.

A natural and important part of this overall lifestyle and communications model is the around-the-clock access, putting the power of information and action squarely with the customer. With a taste of this convenience-first lifestyle, there will be no going back. As we begin to accept, some slowly we should note, this new 24X7 lifestyle, it should quickly be noted that IT is the key enabler. This model is all about the convenience and flexibility of the customer experience, fully enabled by the right mix of tools, systems, devices, and technology.

> *The mission of IT then begins, and it is already under way for many organizations, to make this all look very easy and very natural. And by the way, everything is 24X7 of course.*

Making it look easy is anything *but* easy and takes careful design, planning, and execution. We can fairly say that the easier and more natural the experience, the more work that was necessary behind the scenes to bring this easy experience to life.

IT must recognize this emerging model and, like with so many other things, be proactive in creating the necessary plans and taking the necessary actions now to ensure IT is ready when the business is ready.

> *This mindset can and should apply to much of what we will do over the next decade—ensure that IT is ready when the business is ready.*

If the business is ready and IT is not, we have created a big problem for the organization. A period of waiting, some period of delay, is bad for everybody—measurable in terms of lost opportunities, customers, and revenue. All of this is wholly unacceptable.

Conversely, when the business identifies a need and is ready to act and at this critical time IT has anticipated the need and is fully ready, that is a transformational moment in the business. IT is now uniquely capable of making this proactive model a reality and to create leverage with the systems, tools, and technologies under our charge. This is vital to the success of the business on a broad scale. In the context of this discussion, IT is able to make 24X7 access to services and resources a reality at that very instant when the business needs it, and that instant will be here before many organizations realize. For some, the time has already come.

It should be noted that the model of 24X7 access is about much more than the numbers. We must understand that this model of convenience, putting the power of information and access into the hands of the user and under the control of our customers, builds trust. This model creates loyal and successful customers who will return to an organization time and time again for the products and services they need. Was all this created by 24X7 access itself? Surely not. But was around-the-clock access and always-available-for-me a key to creating this larger perception of trust and value? Absolutely.

This says so much about today and about the future of One IT.

A NEW CUSTOMER

The customer of today bears little resemblance to the customer of only ten years ago. Lest there be any confusion around this point, we should embrace this new customer and see it as an opportunity and certainly not as a problem. It is in fact a big change and a big shift, and with this comes a bigger opportunity for the right business alongside the right IT organization.

Not every business and not every IT team will recognize and understand the needs of this customer, and as such, those organizations that can will enjoy a significant advantage in the market. We have previously touched on the profile of this customer, but it's important and so worth summarizing again some of the characteristics that shape this customer of today and the future:

Insists on flexibility

Expects a personalized experience

Ability to self-learn, self-fulfill, and self-update

Options for other service models if needed

Well educated and very focused on specific needs

Demands a great price with ongoing value

Friendly and intuitive user experience

Able to participate in a customer community

Loyal when receiving a great product or service

Will take the time to research the business

Actively living a new lifestyle balance of personal and professional

Knows what they prefer and what they don't

Appreciates a high level of control

Customer expectations have elements that are timeless and never go away completely.

Figure 13.2 A New Customer

But these traditional customer needs are balanced by the new priorities that have emerged from the market evolution we have revisited numerous times.

The key is understanding both—the long-lived fundamentals of the customer together with the new customer profile born of new and global market realities smashed together with the expectations fueled by new technologies and new business models.

All of these dimensions must be understood, and we need to avoid any temptation to oversimplify. That is just not possible and creates a risk for the business.

Having provided an overview of the new customer, much of which you are likely to recognize through the window of what you are seeing in your organizations today, let's trace back to how the model is enabled in the business. Much to all of this is anchored by the systems, technologies, and tools of IT. Look closely at how customer desires are fulfilled. Behind each is a story or a system or technology or data that is able to bring this model to life. Once again we are reminded of the vital leverage that is held in IT and how only IT can enable the business to first perform and to then deliver what is needed by the market and our customers.

Never before has this relationship between IT and the business been so vital as when we are reminded of what these new and wonderfully impatient, demanding, independent, curious, educated, and always plugged-in customers expect from the organizations they will give their business to in the future.

For this discussion, we are reminded of the intersection of this new customer with IT always being ready to deliver a service and ensure the infrastructure and assets of the business are ready to serve. Seems simple, but yet it is remarkable just how many organizations have not yet reached an understanding of this connection.

The connection of IT assets and services to the business, which in turn is able to service the new customer in fundamentally new ways, is a model that is only new for a short while and then becomes just how we work with our customers every day. This transition time is growing shorter and shorter every year. Improved access and flexibility are no longer enough. We can no longer be comfortable that IT is making improvements year over year.

No, our expectations must be elevated across IT to a new model of always on, and nothing else will do.

QUALITY OF LIFE

Ultimately, the ability of IT to deliver an always-ready infrastructure and services that operate around the clock is not just about this supreme level of availability. It is increasingly about the quality of life of the good people in IT and across the organization, and this quality is then an enabling force to improve the quality of life of our customers. This powerful cycle is about much more than just quantitative measures.

There is a new hunger in our marketplace that is seeking the ability to be productive in our profession while at the same time achieving a new level of flexibility and convenience that delivers an elevated quality of life. The improved performance in business is not enough, and it is only a stepping stone to something much bigger. Now, this should not be confused with a lack of commitment to jobs and to professional success. If anything that is more important than ever because the good people across the organization and a goal held by customers as well is that business success can be achieved with a greater economy of effort, even greater success in many cases, with a dramatically more efficient and more effective model of working which then allows us to enhance our personal lives outside of business.

This has the potential to bring to life
the best of both worlds for the first time
in the modern history of business.

For the past seventy-five years, work schedules, demands, miles traveled, and virtually every measure of effort expended in business have grown steadily. Employee mental health, families, and relationships have been impacted. But this is now changing, and changing with conviction. It's the combination of a new workforce, personal life changes, new technologies that have become integral to our lives, and the realization that we simply can't continue to work tirelessly around the clock to meet the needs of a demanding business.

The brute force approach to business has worked in large part for seventy-five years, but this must stop.

There has been some perception in business that we need to work harder, longer hours, make more sacrifices. More on top of more on top of more. This demanding cycle has shaped our work and the culture of IT for decades. The talented people of IT and the business have made countless sacrifices to support our users and our customers. These wonderful people are willing to do whatever it takes to make the people served by IT successful, and they will never make the decision to stop, or to sacrifice less.

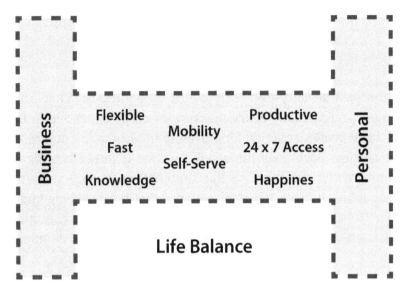

Figure 13.3 Quality of Life

But now, we need to give them some help. The dedicated people of IT will begin to understand and to then appreciate there is a better way that enables them to deliver the same level of service and in many cases even better, while taking on a higher quality of life. A more sustainable lifestyle. A work and personal life balance that we can enjoy for the next ten to twenty years.

> *This highlights another chain of vital connections—this lifestyle shift is not just about the customer.*

This lifestyle change will connect the people of IT to the people of the business, and then in turn we are all connected to the customer and are able to make this new lifestyle a reality for all the people of the chain. All of us together.

There will be no going back to the madness of brute force.

The new quality of life is a wonderfully elegant and powerful model.

Elegant in that it is simplicity in motion. Elegant in that it is all about leverage. Powerful in that we can do more with less for the first time in the long history of IT. We now stand at the threshold of this seismic shift in IT, in the business, and in how we serve customers who will return to us time and time again.

High quality of life for the people in IT will mean longer tenure, a more experienced staff, a happier staff, and then ultimately a better service delivered to the business and to customers. Every element of the chain improves, and this is to the good of all. A happy workforce with a high quality of life is a more productive workforce, and a happy and more productive workforce will inevitably create a more powerful business.

It should not be lost in all of this that an improved quality of life is timely. We need this elevated quality desperately as mental health has been impacted by the growing demands of business over the past decade, but we are also now uniquely able to make this a reality through improved systems and tools. Yes, a need for a higher quality of life is the catalyst, but if we are not able to operate IT and the business in such a way that we can make this a reality, then we have created a fundamental conflict and face difficult choices.

> *Fortunately, those tough choices that could pit the needs of our people against those of the business are not necessary because we can both recognize the critical need for an improved quality of life. Fortunately for all, we have the systems and tools and processes that enable us to meet this challenge.*

For the first time in history, we can consciously deliver an improved quality of life with no loss in productivity and overall business performance. Even better, it is now possible to achieve a significant improvement in quality of life and actually improve business performance overall. This is an exciting development, a real breakthrough for the people of IT who have sacrificed so much in decades past, the dedicated people throughout the business, and the customers who will also benefit from this improved quality of life. This is nothing short of a dramatic shift in the full business model.

It is truly the beginning of a new era where what many thought was simply not possible becomes possible.

I will close this section with a further comment on mental health, which has not been a traditional focus of IT but is now an issue we must watch closely. The stress and general demands placed on the people of IT over the past decade are remarkable and have only grown over time.

> *Mental health is a critical issue and must be on the list of cultural and management priorities for leadership, of course, but also a shared priority for all the people of IT.*

We need to be aware of this issue and watch for signs of mental health risk among our colleagues. Simply being aware of this helps a great deal and then when we do see a colleague in need of help, we can offer some assistance as best we can and encourage them to get further professional help through the resources of the company if needed.

Every person will appreciate this support, understanding, and empathy, and it will further strengthen our culture and our business.

We are so strong together.

BUSINESS VELOCITY

The commitment of IT to always being on and always being available will create an opportunity for increased speed, starting in IT and then providing an engine for increases in speed across the business. This can make everything move faster as we now have the opportunity to complete tasks at any hour of the day, which is itself very valuable. But it's important to recognize that this benefit starts a chain reaction that carries over into the next day and beyond. The flexibility to complete work or to execute automated tasks (an increasingly critical element) at any time stimulates the completion of work in the next twenty-four-hour period that would not otherwise be completed. This has a positive effect on the overall cadence of the IT organization and the business.

Everywhere we look across the organization, we have both the need and the opportunity to create speed of performance, an improved velocity for the business. This is an increase in speed, a reduction in the elapsed time required to complete every meaningful action across the organization.

The IT organization should view this improvement and the chain of dependencies and actions as starting within the IT organization and our people. The people element of this should not be underestimated. The link is vital.

Of course, there are other opportunities to improve business velocity throughout the complete organization, but IT can be the catalyst and can unblock many improvements across the business that only become possible when IT makes fundamental improvements to assets, infrastructure, systems, and tools that then make new levels of performance across the business. Better yet, these actions taken by IT send a signal to every person in the organization that speed is a focus; we are creating business velocity every day and this must be on the priority list for everybody across the business. IT is leading this change, this revolution, in many regards.

Business velocity is not just something that happens as a convenient byproduct of other work that is occurring. It is very much the opposite—speed in every action of the business is the result of careful design, planning, and execution that is precisely targeted at these speed improvements. Velocity occupies a place in the top tier of our priorities, and IT will make investments that are all about increasing business velocity.

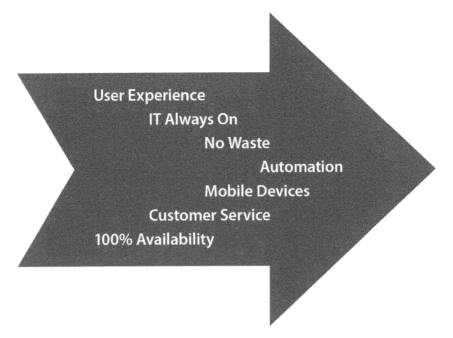

Figure 13.4 Business Velocity Created by IT

This is a good time for another reminder of the vital connection between the customers we serve and the velocity of the business. This new generation of customer, demanding and impatient but willing to invest when their requirements can be met, can be served better and likely much better when IT delivers improved speed and business velocity. Yes, the business itself has some control of this speed and in particular with those processes that are largely manual. But ultimately a large leap forward in speed across the business must come from the tools, technologies, systems, and infrastructure managed by IT. Speed improvements we make here then have an immediate impact in every element of the business. Every element of the business can benefit.

> *By moving IT to this powerful Always On model,*
> *we open up the capacity of the organization*
> *in ways that were simply not possible before.*
> *It changes the physical motion of the business*
> *but also changes how people think.*

What was not possible before now becomes possible. The clock- and calendar-related limitations of the business that have existed from the very beginning now fade away, and the time of day or the day of the week won't slow us down. Our approach to how we get things done evolves and is encouraged by the new around-the- clock model. This is a much-needed boost to the business that IT is uniquely able to provide.

Much of our improved business velocity will come from tangible system improvements and from harnessing new and improved technology. Automation comes to mind as a great and very real ex- ample. The first generation of automation will have an impact dur- ing normal and then extended business hours. Then, IT will create a more powerful second generation of automation through auto- mating additional tasks, by delivering more intelligent and learn- ing automation, and by complementing this with making all the automation capabilities available at all times, no exceptions. Both around-the-clock resources and 100 percent availability of systems becomes the norm. This brings us remarkable leverage and will fully touch every person in the organization.

It is fun and easy to focus on technology and systems, but we will also look at how we work every day, and that calls attention to another great example of the people and process side of improvement—the streamlining of the organization through the elimination of waste. I address this particular topic throughout the book because it represents such a tremendous opportunity for improvement and it is fully under control. No miracles needed here, just some thoughtful review and hard work.

This is good stuff.

A good balance of people and process improvements, even small steps, along with the IT Always On initiative and the growing automation across IT together fundamentally changes how our people work and especially how much work can be completed in a day and how quickly tasks and business processes can be executed.

It should be emphasized that IT Always On is a necessary enabler to the Business Always On. The first beneficiary of this full availability model will be those people closest to the assets and systems—the people of IT. This in itself has big benefits because the IT organization is then able to better service the employees of the business. Then, a wonderful thing happens. The people of the business are able to work differently and better, bringing agility and scalability to life. These are important principles in the business that we revisit many times because they are so important, and so important to creating leverage. With this enablement of the people across the business, momentum quickly spreads to our serving customers in new and creative ways. The business is able to offer enhanced products and services that were simply not possible before. This simple Always On model is born in IT but has no boundaries in the good that it can create. Along the way we are doing another important thing, and that is making our people and our customers happy and empowered.

*This is a powerful and wonderful mix
with a virtually unlimited upside.*

CHAPTER 14

TRANS IT AUTOMATION

The traditional model of IT has evolved around thinking in terms of local functions and the people who make up these functions. The organization is then further shaped around these functions and people, and the model has then shaped all the extensions that drive what happens in the IT organization every day. This complete multifaceted structure will also commonly be called a silo.

This has many implications. As we think locally, we then tend to build tasks and business processes and ultimately automation models that are localized within this model. Limited in scope by definition and to a degree, preordained. This is a fundamentally flawed model that will limit the value, speed, and scale we have the potential to create with what is a more natural and superior model.

The time has come, for many reasons, including improved technology and automation tools, to review all the business processes, workflows, and any automation in place today to carefully evaluate the scope of these business processes.

*What we are looking for is the Natural
Beginning and the Natural End to these
processes. This beginning and end is a
business trigger that launches the business
process and then the final completion of
the work that supports this process.*

This is a vital distinction. What we will find in many cases is a business process or workflow that has been designed around an organization structure, or the scope of an existing application or the boundaries of a silo. This happens all the time but creates some major challenges, including:

Artificial business process design

Workflow that is broken into unnecessary pieces

Unnatural starts and stops in a business process

Potential delays in the business process

Unnecessary integrations designed into the workflow

Significant risk in the execution of the business process

Business processes and workflows that don't reflect the business

Confusion is introduced into the organization

Business processes that don't reflect how people work

And this is just the beginning. It becomes clear quickly that the design of business processes and workflows becomes greatly twisted and fragmented when our focus is the current IT organization, the ability of current tools, or the structure of our functional silos.

We are missing the point when what we
really should be creating are business
processes, workflows, tasks, and rules that
reflect how the business works every day.

It's not an exaggeration to call this alignment critical, and at the same time recognize that it does not exist in many IT organizations today. Our examples to this point have been the business processes and workflows themselves because this is the work that is performed every day and creates the work product that IT delivers within IT and to the business.

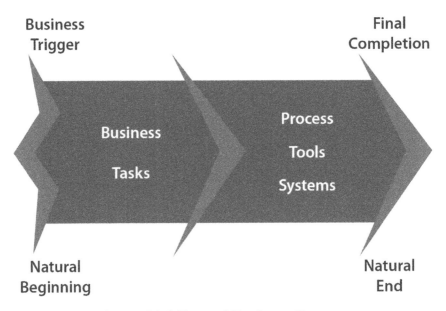

Figure 14.1 Natural Business Process

These business processes are then the model of what we automate with automation tools, which is the fabric of work that will be done in the next ten years. Based on my experiences with many IT organizations in the past few years as automation has begun to be incorporated into the daily operations of IT, approximately 20 percent of the work performed in IT is automated. However, we stand at the threshold of a dramatic surge in the level of automation across IT over the next decade. The goal for IT organizations today is to push for an achievement of 90 percent automation in the next five years for the standard and consistent work performed in IT every day. I address this topic in more detail in Chapter 18, The 90/90 Rule, but the essence of this theme is a revolution of automation that is being driven by an obsession with serving our customers better, which in turn creates a critical need to work faster, more consistently, and to enable customers to service themselves when so desired.

> *There are of course many more benefits to automation, but when we look at the very short list of the things that can change our lives in the world of IT, automation certainly makes this exclusive list.*

The topic of automation arises repeatedly throughout the book in a number of different contexts, and given its strategic nature, this makes sense and it needs lots of attention. For the purposes of this chapter, we are looking at the motion of IT business processes, the scope of these processes, and how we extract the maximum possible value and impact for the automation of this daily work. This very central theme is fundamental to the success of IT over the next decade, building a new unified IT, bringing to life the singularity we must live every day, and the alignment and coming together of IT and the business that will shape the organization of the future. This model is the backbone of the successful business of the next ten years and beyond.

NATURAL BEGINNING TO END

Fundamental to the design and operations of Trans IT Automation is the concept of natural beginning and end as touched on in the opening of this chapter. The distinction we are making here is the difference between the artificial design of business process and then automation based on organizational structures, the ability of applications and tools, or the scope of existing IT job functions. This is a fundamentally misguided design, although a very common one today based on the anatomy of the traditional IT organization.

A far superior and far more natural model is to take the time to identify the true and natural beginning and end of each business process and workflow. It requires a bit of investigation and forensics but all the answers are there for the people that take the time to look and think about what we are finding.

Every business process and workflow will have a trigger that initiates the process based on a business need. This is typically driven by a clear and identifiable business requirement.

This is the one and only beginning.

Then, each business process or workflow will be executed until such time as all work is complete and the original business requirement has been fully satisfied in the judgment of the customer or user. As with the beginning, there will normally be a clear deliverable or work product created at the end of the business process to a specific group of users in need of this deliverable.

This is the one and only ending.

The investigation and review of each business process is necessary and important work (see Chapter 7, Business Process Design and Chapter 9, Elimination of Waste) to both eliminate waste that has accumulated over the past twenty-five years in many cases, along with simplifying the process and validating the work and its deliverables are required today and have an understood value. This work is necessary in that it is long overdue, will help to ensure the precious resources of IT are invested in the right things, will benefit the manual work that is done every day, and is critical to cleanse all our business processes before we take on more automation work. What is likely to occur for most IT organizations is the automation process will continue for the next five to ten years as we work toward the milestones of 50 percent, then 90 percent, then 99 percent automated, which is where we expect IT organizations to be in ten years. Each of these phases will require the automation of an additional block of business processes, and these processes and workflows can only be automated when there is only necessary work and no waste being taken forward.

The importance of this can't be overstated— the cleansing of all business processes and workflows is a necessary and powerful predecessor to the work of automation that is so critical to IT over the next ten years.

With this investigation and understanding complete, we now have what we need to define a business process or workflow that is aligned with a true business need, and does not include any unnecessary starting and stopping, integrations, waiting times, queues, or delays. Each of these elements is common today and each introduces a level of risk, complexity, and cost. There is even more at work here in that where these elements exist there is also slowed performance and waiting.

> *These things related to slowness in all its forms*
> *are poison to the IT organization of the future.*

So, our mission must be to identify these natural beginnings and ends, and then if necessary to either design new business processes and workflows based on the definitions or to redesign any flawed or fragmented business processes that exist today.

Figure 14.2 Benefits of Trans IT Automation

This is vital work because what we need to create is a new generation of business processes and workflow that are aligned with true and complete business requirements, and the breadth of scope of these business processes match the business. In many cases, this will mean that the workflows span several functional areas of IT, several silos, and this will be an extension of what these workflows would have been modeled as before. The new version of these business processes will be a more accurate model, now lined up with the business, and will allow work to be completed faster and likely bring with it some cost savings.

In many cases, redesigning the business processes across IT will for the first time create Trans IT business processes, which then clear the way to create Trans IT automation. This is a natural next step and will change so much of what happens in IT every day. Benefits of Trans IT automation include:

Improved teamwork

Continued erosion of any existing silos

Improved transparency

Significant increase in business process speed

Reduced number of integrations

Big reduction in organizational waste

Elimination of most waiting times and queues

Creates a unifying force across the IT organization

Drives a natural alignment with the business

These exciting benefits are virtually without limits.

Teams that have not done much work together now will, communications will improve, transparency will improve, and work will be completed faster in almost every case.

These improvements bring us benefits at a strategic level, at the operational level, and of course accelerate the unification of IT and the business. IT should not be lost in all this. The alignment of IT with the business will take a big leap forward, and we will begin to work more naturally with key business owners to ensure *the work of our business* is completed every day in a more natural and leaner way.

NO WAITING & NO WASTE

The design and operation of many existing business processes and the automation that reflects this work are often fragmented due to organizational structures and silos. Fragmentation does not reflect the natural scope and structure of the true business process, and as such these business processes are in fact only pieces of the true business process when viewed strictly from a business perspective.

With this structure there is a level of waiting and waste that has been designed in to the IT business processes of the past and today. It is now time for us to carefully and completely scrub our processes and workflows of these delays and waste.

> *The impact of this slowness and unnecessary work is huge—it places a tax on all of IT and makes every action we take harder than it needs to be. It makes agility all but impossible.*

We should view this as a positive thing, not as fixing a big problem but rather taking advantage of a big opportunity that is right in front of us and completely under our control.

So, we take on this important task of focusing on delays and waste in the largest context of Trans IT Automation. This is a natural pairing, and we would not do our best with building this new generation of automation that spans IT in many cases without taking the time to ensure we have eliminated any slowness, delays, or queues at the same time. Every second counts. We can't tolerate anything that slows us down. Raw speed is a key to the future of IT and to the future of the business, and achieving the next level of speed is possible right now. We build the speed we need with small steps, and with small steps anything is possible. But this needs to be a focus or we miss the opportunity to extract every possible second.

It is also a time to take a hard look at any manual steps in our business processes, including any manual approvals, which are a big source of waiting and delays. Our first goal is to eliminate manual steps and approvals entirely when possible. There should be a lot of pressure on the organization to validate why manual work or approvals should be taken forward. If the case is there, then fair enough. But often we will discover that manual work or approvals can be eliminated altogether. This is always the best result and brings us the most benefit. If the work or approval is necessary, every effort should be made to automate what is manual today, including the automation of approvals, which is very much within our reach.

> *Taking this a step further, any approval in a business process should be modeled with a specific and brief waiting period and then routed to a secondary or tertiary approval.*

Doing so is very effective and can save us lots of time. It is remarkable just how much time in IT has been wasted in the past waiting on an approval from an approver who is unaware of the request, out of the office, or traveling. This just can't continue. We must design a process that compresses approvals that previously took days or weeks into a window measured by minutes. This is the new standard.

Even more to consider—any manual work product impedes our ability to build scalability and agility into everything we do in IT. These two themes should always be on our mind when we launch new initiatives—how can we design scalability and agility into this process or system? When evaluating commercial systems, how does the system perform with regard to both scalability and agility? This has everything to do with the useful lifetime of our systems and the ability of our systems to deliver value to the business.

These priorities should go to the top of a new scorecard we use to review and evaluate commercial systems to be purchased and deployed across IT in the years ahead. Software applications that are common across IT today in every element of the organization look more and more alike from a user experience and functional requirements standpoint. This is typical for maturing markets—products tend to commoditize over time. But we need to look more closely through this lens of scalability and agility, and in this regard, tools and systems can be very different.

The attributes of scalability and agility will often be assigned a greater priority with traditional functional requirements.

> *The systems deployed today in IT organizations*
> *globally that have proven not to be scalable*
> *or agile are likely under review to be replaced*
> *or retired. This scrutiny is long overdue.*

As we follow this path of thinking—very much aware of the need to eliminate waiting and waste across IT and to then take this momentum across the business—we develop a growing appreciation for the ability of our IT systems to scale and to respond quickly to change. Clearly, Trans IT Automation is a significant enabler for these strategic qualities. Then, as we are increasingly successful with Trans IT Automation, we quickly create a growing influence across the business, our automation rapidly makes inroads into the business, and it is increasingly difficult to see or identify any boundaries or divisions between any element of the business and IT.

Why? Because our focus has shifted from an internal-first and structural operational focus to a focus on the customer, business outcomes, and external-first influences, including the market-place, and business performance, including growth and earnings. Certainly our growing focus on these business performance and business outcome measurements has existed in some IT organizations globally, but it would be fair to say it is more the exception than the rule and more limited to exceptional and visionary organizations.

In the years ahead this vision will spread quickly across hundreds and then thousands of IT organizations globally, and the connection between these IT organizations and their businesses will benefit immediately. The singularity of IT and the business is sure to follow, and we have then created a new and remarkably powerful business model fit for the next decade and beyond.

I frequently refer to the next decade as a period of great change, and it must be.

However, the new models for IT and the business, and the ensuring unification of IT and elements of the business, then create a rebirth of the complete business as we know it today, and this force will sustain organizations that emerge from this transformation and create a new generation of market leaders.

TIME COMPRESSION

To ensure there is no confusion around the use of the term "compression," it is used here to describe a reduction in the total time required to execute a simple task, a series of tasks, or a complete business process regardless of size or complexity. Every unit of work both large and small is in play, and every segment of work is reduced, either from the beginning, from the end, or from a compression that begins in the middle of the segment itself.

This is an overall increase of speed, but it originates from within the work conducted every day. We view these work elements, whether they are executed in seconds or days, as the building blocks of the operations of IT.

Every minute of work represents a physical and virtual block of work that together make up the daily operations of IT and the business. These work blocks make up every workflow and business process across the organization. There are no boundaries here, and this is very much the daily output of the organization from top to bottom.

Figure 14.3 Time Compression

Trans IT Automation will bring us many benefits in the next five to ten years, and among the most impactful will be the compression of time in every action that occurs every day—what will become a redefinition of time as we know it today. The expectations that govern IT today will change, and new expectations will emerge that all business processes and workflows and tasks will be completed faster, then much faster and with a greater degree of precision and reliability. This time transformation will occur faster than what we might think, much faster in many cases.

The process of designing, validating, implementing, and then operating Trans IT Automation will drive a number of significant benefits with regards to time:

Compression of existing tasks

Compression of sequences of tasks

Connection of tasks that are not connected today

Creation of new business processes that are new combinations of disjointed processes in the past

Acceleration of information flow

Rapid growth in the breadth of business processes

Boundaries of the organization are broken down

Multi-function business processes become common

Single-function business processes become uncommon

Business processes push beyond the boundaries of IT

A significant reduction in time required to deliver IT services

Increase in user satisfaction and productivity

**This list of improvements is exciting enough
but really only the beginning of what we
can accomplish with Trans IT Automation,
and it is very much about the compression
of the virtual and physical yardstick we
use to measure time in the business**

The remarkable thing about changing expectations and perceptions around the time of IT is that with each improvement, what we thought was impossible before becomes possible. We create an unstoppable force in the unified culture of IT.

The strategy of Trans IT Automation is so important because the greater the scope of the business processes we create, the greater the opportunity for time compression and overall speed gains, along with waste savings. Put another way, single-function automations are common today, but when we create multi-function automations, we can connect several single-function automations of today and bring together what was previously separated and should be combined to reflect the natural way IT works. Each of these combinations brings us a speed improvement, a savings of waste, and an economy of motion and effort. Each of these combinations helps to free up IT and the business and better aligns how automation works for us with how the real work should occur.

All of these steps and refinements go together and are inseparable in a wonderful way.

> *This is a vital cycle—as the scope of our redesigned business processes grows, these same processes will be better aligned with the business, and at the same time we are enhancing every process to be leaner and to scale more effectively.*

We are stripping away any artificial structure, handoffs, and transitions. Never underestimate how important and impactful it is to shed each one of these unnecessary steps or transitions. There are countless numbers of these in IT today, and we should strip away each one in the months and years ahead. This work could continue for years for larger and more complex organizations but is absolutely necessary.

All of this then begins to look perfectly natural and perfectly reflective of how the business operates every day: in alignment and harmony with the living organization and our people. With each improvement we also create savings in many forms, including the time compression of this current discussion but also cost and resource savings.

RELIABLE & SCALABLE

As we create new Trans IT Automation sequences—either through organic construction or through the combination of currently single-function or segmented automation—we are naturally creating more reliable and scalable results. This new generation of automation will greatly reduce our reliance on queues, pauses, waiting periods, approvals, and integrations. All of these things fundamentally slow us down and create risk. Where there is slowness of action and risk, there is poor reliability and scalability.

The profile of Trans IT Automation benefits should explicitly include simplicity because it becomes clear that simplicity is here as we are describing the attributes of a natural and broader automation.

> *Simplicity is a natural ally for reliability and scalability, and we bring along with us all the other benefits of natural and more consistent automation. Simplicity emerges from the work that is done to design the new Trans IT Automation models.*

As these more complete automation models are designed and implemented, we begin to see the thinking and work patterns of our people change as well. The tools of automation help to pull us forward both in how we use technology and in how people work together.

We have discussed the benefits of cross-functional teams throughout the book as a powerful way to get work done—the only way to get work done in the future of IT. The new models of Trans IT Automation are similar to cross-functional teams in that they are creating our first generation of cross-functional business processes that have a similar set of benefits as do the people side of cross-functional teams. Reliability emerges from our work on Trans IT Automation because we have carefully evaluated and re-evaluated every step in the business process to ensure that what remains is necessary, clear, and accurate. There is a level of precision here that simply did not exist before in our business processes. This work and what emerges from it is very much in line with what we would do with the singular goal of creating reliability.

So, we enjoy the dual benefits of creating our new Trans IT Automation models and delivering these new business processes for both IT and the business to operate what are fundamentally more reliable models. This then improves the availability of our services, which in turn raises user satisfaction, which in turn has a positive impact on customer happiness and loyalty. We have elevated the performance of this wonderful, fundamental chain that exists in every business today through the new generation of Trans IT Automation sequences and all the good that they bring.

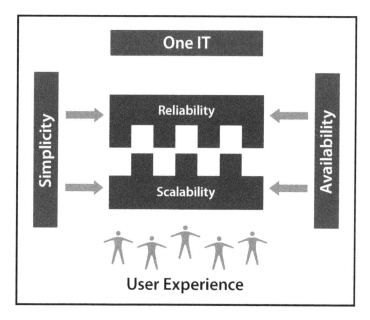

Figure 14.4 Reliable and Scalable IT

Again, IT is changing the business and bringing value from the inside out, but by running IT with outside-in thinking.

> *This is nothing short of a fascinating and sublime cycle that begins with IT committing to an outside-in strategy, operationalizing this strategy, and then delivering these new operational models to the business from the inside—bringing the best of customer and market influences to all of the business.*

This is exactly what the business needs, although it's coming from an equally unlikely and surprising source. It is even likely that as this influence begins to impact the business from IT, it is not recognized as such. Key business owners will only have the recognition of the immediate help that IT is bringing in our daily work, and the understanding that innovation and customer influences are behind this will come later. That is all fine. What matters is that the results are improving and the business is getting stronger and better.

As these waves of supremely reliable business processes begin to impact the business, we are now in a superior position to scale. Fundamentally, reliable systems will scale far better than unreliable systems. Unreliable systems are more likely to fail with current loads and as such are certainly more likely to fail as loads and volumes are increased. This is unacceptable and will hamper the business when the opportunity for growth comes.

What the business needs from IT—and possibly far more than it understands today—are business processes that are lean and simple and will scale if necessary. Working to improve reliability and scalability can't be done when an opportunity presents itself to the business because at that critical time it is too late. At the speed of business today, it will be far too late. There will never be enough time for IT to circle back and make all of these comprehensive improvements. It will take too long and the opportunity will be lost. So, IT must demand of itself and make it a fundamental part of the IT strategy to conduct these reviews and to make these changes and improvements now.

IT can't wait for an urgent call from the business. By then we are facing a significant cost in terms of time or a large resource shift to catch up. In terms of the business opportunity, the delay could be far more expensive than even a very large resource investment to recover some of our timeline.

Self-examination of all IT business processes and then leaning out and creating agility and the ability to scale—a great example of IT being proactive and thinking ahead.

We are "firing ahead" of the business and anticipating where the business will be in three to five years and then taking actions in IT that will be important at that time. It's a great mindset of IT to have and will transform IT from a perceived laggard to the organization that becomes the fastest of all.

CHAPTER 15

HUMANITY AND TECHNOLOGY FOR BUSINESS

A wonderful and remarkably powerful alliance is emerging between humanity and technology, and the biggest beneficiaries are the business and our customers. In many ways, this alliance is now possible for the first time, and our need to leverage this alliance is anything but casual. And it's definitely not optional. Our focus on leveraging this unlimited value is urgent and critical. In this section we will look more closely at this model and how it will be shaped. Many of these actions need to be taken now so we are again ready when the business finds itself in the position to create a competitive advantage, enter a new market, or capture a significant segment of new customers. And this is just the beginning.

Some organizations will simply not understand this, and that this very partnership could very well mean the difference between a business surviving and not surviving—then the difference between the business simply surviving and thriving. Between the common businesses of the future and the new market leaders. The organizations that become the standard by which all others are measured and are discussed in households, coffee shops, and offices everywhere.

> *The very essence of this model is enabling technology to do what it does best and more importantly to enable humanity to do what people do best.*

This is just not the case today, not even close. In many cases we find technology deployed on tasks that it is not well suited for, and the very same thing can be said of people. Humanity is remarkably good at performing some tasks and very much not equipped to perform other tasks well.

We as the professionals of IT have a natural affection for technology, so let's take a look at some of its advantages, in particular the new generation of intelligent technology, robotics, and AI, as this will become such an important part of our daily work over the next decade.

The strengths of intelligent technology are extensive. Intelligent technology is:

Capable of perfectly consistent execution

Supremely fast

Remarkably strong

Never fatigued, no sick days, no vacation

A natural fit for around-the-clock operations

Virtually unlimited ability to handle large volumes of work

Well suited to evaluate high volumes of data

Great at following orders

Designed for automation

No bad days, no attrition

Increasing ability to learn

Complete lack of emotion

As with the wonderful attributes of intelligent technology, we are reminded of the equally compelling strengths and advantages of our people, of humanity:

High capacity for empathy

Sense of humor

Advanced ability to learn and adapt

Ability to negotiate

Broad range of emotions

Ability to create strong relationships

Advanced problem-solving skills

Ability to solve unique and dynamic problems

Verbal and written communication skills

Very much human

Unique capacity to mentor

Looking at these lists if only briefly, we can't help but be struck by

the wonderful range of talents, attributes, and strengths both intelligent technology and humanity offer. But even more than that,
look a little more closely and we see that these lists are not the
same but very much complementary to one another.

> *It's an opportunity for intelligent
> technology and people to help one another,
> to form a remarkable and virtually
> limitless new partnership if you will.*

This is the very concept and strategy we will explore in the following pages, a partnership that can help to shape the future of IT and
the future of business for the next fifty years and beyond.

A NEW KIND OF PARTNERSHIP

The continued progress and evolution of technology have now brought us to a place where we can contemplate making significant changes to how we operate every day and how we perform better. The outline of the respective strengths for people and for technology presented in the opening overview brings to mind some exciting possibilities. Our people can't do everything well, of course, but we have never had a worthy partner to complement our people in such a way that we can focus them on what they do best and leave the rest to a capable partner—one that is able to do what our people are not naturally great at.

This has now changed for the first time. Consider just how far automation has come and how far AI and Machine Learning and other intelligent technologies have advanced in the past ten years, and we can now dare to think about pairing up technology and our wonderful people in such a way that everybody gets better. Out of respect to technology, I have included it in the "everybody" category, to make our partners feel truly like a part of the team!

Figure 15.1 Scorecard for Technology

Technology can shine in new roles that it is especially well suited for, and we can offload our people in such a way they can shine even brighter.

Yes, our people will be the real stars, as they should be, when we allow them to do the things they do best and are uniquely and supremely qualified to do.

The high-value work we want to focus our people on will highlight their remarkable empathy, communication, relationship, negotiation, and advanced problem-solving skills.

There are many levels of work that occur every day in the world of IT and business. In the long history of IT, we have largely required people to take on virtually all of this work, regardless of the type of work or the abilities required. People were our only real option to get the work done day in and day out. In the past five years, we have begun to assign some selected segments of this work and the tasks we can break the work down into, as technology has become better and smarter and more consistent. For the sake of this discussion, we will use simple business rules and automation blocks as an example. IT is now able to automate small blocks of work that are well understood and well defined and with well-structured work sequences, inputs, and outputs. Although automation has gotten better—much better by many measures—we can't yet call automation highly advanced or elegant. That day is coming but is still somewhere ahead of us in the technology journey.

Figure 15.2 Scorecard for Humanity

Tasks like delivering an application to a laptop securely while ob-
serving defined rules, watching an email box for incoming email,
evaluating each email and routing it to the correct destination, or
interacting with a caller in the phone system and delivering the call
to the right person with the right skillset are all tasks we can count
on technology to manage well today and to perform consistently
and reliably. Yes, these tasks are somewhat simple and primarily
tactical in nature, but the work is helpful and valuable within a giv-
en scope and a given role.

Every task we can lift from the shoulders
of our people makes a difference.

But more help is on the way, and technology is poised to take a quantum leap forward in the next five to ten years. The work we can assign to technology will rise to the next level and will be far more complex, more strategic in nature, and broader in scope. We will count on technology to learn, to get better every day, and to bring an increasing level of value at a staggeringly rapid pace.

What makes this partnership interesting and not just a token thing, not just the next thing, is the growing power of technology and how much more of the work technology can take from our people. What makes the partnership a true partnership is technology now bringing capability to the table that is superior to what our people can do.

This contribution from technology is a
very good thing. It allows our people to
shift onto work that humanity is the very
best at and likely better than technology
for the next fifty years and beyond.

This elevates what we can do in IT and what we can do for the business.

The ultimate value of the partnership is maximizing the contribution of technology just when technology has become significantly more capable, and the corresponding refocus of our people on the critical tasks that our talented people are capable of.

This human work includes enhancing
customer relationships, innovation,
negotiating strategic alliances and contracts,
enriching IT and business strategy, and
nurturing the careers of our people.

The organization is made stronger by these very human actions, made possible by the partnership with technology, whereby technology offloads the very people with advanced skills who are able to perform these strategic tasks.

Technology is better than ever, people are better than ever, and the business is better than ever as a result. We can't get there with technology alone, or people acting alone.

LEVERAGING HUMANITY

The single biggest value this new partnership creates is up-valuing humanity.

This is a crucial point to get us started on this topic—technology enables us to maximize the priceless value of humanity that has been muted by much of the daily routine work that has taken so much time from our people for decades.

We need to appreciate the multidimensional value here.

The first dimension is IT operations and the multitude of related tasks that necessarily involve a large number of operational and tactical activities that must be performed consistently and in many cases every day.

This is the nature of managing technology and managing infrastructure. It requires care and attention in order to keep the assets and infrastructure of IT healthy and performing at its best. This work can't be ignored and so it takes a certain amount of people time today. With this need, the first opportunity is created whereby the use of technology to offload this operational infrastructure work will create new time for the people performing this work today. We should never underestimate the value of every minute that can be freed through technology taking on this work, and the option of this today is more real than ever.

The second dimension is the services that are delivered by IT every day.

Most organizations offer a broad range of services that continue to grow every day, and this work continues to be performed largely by, or entirely by, people, which is okay in cases where people are uniquely qualified to deliver a service. In some cases, the service is a very simple thing and the delivery cycle is very short. For example, resetting a password, which happens in virtually every organization of any size every day, is an excellent candidate for work that can be automated with no loss in capability or the result. When done well, we can automate the reset of a password, which in turn saves money while creating a happy customer/user. This is a good thing for everybody, and this simple task can make up 20 to 30 percent of the volume of issues coming to the service desk. Remember, every task we can automate will then free up our people to focus on other things that humanity is more qualified for and bring more value to those we interact with. While this particular service can be automated, there will be others that can't be automated today. Highly interactive, complex, or variable tasks will continue to be performed by people until such time as our partner technology advances further and can take more of the load. But for now, technology can take a nice block of this work and execute it well in order to free up our people to focus on key services or on the third or fourth dimension of work.

The third dimension is the motion of escalations and service interruptions and their identification, response, and resolution.

This is a simple fact of IT operations, and this work will never completely go away, certainly not in the next fifty years and potentially beyond. We might be able to greatly reduce these occurrences, but not completely eliminate them because there will always be risks that threaten our operations and failures of many different variations. The types of failures that create escalations and interruptions will change, but failures will occur at some point. In this dimension of urgent work, people are often the best qualified to perform the work, recognizing it can become more complex and more emotional. This work can require some level of technical expertise, communication skills, and negotiation.

> *The fourth dimension of work in IT is advisory and consulting with the IT organization itself and with our colleagues in the business.*

This activity occurs in every IT organization as well and is a good fit for the unique mix of skills held by people. This dimension could be called the most strategic and most impactful of the four, but today it is also the dimension IT spends the least time on because the first three dimensions demand most if not all the capacity of our people.

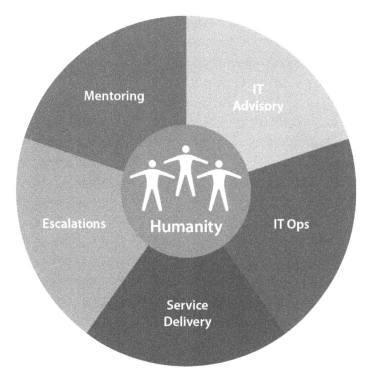

Figure 15.3 The Power of Humanity

We are simply fighting to keep the first and second dimensions intact hour to hour, day to day, which has been the case since the
beginning of the IT organization—focused on managing assets and
delivering services. In most cases these services are the standard
and tactical collection of services that are focused on the immediate needs of IT and the basic needs of the typical employee. The
category would include the break-fix cycle which demands immediate attention.

While IT has been caught in this reactive and tactical cycle since the beginning of the IT organization thirty years ago, we now have a capable and scalable partner that can take this yoke from the shoulders of IT and enable our people to spend more time on the third and fourth dimensions of work for the first time.

Our partner, of course, is technology, and its impact is hard to overestimate. There are many streams of value here, as humanity can delegate much of what transpires in IT every day to technology which in turn allows us to begin the shift of time from the first and second dimensions of work onto the third and fourth. The most impactful and strategic work is awaiting us in these third and fourth dimensions, and it is exciting that we now have the opportunity to focus our talented people here where they will have the most impact.

Even better, I can envision a fifth dimension that will emerge in the next decade in the form of humanity mentoring technology. This suggestion might come as a surprise initially, but it makes perfect sense.

The fifth dimension is a transformational alliance within the broader partnership and brings a new level of strategic value and innovation to the humanity/technology partnership. As technology becomes faster and more capable, as the capacity of technology to learn and adapt advances, a shrinking set of skills and capabilities will remain beyond the reach of technology without some assistance from talented people, the potential mentors for technology in the future.

Only our wonderful people are capable of lifting technology up to the next levels of advancement. This is a highly refined and elegant set of skills.

These skills include advanced problem solving, complex reasoning, empathy, specialized consulting, humor, advisement, and negotiation skills. Technology is all but helpless on its own and must rely on humanity to help develop these more advanced skills. These skills and emotions are remarkably complex and advanced, so it will take time. There will be long learning curves, and we need to be patient with the new model for human mentorship of technology as both a baseline to get us started and to continue the mentorship for years into the future in order to develop and then refine these elite skills.

THE TRAJECTORY OF TECHNOLOGY

The new partnership between humanity and technology is a fun and necessary topic to address, as the partnership is now more interesting and practical—in large part due to the ascension of technology. Technology has simply gotten so much better in the past ten years that we can now dare to think about new possibilities and the impact of this dynamic partnership on IT and the business.

The truth is that technology could not bring much to the table for this partnership as recently as five years ago. But today we are witnessing a remarkable acceleration of technology and the usefulness it can bring to the daily operations of IT and, more importantly, to the new shape of IT strategy. This is a real and tangible benefit that can be delivered today. We can now envision both a new operating model and new strategic contributions that were not achievable in the recent past.

Automation is a great example.

Advancements in technology have created flexible and robust automation designers and execution engines—able to capture much of the business rules and workflow steps that occur in IT every day.

When we use the framework of automation to describe and capture business rules and the combinations of tasks that form business processes and workflows, we are able to do this accurately. With this, the execution of business process brings a new level of consistency to operations and decision making. Automation enables us to do this accurately every time. Once properly modeled, automation is able to improve on the consistency of execution as performed by our people. Of course, building the right models is not a simple thing, but once in place they bring us a big return on this investment.

While automation is powerful and exciting in its own right, intelligent technology and AI bring a whole new dimension to technology. Even better, intelligent technology is a natural complement to automation, making automation smarter and more aware, more adaptable, and more scalable. The possibilities of automation that can learn, adapt, and be quickly shaped to meet new business process requirements is very exciting.

> *As we will use measurements of speed, agility,*
> *and scalability in all we do in the future*
> *of IT, the ability of intelligent automation*
> *to be agile and to scale with little to no*
> *human intervention is very exciting.*

This capability was a distant dream just a few years ago but is now within our reach. Think of it in terms of AI enriching other technology areas, helping to advance other technology areas even faster, and much faster than they are able to advance independently or with human assistance. AI can carry these technologies forward and over obstacles currently in our path today. These other technologies could be anything, but in this example we look at automation—there is so much automation will do for us in IT over the next ten years, and it is always an easy and timely example. AI is uniquely able to make automation better by addressing the limitations of what automation experiences today and removing some of these limitations to further grow the value of the technology.

In many ways intelligent technology, including AI, is a great example of how we have altered the trajectory of technology. This fundamentally alters the curve of technology evolution. The trajectory has been moving forward in a largely linear fashion for many years, but automation, in combination with AI and other intelligent technologies, has accelerated this progress like never before. This is good news for all of us as it enriches the contribution of technology to the technology/humanity partnership. Just as technology has improved, so has humanity.

The accelerated trajectory of technology now expands the potential of the partnership, making a broad range of more strategic work possible.

> *This partnership would not be interesting or valuable without an increased contribution coming from technology. The IT organization needs technology to step up more than ever and go beyond the tactical roles of technology in the past.*

Both technology itself and the partnership will lift many of the limits we have assumed for technology in the past and will move technology into valuable, strategic new roles in the next ten years.

Make no mistake, we need the tactical and operational contribution of technology as well. It helps to improve the speed at which our tasks are performed across IT, improves the consistency and precision of our work product, and enables IT to offer an increasing range of services around the clock. These simple examples should not be underestimated. The value is clear: simply freeing up some of the capacity of our people while at the same time driving significant improvements of speed across IT and then leveraging automation to offer services 24X7.

It is a strategic fit with the future agenda of IT, the transformation of IT, and it all becomes possible with automation.

> *My frequent (and always fun) informal polls with IT professionals in the past year put the current level of IT automation at between 20 to 30 percent. Your organization might be a bit higher or lower, but this should be pretty close, and with this we discover another compelling opportunity.*

To put the impact of automation in the proper perspective, if we could only automate 50 percent of the work performed today across IT, versus the 90 percent we will define in the following chapter on the 90/90 Rule, over the next five years, which should be very achievable, and then make these elements available and performing 24X7, we have had an enormous impact on IT. There is now a domino effect of the very best kind across IT with respect to what our people can now do with the time savings and the increased speed of execution. We will find layers and layers of value now possible.

Note that automation is but a single example of this trajectory for technology and what it brings us. You might have a better example, but we should all be able to agree on the unlimited upside automation brings us in the decade ahead.

As people who naturally love technology, this is exciting stuff.

THE IT INTELLIGENT ASSISTANT

The advancement of technology will create exciting and impactful possibilities in the future, and in the not too distant future as well, which is even better. One such example is a new role we will call the IT Intelligent Assistant.

These virtual assistants will provide a set of capabilities we don't have readily available in individuals among our people staff today and will dramatically change how we work and the rate at which daily operations are performed across IT.

First, the IT Intelligent Assistant will provide a conversational interface; this simple advancement will create exciting new possibilities. The assistant will be able to have a conversation with a person, to answer questions, to make comments, and to provide recommendations. In the beginning, the scope of intelligent assistants will be limited and very focused. Over time, however, the scope and the depth of knowledge will grow. Then we add another layer, including the ability to learn, to take and perform actions, and to problem-solve and make recommendations, and we have a technology that can change the daily operations of IT.

*The IT Intelligent Assistant can become the
interaction that begins and often ends our
normal day in IT. Even better, the IT Intelligent
Assistant will likely become the first place we
turn to when there are significant challenges in
IT—an outage, a major customer escalation, or
a strategic service interruption, for example.*

We will call this Intelligent Assistant Susan, and the discussion with Susan can quickly give us an update on the current status of the IT infrastructure, any new outages, security issues, customer escalations, key meetings scheduled for today, the results of any past actions, key deliverables due today, and much more. Even better, the IT Intelligent Assistant can answer questions quickly, take actions for follow-up, and provide comments and insights based on advanced reasoning and problem-solving skills. This model is very much within our reach, likely about four to six years away at the time of this writing in 2018.

This interaction would be a very productive way to start the workday and a fast vehicle for getting the information we need.

Then imagine that during the day Susan follows up on the questions asked during the top-of-the-day briefing and provides the additional answers needed. We can talk to Susan about this, or she can send texts or email updates. Within a few hours we will have all the questions answered. But there is still more—in our morning briefing Susan took a number of actions and has been working those actions throughout the day. Many of these can be completed today, and as they are completed, Susan will once again follow up with us through a phone call, answer our phone call, or send a text or email. Everything will be done faster than what we are accustomed to.

There is another important element: the perfect execution displayed by Susan as the questions and actions from the morning meeting are systematically completed, every time without exception. Nothing is forgotten, nothing is overlooked.

We then quickly come to expect this from Susan and from the other Intelligent Assistants deployed throughout IT, which in turn raises the expectations of the organization. This standard will be noticed by everybody.

Our Intelligent Assistant will show an increasing capacity to learn, something that will be evident when we have the next morning briefing with Susan. She will remember all the questions asked in our meetings; she will anticipate these questions being raised again and over time will be ready with answers to a growing scope of questions. Susan will not only anticipate these questions but also variations of these questions and new permutations of similar topics. It will be increasingly unusual for us to ask a question that Susan is not ready for. We might even have some fun with this...I know that I would. What can we ask Susan today that she will not be ready with an answer for? In a twist of irony, the more we extend these conversations with creative and unusual questions, the more quickly we provide the fuel for our Intelligent Assistants to pattern and predict our thinking and needs for more information. This is of course a good thing and enables us to have access to all the information we need more quickly.

By now we get the idea that our Intelligent Assistants like Susan will create a new sense of productivity in our day and greatly reduce the time spent chasing information and looking for answers to questions that will now come to us immediately in most cases, and very quickly in the remaining cases. This time savings enables our people to spend more time on thinking, problem solving, and creative solutions to the challenges that occur every day in business.

As time passes, we begin to develop an increasing sense of trust with Susan and appreciate the new levels of productivity and the accuracy and timeliness of information now available to us. It will be a remarkable experience.

Now, let's take this one step further. Susan will of course not be the only Intelligent Assistant operating in IT. There will be others and then many others as the designs of these intelligent elements are improved, the cost is reduced, and the daily performance is validated.

> *The evolution of Susan and her peers will create a community of Intelligent Assistants, and as such Susan will rely on her colleagues in order to get answers to questions and to have access to information even faster.*

Intelligent Assistants will create a virtual social and intellectual web of learning and insights that will quickly be leveraged by our people. And so the pace of business grows even faster, and all our information arrives more quickly and is of higher quality. Decisions then continue to be made ever more quickly and the quality of our decisions rises. This will be a remarkable cycle that will impact IT and the business. Yes, due to the affinity for technology we have in IT, I expect Susan and the first generation of Intelligent Assistants to appear in IT, but they will quickly have an enormous impact on the business and become increasingly more common—changing everything yet again.

HUMAN MENTORS AND BEYOND

We touched on this wonderful topic earlier, and it is an important one, an important strategy really, so we come back to it here. It might be a bit confusing for some people, so let's take a closer look, remove some of the confusion, and try to shape the approach.

Most people are familiar with the concept of mentors, and for many of us our career development was assisted by some number of mentors throughout our lives and our professional work. These kind and generous people had a wealth of knowledge they willingly shared with us in order to help us grow and develop. With the help of a mentor we were able to learn more and learn faster than what we could learn on our own—in many cases, much more and much faster, but always more. Our memories of mentors are almost always thankful and apprcciative as we recognize how much they did for us, with some of this only becoming clear many years later.

Until now, we have all thought of a mentoring model as very much a human thing, all about two people.

In the years ahead, the mentoring model will change, and we will see technology join this wonderful pairing and become part of mentoring. Mentoring is valuable and timeless—but the parties that participate in mentoring will change. They will evolve.

We will discover that as technology advances, and intelligent technology in particular, it will develop a powerful appetite for information and for learning. This appetite is important and necessary because it will drive the continued development and maturity of technology. The very longing for information will help to ensure technology continues to improve and take large leaps forward in terms of intelligence, capability, and the ability to contribute to the business. We all want technology to get better and better, smarter and smarter. This very cycle is a key element of how technology will bring so much to this new partnership.

Technology can't satisfy this need and this growing hunger on its own; technology needs the help of our people, creating a new and what would have been considered an unlikely alliance. But the time has come and our world has changed.

The needs of intelligent technology to learn,
and to learn more advanced skills, have grown
to the point that today only knowledgeable
people are able to satisfy this need.

One interesting dynamic here is that technology will be limited in its growth without the mentoring of our experienced people, and with this very mentoring, technology will pay back to our people by offering an increasing amount of help in IT and the business every day.

People mentoring intelligent technology just as we would younger, inexperienced workers, in order for it to grow and develop to the point where a more meaningful contribution is possible. This is a completely new model, but a model that is now necessary and critical to the long-term value of AI and intelligent technology. We need to build this time and this priority into our future plans for IT.

It is important we recognize the mentoring model as a new reality of IT and the business that is likely to be with us for the next ten years and beyond.

We will discover that intelligent technology has a voracious appetite for information. As our people share insights, knowledge, and problem-solving skills among others, this investment of time pays back to us many times over as intelligent technology quickly takes on more and more of the daily work of IT, thereby freeing up the time of the very people who have served as mentors. This recognition will help us to support the investment of time required for mentoring and recognize this investment will pay to us immediately.

Earlier we discussed the IT Intelligent Assistant—one example of an intelligent technology worthy of our mentoring. This entity will be working closely with our people, including our leadership team—for example, it is easy to see a plan where senior leadership, including the VP IT and the CIO, will be among the first people to work with an Intelligent Assistant. The technology can bring an immediate time savings and relieve some of the immense pressure on the daily schedule and work of these people. Mentoring the IT Intelligent Assistant is therefore a good investment of our time because it can have an immediate impact on the leadership of IT and begin the cycle of offloading some amount of work every day for our people. Beginning with IT leadership, we maximize the leverage of this time savings.

The mentoring model between people and technology will expand over time, and the population of intelligent technology entities will grow over time. The investment of our people to patiently share knowledge with this intelligent technology becomes increasingly well understood and common. Once again, we will see a compelling payback on our investment, as technology will learn far faster than people. With this, the investment of time comes back to us quickly, and our people will be surprised and impressed by how quickly intelligent technology learns and applies the information shared.

We will soon have this powerful cycle of people mentoring intelligent technology established and widely accepted—something everybody understands is important and we freely give our time to.

> *Then a remarkable thing happens—intelligent*
> *technology begins to mentor and guide*
> *more junior intelligent technology, opening*
> *a completely new and virtually unlimited*
> *capacity of mentoring for the future.*

This model of technology mentoring technology does not replace the model of people mentoring intelligent technology. But it does impact the areas our people will focus on with the continued teaching and learning of technology. Our people will begin to focus on more advanced areas, including empathy, humor, and advanced problem solving. These areas require a bigger investment of time and, in return, will provide a bigger value back to the organization as skills develop over time. It will take time, but now our people will have more time to give.

The evolution of moving to the new possibility of technology helping technology is a case of great timing. It once again offloads work from our people as technology can now tutor technology on the more basic skills and the more tactical business processes—enabling our people to double-down our teaching of intelligent technology on the more advanced skills. This then accelerates our progress in those areas, which in turn brings us more value and yet more assistance with our people, who can increase the amount of time spent on strategic and customer-facing activities in the business.

SUPERIOR CUSTOMER SERVICE

In exploring this wonderful and rich tapestry of what humanity and intelligent technology can offer us, we should not lose sight of why all this matters and what this should be about. The value we create and the focus that takes us forward should always start with how we can improve the service and products we deliver to the customer. Without a tangible value delivered to the customer, our efforts don't have the right focus or the right guidance. This simple idea, how can we better serve our customers, is a good reminder of why we are doing all this work with technology anyway. Otherwise, there really is no point. This is certainly not about the technology itself, or small efficiencies within IT. Even saving a bit of time in our daily work is not valuable if that time savings is not connected to our customers.

This is very much about yet another reminder of why any improvements we make in IT are truly important and changing our thinking from the historical inside-out model to the new outside-in model that will take us forward.

The impact of intelligent technology from day one should always be framed in real terms and terms and measurements related to customer service, customer loyalty, and customer happiness.

Imagine a very specific description of these connections between intelligent technology performance and the customer—connections won't always be directly with the customer, as that might not be sensible, but rather might be a case of enabling a team of people to better serve a customer. Intelligent technology can be the enabler behind the scenes, which is great. All that matters is the result. Let me say that again slightly differently—a significant impact of intelligent technology in the next ten years will be the ability of this technology to lift some of the noise and some of the daily work from the shoulders of our people. There is a great deal of this daily and weekly swarm that demands attention of our people, and it is normally highly or completely manual work. Some of this is basic and far less than advanced, and a great fit for the contribution intelligent technology can make in just the next few years.

> ### *We will call this an assist that intelligent technology can give to people and humanity as a great and meaningful step forward.*

What then happens is far better than just swapping a task for a task. It's a multiplier of sorts, where technology can automate or manage by some other means a slice of the work that is currently being done by people and then taking every minute freed from our people every day and directing every one of those minutes onto an activity connected to customer service and improving the customer experience. There is a remarkable amount of customer-connected work readily identifiable today, but necessary work, mostly tactical, stands in the way of moving our people onto this work that drives customer happiness. Intelligent technology is now in a position to take this work, and not just that, but to perform the work well and in some cases arguably better than it is being performed today.

> *Remember, the greatest abilities of our*
> *people are on display when they take on the*
> *most complex and dynamic work, the most*
> *advanced problem solving, negotiations*
> *of strategic issues, and creating a very*
> *human relationship and connection.*

The time for this work is too often limited as people are pulled back to the highly repetitive and tactical tasks that don't fully take advantage of their remarkable skills and experience. So we now can take the opportunity intelligent technology creates by delegating a significant block of our daily IT tasks and deliverables and moving this work over to automation and other technologies. We should do this with some thought and planning to specific connections to key people who have the customer-facing skillset and can be moved onto more customer-centric work. This two- or three-step process creates leverage of the best kind when the final step of the process is reassigning the right person to customer-oriented work. The quality of the customer experience is elevated and our customer relationships are strengthened. Often, the improvement is significant and will have an immediate impact.

Customer-focused work can include customer advocacy across the organization, filling the roles of IT Concierge. In many cases the role would be staffed for the first time, improving customer communications, developing the customer community, filling the role of IT Business Management with an emphasis on the customer relationship, focusing on customer-focused innovation programs, facilitating customer engagement on new services offerings, working with customers on business roadmap planning, and much, much more. This is just the beginning. Once we create the opportunity for our people to focus on customer success, we will find that good ideas start to come and just keep coming.

*The people of IT will have a remarkable
number of ideas on how we better serve our
customers—ideas there and waiting to blossom
that just need a little time and encouragement
to come forward—with intelligent
technology being another unlikely source of
encouragement by lending a helping hand.*

Once this process has started, it is unlikely to slow down and is carried forward by the natural passion our people have for the customer. It just needs a nudge from both the people of IT as we shift our culture to be more connected to and more focused on our customers, and intelligent technology that is able to extend the new partnership with our people and contribute something meaningful by taking something along the lines of 20 to 30 percent of the manual work currently carried by our people. This range of numbers might be a bit low as we can very well be underestimating how much intelligent technology can contribute in the years ahead. Let's consider this the three- to five-year baseline; the number will grow beyond this baseline and likely reach 60 to 80 percent of the work in IT managed by intelligent technology in the next ten years. Note that I'm making a distinction here between intelligent technology as a subset of the broader category of automation, where I expect the share of work to reach 90 percent in the next five to six years and close to 99 percent in the next ten years.

We can argue about these numbers, but the trajectory is clear. The impact on customer service will be remarkable and drive the creation of a new model for customer value aided by intelligent technology and lifted up by our talented people.

CHAPTER 16

THE 90/90 RULE

To avoid any confusion, the 90/90 rule is all about the two strategic initiatives of SPEED and AUTOMATION. These elements of IT are critical to the unification of IT and the business, and the transformations beginning within IT and spreading across the broader organization are simply not possible without dramatic improvements in these areas.

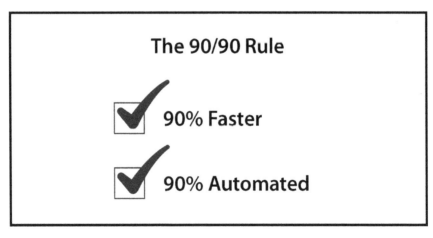

Figure 16.1 The 90/90 Rule

Because the book is a look at the future and about the transformation and simultaneous and complementary unification of IT, a lot of our discussion focuses on strategy, goals, and planning. This is understandable and necessary in order to shape the future of IT with today as simply a baseline, but that's not always a reflection of where we need to take IT in the future. Or, to thoughtfully navigate IT into the future might be a better description.

Any discussion on strategy is good and much needed, because the culture of IT today is all too often NOT about strategy. But in specific cases the addition of numbers to help us quantify the journey and to monitor our progress is helpful. It's a long journey, and there are times when we need to calibrate how far we have come and to be clear on our targets. This is particularly helpful when we are considering some of the key aspects of bringing IT and the business closer today, creating the unity and singularity that is so critical to our future.

This chapter provides one such set of examples in terms of how we increase our speed and the level of automation across IT. Both are vital to our journey and both performance areas are strategic.

> *These are transcendent measurements*
> *and so we need to establish a target*
> *for future improvements.*

I have given a simple name (simple is good of course) to this pair of performance titans, and we will spend this chapter looking far more closely at our goals for improvement and how we get there. What we will provide is a benchmark, a quantified target that represents a good starting point for most organizations. It can be an initial goal, but with the understanding that every organization is a bit different and on its own journey. Countless variables shape the stages an organization will move through in the pursuit of speed and automation, and these are strategic enablers—nothing less than pillars in the transformation of IT. Better yet, these pillars are firmly under our control, and as such IT is able to create and then implement plans that can benefit the full business and in ways we can't imagine today. This is only the beginning.

Detailed plans for speed and automation improvements across IT may be in place today in our IT organization, and if they are, that is great. Does your IT organization have specific milestones and goals for these initiatives? If so, that is even better. The next step will be to cross-reference your goals with what I provide in this chapter and determine if they are aligned with the measurements provided here.

> *I believe these targets now represent the new standard most IT organizations should plan for. In some cases that reflection on the current state of IT might require a review of timelines, priorities, resource assignments, investments, and goals.*

That is to be expected. We should all understand that the bar is being raised in the market for many reasons, and IT is a necessary enabler for the business—as ultimately speed and automation are key business initiatives and will help position the business for future success, regardless of company size and market.

If specific plans for speed and automation initiatives are not in place in your IT organization today, now is the time to put more focus on these areas and create structured plans and timelines. It is likely that even with a structured plan missing from the IT organization today, some automation work is occurring. Now is the time to bring that work together and ensure the right level of focus, coordination, and investment is occurring. This is too important to trust that some loose activities will be enough to improve the state of automation such that it can help to power the business in the next five to ten years.

Speed is a bit different, and less likely to have a structured initiative in place today focused on speed specifically. That is not unusual, but the time is now here for us to elevate the visibility of speed, and to create a new set of plans and investment to drive speed forward. When we look at speed more carefully, it becomes clear quickly that there is much more to speed than what might be apparent initially. Speed helps the organization to scale, improves agility and the quality of customer satisfaction, saves money, and enables our people to work more strategically because the load of manual and tactical work across IT is compressed.

> *With a combination of focus, plans, and*
> *investments around both speed and*
> *automation, we can begin to change*
> *the daily cadence and motion of IT.*

Every day becomes better, and we create leverage that did not exist before. We create an engine for the business that brings IT and the business closer together, nurtures the sense of singularity that is so vital to our future, creates loyal and happy customers like never before, and directly supports key business outcomes. This is the difference between IT gaining visibility to key business outcomes, which in itself is an important step forward, and then directly improving the performance of these outcomes. This connection and improvement is a good example of the changing relationship and the growing partnership between IT and all elements of our business.

90% FASTER

Most of us would agree that IT must be faster—faster at virtually everything we do—but how much faster? Is 20 percent faster good enough? What about 40 percent? That seems like a lot and would not be easy to achieve. But these improvements although helpful do not elevate speed to the level of a strategic force. Every speed improvement helps of course, but it is necessary to push speed beyond the threshold of a tactical improvement to that of a strategic advantage. This advantage spreads across the IT organization and across the business and ultimately reaches our customers, where it has the greatest impact. Make no mistake, our customers will instantly recognize speed and appreciate these improvements. This is the bottom line in every speed improvement we make in IT—enabling our business to pass speed improvements on to the customer, which in turn provides a boost to the ecosystem of our clients.

> *Recognizing this need to cross a performance threshold with speed, we set a 90 percent improvement as the goal for IT over the next five years. Our customers will instantly recognize and appreciate this improvement.*

Some organizations will come close to this mark but not achieve the number entirely in the next five years, and that is okay— because likely we will create a virtual momentum of speed born of this focus and momentum in the culture and with our people, and as such it will continue to bring improvements. Ultimately these organizations should achieve the 90 percent speed improvement shortly after the five-year window. This is important—that we continue to seek speed improvements in everything we do and recognize that every second saved brings value back to IT and to our business. In fact, some organizations achieving the largest overall time savings will start slowly and might not achieve the 90 percent target in five years but will overachieve on the 90 percent in five to seven years. These slow-starting organizations might build the biggest momentum and have the largest potential for speed improvements.

Every organization is different, and it will take time to shift our focus to speed and dedicate the necessary resources and then align our priorities and people around this initiative.

> *The important thing is that we make the commitment, because with this commitment to speed, every organization, regardless of its current condition, will be able to make significant speed improvements.*

The waste, unnecessary delays and work, and the legacy business process are there to be found.

Back to timing for a moment—it is good to keep our focus on the five-year window because this is neither a short-term nor a long-term window. It brings value back to the IT organization in a reasonable amount of time. The horizon needs to be achievable and reasonable, so five years is about right. But of course, this is not the end.

We are creating a cultural shift that coincides with this focus on speed, and that cultural shift will be permanent. It will never stop; it will change how we think and how we act and ultimately how we view the dimension of time in everything we do. This becomes a relentless focus, and we never stop looking for ways to save time and to build speed.

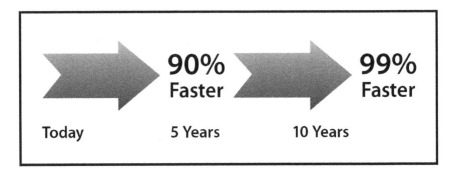

Figure 16.2 The Progression of Speed

Our focus needs to be squarely on the 90 percent goal and the five-year horizon, but there is another goal beyond the five years—that is the goal of 99 percent automated for the IT organization in ten years. So, while our focus is on the gains we will make over the next five years, it does help to understand the next stop on this journey. The good people of IT are beginning to understand we will get a lot of help from automation and from Intelligent Technology over the next five to ten years, and this will give our people a boost in achieving the 90 percent and then the 99 percent target. We can't get there through manual work, not even close. Automation will be fundamental to achieving this target along with a big assist from eliminating waste and simplifying how we work every day. Our work on these speed improvements will also have a big impact on scalability and agility.

*This is a remarkably powerful trio of value
for the IT organization of the future—the
elements of speed, scalability, and agility will
change everything, starting in IT and then
quickly bringing an influence to our business.*

Back to speed. The goal of 90 percent in itself is a very big deal. It changes the cadence of IT every minute of every day, and everything gets done faster—so much faster that everybody notices. This machine throws off all kinds of new opportunities, including the ability of our people to change the mix of how time is spent every day. It is a fascinating cycle that every bit of time saved through speed frees up our people to focus a bit more on finding the next time savings. With this we are able to find the next improvement that enables IT to complete tasks and business processes faster, which then creates more time to both find the next time savings and to also focus on strategic initiatives like innovation.

Key IT initiatives, including innovation and customer engagement, might be recognized by all our people as important, but if we can't create new blocks of free time in the day, our people will never have the opportunity to focus on this important work. Speed does this for us—it offloads daily tactical work from our people, much of which has been in place for decades and occupying generations of IT staff—and enables us to shift people onto a more strategic set of activities.

This changing mix then continues to advance our alignment with the business and the unification of IT. Amazing when we realize that alignment and singularity are made possible by saving one second or one minute at a time.

90% AUTOMATED

The elements of automation and speed are inseparable. We can't achieve one without the other, and one can't advance by any meaningful amount without the help of the other. We could achieve some level of speed improvement through working smarter, eliminating waste, and simplifying tasks and business processes. But these manual improvements would only bring us incremental improvements, and we would never be able to achieve our 90 percent faster goal. The talented and dedicated people of IT can only advance so far on their own.

But with the help of automation, there is virtually no limit to the improvements we can make, and we can achieve the 90 percent faster goal and potentially do even better. Some organizations will do much better in fact, and achieve the next goal of 99 percent faster inside the ten-year window.

If we were to look at the highest performing IT organizations, we would likely discover two things—the people embraced the cultural changes necessary to drive big improvements in speed and at the same time created a commitment to and competency around automating the work performed in IT every day. I clarify "every day" because the large blocks of work that are repeated across IT every day and every week are the best candidates for automation; these tasks are likely well understood and bring the biggest potential time savings.

Expanding our thinking a bit, the synergies of speed and automation then bring us another goal that supports the target of 90 percent faster, and that is moving the daily work of the IT organization to 90 percent automated.

> *Every step of successful automation will bring us another corresponding step of speed. We effectively enjoy the dual benefits of these improvements because although the benefits of speed and automation are similar, they are not exactly the same.*

For example, a big benefit of automation is perfectly consistent performance. This is important in its own right for many reasons, and is not a given with speed alone. Consistency is important as it delivers the excepted result every time and removes some of the variability that we naturally see with people performing the same tasks. Another benefit of automation is scalability, which directly benefits our ability to scale and to scale quickly, much more so than speed alone. This is an important attribute of automation because we are automating the work in front of us today, which is in itself a strategic improvement to the IT organization. But it is about much more than what faces us today. Automation creates a foundation for the future and creates a degree of readiness for what might come. This is a great proactive enablement that IT can perform for the business and very much in line with what the business is expecting in the future. Often, the biggest and best business opportunities come quickly and require immediate action. When these opportunities do come, IT will have little time to react and virtually no time to make major changes to IT infrastructure, processes, or systems. Either the larger model of IT is ready to support a strategic move—we can fairly call this a strategic strike executed by the business—or IT is not ready.

Automation can make the difference
between the answer to this important
question—IT being ready for a strategic
business move—being a yes or a no..

It is critical, starting now, that every IT professional develop a new and strong appreciation for the difference between a tactical and reactive action, and a strategic and proactive investment. This is not intended to imply that we have had no appreciation for this in the IT of the past. There has surely been some awareness in the past, but it has been isolated and limited, not at all widespread and commonly on display. But with a new focus on the need for strategic investments, we can ensure that a number of these are protected in the budget planning and resource allocation process in order to further ensure that strategic enablers are being developed across IT so that when the business does have an opportunity, IT will be ready. This creates a powerful shift in the business.

It is easy for the people and budgets of IT to be consumed by the daily demands placed on IT. It dominates the daily agenda and with good reason. But now we must protect a few of the right investments, and automation should be one for most IT organizations.

Another advantage of automation is the enablement it brings us with supporting and driving 24X7 operations and enabling access to systems and services around the clock. This becomes another driver that reaches far beyond the IT organization and provides more flexibility to our employees, which in turn enhances how we support customers. Around-the-clock operations and the offering of services are increasingly assumed and expected by our customers, and if we follow the path from the systems and services back to their roots in the organization, back to where they are anchored, we find that it is often within the IT organization.

This is yet another element of the case for automation, and in combination with scalability, consistent performance, and speed, we begin to see a strong pattern of what can be enabled by automation.

> *The closer we look at automation, the easier it is to appreciate the multifaceted benefits it provides at both an operational and a strategic level in the organization.*

With this, we set our sights on the 90 percent automated target for the next five years as the goal the best IT organizations will achieve as a new baseline for the next decade.

This should not be seen as an option. With the benefits we've discussed and the boost given to the business, we can't afford to question the importance of creating an aggressive goal in this area.

Even better, a full commitment to the 90/90 target for automation and speed will be increasingly seen as a key element in IT Strategy for the next five years and beyond.

ESTABLISH THE BASELINE

With our sights set on achieving the rule of 90/90 through the next five years, it is necessary to have a baseline for where the organization is today. It is not possible to understand, quantify, and then measure progress in the absence of a good baseline. This should happen at the very beginning of our improvement process because attempting to measure this later can dilute our results or, even worse, provide an inaccurate number that makes it all but impossible to measure progress and the impact of our programs.

A useful baseline will require some careful review of how IT is operating today and the performance of our systems and our teams.

The expectation should be set from the very beginning that this is not a grading process, and there are no wrong answers here.

The only thing that matters is getting an accurate measurement of the current state so we then have a performance baseline from which to improve. We must take the time to carefully communicate with our teams what we are doing with this effort and why we are doing it. All that matters is an accurate representation of where we are today, and even uncovering significant challenges in the speed and automation of our work today is okay and, to a degree, to be expected. We should send a clear message that the good and the bad of today need to be understood in order to drive the big improvements we can make in the next five years.

There will be no judgment of what we should have corrected previously, or why our current state is not up to the expectations of some.

It's all about accuracy, honesty, and openness.

In fact, it is a good example of the improved cultural model for the future of IT and in creating the unity of IT that is so important to our future.

We have two areas that require a baseline—speed and automation. Both will be measured carefully, providing a starting point from which we can show improvement. All of this is important, both the measurement process and the improvement process. Every step, regardless of what we find, should be documented, because over time this is an important reference for our teams. Don't assume we will remember the numbers and don't assume key findings will be widely understood because that is just not the case. The people conducting the work might take new roles, leave the organization, or just not remember the details over time, which is natural. The documentation need not be detailed or formal, just a simple summary of our findings.

Establishing a baseline is also important in that we can create some focus around mobilizing this effort, and we can use the measurement of the baseline itself as a way to launch the initiative and get our teams energized.

This is the first step, and we should be excited about the opportunity in front of us.

The first baseline is around speed. We begin with the tasks and business processes that are performed on a regular basis. This is at the discretion of the team performing the measurements, but regular can mean anything from daily to weekly to monthly. Depending on the organization, the number of units to be measured can range from a few dozen to hundreds of items—both tasks and business processes.

We are measuring the total elapsed speed for each. From the clear beginning to full conclusion. No skewing the number, no judging, just an accurate measurement of the elapsed time.

Remember, both the common tasks and the more complex business processes are important. This is the bulk of the work that occurs every day across IT, ranging from things like upgrades to email, standing up a new server, onboarding a new employee, resolving a client escalation, delivering patches, or fulfilling a service request. Any of these and much more should all be measured.

The measurement process should apply to both manual work and what has been automated because what we are focused on is speed, and we can find opportunities to improve speed in both types of work. Yes, the opportunities are likely bigger and more available for the manual work, which is to be expected, but the automated work can include simplifications and other opportunities that can save time. As we learn in going through this process, every second counts, so we are looking for small gains and big gains—everything helps.

When possible, we should measure the average time to complete the work if the task or business process has a higher degree of variability with regard to elapsed time. Some units of work will be consistent in the amount of time required for their completion, and this is great and will save us some time. But for those with a large range of completion times, an average should be taken.

The process of measuring the baseline is an important one because we will learn more than we might expect in just going through the process. Some work will take longer than we would have guessed, and some work will take less time than we might have guessed at the start of the process. All that matters here is accuracy, and capturing the elapsed times for each. Another key point of learning will be capturing key assumptions and issues as we are working with the teams performing the work.

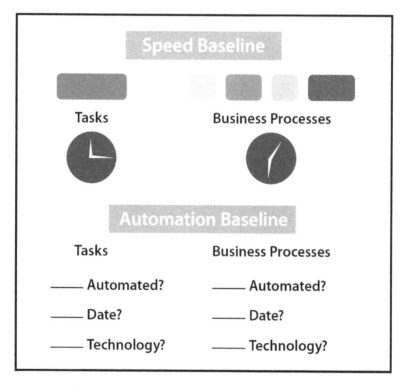

Figure 16.3 IT Performance Baselines

For example, some people performing the manual work today might immediately point out a possible improvement/simplification/time saver as they become aware we are making these measurements to create our baseline. This is a good dialogue and only natural when the attention comes to what a team is working on today.

*Dialogue should be encouraged and all this
feedback captured. We do not, however, want to
implement any of these changes immediately.
We need a clean baseline, and we need to stay
focused on completing the measurements—
everything is on the stopwatch for a while.*

At the end of the process, we have an accurate measurement of elapsed time for all the tasks and business processes in the scope of the exercise, and this becomes our starting point. The report should be published as widely as possible because it will be valuable and interesting for most of our people across IT.

The report will get lots of attention, so take some time to do it right and keep it simple. Also, be sure to include a clear description of each work element being measured to avoid any confusion.

Remember, lots of people will be reviewing the report, so we should anticipate the items people will naturally focus on and anticipate the typical questions we will receive.

This is our speed initiative baseline.

The second baseline report is the automation baseline. This is similar to the speed baseline report but with some differences. The automation report will document each task or business process automated within IT today, and what is not currently automated.

*The scope of tasks and business processes
should be the same as the inventory of work
shown in the speed report. This list will
be used to cross-reference both the speed
improvements and progress we take on
automating our common tasks and workflows.*

There is no measurement of these elements in the automation baseline as part of this report; we are simply trying to capture what is automated and what is not. So, this is a complete inventory of our IT tasks and business processes and what is currently automated and what is not. It is helpful to indicate when the process was first automated and what technology is used for the automation. If we have the information available for the improvements in speed for when the automation was done, it would be helpful but is not required.

It is also helpful to indicate how often each task or business process is executed. This should be an average per week or per month given the natural variability of many blocks of work. This volume of execution is then a helpful reference when given the planning necessary around increasing the level of automation across IT.

> *With these elements included, we now have our virtual arms around the tasks, business rules, and business processes to be automated and the volume of execution for each.*

There should be some additional judgment around the strategic impact of each and other intangibles. These other factors can ultimately help to shape where we start the push to increase our levels of automation and can also put some structure to phases and the like.

The main thing is capturing everything.

EVERY SECOND COUNTS

Every second counts.

Every single second counts.

Every second makes a big difference.

Every second gets us closer to 90/90 being a reality.

Every second should be celebrated.

Every second should be recognized.

Always search for that next second and never grow tired.

Every second is as valuable as the previous second.

"Every second counts" is an important mindset to reinforce for every person across IT as we set about achieving the 90 percent faster and 90 percent automated goals—the reality of how we get there is one precious second at a time. Yes, big time savings and big blocks of automation are fantastic, but we can't count on these big leaps forward to get us to our goals.

*IT can achieve the 90/90 goal by rolling up our
IT sleeves and doing the hard work every day
to find these seconds—and these seconds then
add up to be something much more and have an
enormous impact on changing the business.*

Paying attention to the details and finding every second is what prepares us for the journey that will be necessary to reach our speed and automation goals.

If our teams carry the perception that a lot of huge time savings and glaring opportunities to save time along with big blocks of automation are waiting for us just around the corner and this whole thing won't be all that hard, well, we will be very disappointed.

It is important that we set an expectation with our teams from the very beginning and then every step of the way that this is all about the details and every small time savings and every small block of automation.

*The small steps and the little details are how
we build a great result—not by finding great
and spectacular blocks of speed or automation.
The approach of small steps might seem a bit
unlikely, but it is exactly how we get there.*

With the right mindset at the very beginning, anything becomes possible, and we won't be disappointed. Our teams will begin to see the results of this careful management of the details, which will then give our people more encouragement and more energy to continue on the journey.

The leadership of IT should reinforce just how important this work on speed and innovation is to IT and to the business. We truly are changing the business with every step we take and, at the same time, protecting the very future of the business.

As an extension to the value of seconds in our pursuit of speed and the leverage we can create through automation, it is a powerful cultural shift to reinforce the importance of minding the details, of being good at the little stuff, of executing well. This is an organizational discipline lacking today in many IT organizations and in many businesses. We change culture from the top down and from the bottom up, which are equally important. We should think of this as applying pressure from all our sides on ourselves—this is coming from within IT to fundamentally change IT of course but to also bring life to a chain of change that is connected to the business.

> *A focus on the details enables us to change*
> *IT from the inside and then change the*
> *business, and to then bring IT and the*
> *business together as Our Business.*

A unified IT is the only model for the future—a unified IT is only a stop on the way to a unified business, the singularity we visit repeatedly throughout the book, Our Business. This is a business that we all own, that we all drive, that we all focus on as a massive and energized engine to create value for our customers. Delivering to our customers, meeting or exceeding expectations every day, delivering what our customers can't get from any other organization in the market—these are the only things that matter.

This is a remarkable stack of dependencies that fuel and enable one another—a focus on saving every possible second, which in turn transforms the performance of speed and automation across IT, which then creates a new and Unified IT, which then pulls the Business and IT together into Our Business, which then empowers Our Business to deliver a new level of performance and value to our customers every day.

It all starts with and is made possible by the pursuit of saving every second in how we work every day and how our systems perform every minute across IT.

This single atomic unit of work will ultimately change IT and be a catalyst for the chain reaction that creates Our Business.

ACCELERATE THE CUSTOMER

Let's continue/revisit the remarkable theme that is the connection between the 90/90 rule and what it can create in terms of our speed and automation.

There is a necessary element of unifying IT and transforming how we work every day that is an elemental ground-up change across IT but at the same time working toward strategic goals.

Let me explain. IT is fundamentally made up of building blocks of technology, systems, tools, and data. These are the assets of IT, if you will, and they are leveraged every day by the good people of our organization.

> *The people of IT and our actions bring these*
> *assets to life—all these things that make*
> *up our infrastructure are inert on their*
> *own, powerless to provide any value.*

But with an assist from the people of IT, these assets come to life and are capable of performing remarkable things in the hands of and under the direction of the right people.

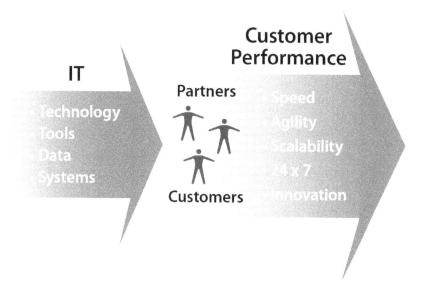

Figure 16.4 Accelerate the Customer

Because there is and always will be a connection between IT and these very assets—the technology and tools and systems we use every day—we must then recognize the connection between any vision and strategy at the highest level and the assets that represent ground zero of the IT organization. This is where it begins and what we must bring to life. As such we can't transform or unify IT without an understanding of a connection to this level of technology. Embracing this essential truth, we must have an element of our plans that drives performance from the bottom up.

At the same time, the ultimate value of speed and automation is with the business, and the ultimate value this generates across the business is only what can be translated directly to customers. IT must be the engine that makes this connection possible with the customer, which is where the value chain both begins and ends. By beginning we mean that the key requirements of any IT initiative must originate with the customer, and with the end we mean that the only possible acceptable outcome is with some measurable results realized by our customers. This is an important distinction, as the business should not be seen as the equal of the customer. Yes, what we do in IT to enable the business is important, even vital, but it must all be framed by the impact we are able to deliver to the customer.

The business sits squarely on the path to the customer and the path back from the customer, a bidirectional facilitator of value, if you will.

But if the value is not fully delivered to the customer and is somehow lost inside the machine of the business, then we have failed.

Every second of speed gained and every element of manual work that we manage to automate are all about how we as IT and the business have jointly delivered these improvements in a leverageable form to the customer.

This remarkable chain of value must begin with IT. The acceleration of the business and of the customer must begin with IT. We start with a simple recognition and understanding of this connection, a vital connection, and all the initiative and innovation investments become more clear and compelling.

The 90/90 rule is a great example. These advancements in speed and automation are difficult to fully appreciate in terms of the impact that can be delivered to the customer, as IT is able to make these strategic advancements in speed and automation together. Each makes the impact of the other larger, both creating leverage that would not be possible with just one of the initiatives.

Although the translation won't always be clear, every unit of improvement in speed and every element we automate will convert to some amount of value with our customers. This takes a few forms:

A direct translation of speed or automation in the business of the customer

A fundamental change in how the business supports customers

An indirect translation of speed or automation to the customer

The ability of the business to offer new services to customers

The ability of the customer to offer new services to their clients

Each of these value examples is important and each contributes value in different ways. Remember, each is only possible with the roots of value living inside of IT and with every gain in terms of speed and automation.

We highlight speed and automation in the 90/90 Rule because we need to have some quantification of the improvements the organization should target; these improvements are achievable for the majority of IT organizations today; and speed and automation have such an impact on the business and then on the customer. Both speed and automation are great examples of highly leveraged investments that have a wide circle of influence. There are other investments that fit this profile, but speed and automation are easy to understand, easy to target the improvements, and not risky to implement. All of this combined makes this pair of investments on our short list of what requires immediate attention.

Strategic improvements are born of technology and how technology is leveraged by our people, and this always brings us back to the baseline that lives inside of IT.

Born and conceived in IT, only in IT, to ultimately better serve or bring new value to life for the customer.

CHAPTER 17

THE INNOVATIVE BUSINESS

The ability of a business to rise to a leader in any market will be very much about the organization creating a sustainable ability to innovate: a culture that values innovation and fundamentally places innovation at the center of the organizational strategy. This does not happen by chance, nor is it a part-time interest. Innovation can only occur through real cultural change and cultural focus, beginning with the leadership of the organization and then understood and embraced by every employee. It becomes part of the DNA of the organization and who we are. Innovation is not a project, a program, or an initiative.

Innovation just becomes part of who we are and what we do every day. Innovation is no more a program or a project than breathing is.

Today, we have a remarkably powerful mosaic of technology and information at the ready to help propel the organization forward unlike at any time in the history of business. In many ways, this is what we can fairly call a quantum leap forward in technology that will forever change how we work every day.

The reality and potential of technology today are helping to drive our renewed focus on innovation across IT. The importance of innovation is certainly not new; it has been on the agenda of business for some time. But often, the responsibility for innovation was scattered around the organization, diluted, and not always clear. There has been no easy answer to this complex problem.

While the broader organization will continue to search for clarity around this issue, IT should not wait. IT is now in a position to lead, to bring real solutions to the business, and to be proactive in creating a new center for innovation that will change IT, the business, and how we work with customers. In most cases IT won't be given this mandate by the business, but that is not a reason to wait. It is not a reason to see this as NOT the responsibility of IT. If anything, it's a great reason to take this action and begin to expand the scope of what IT owns going forward, and to be proactive in building a new generation of innovative ideas and solutions into our IT initiatives for the next five years.

> *The timing is perfect for IT to make this strategic investment in innovation, under its own initiative, and on behalf of the business and our customers, who will ultimately benefit the most.*

Although the beginning of this investment and cultural change around innovation will be taken on by IT, we will quickly engage key business owners across the organization after IT has created the platform and process to help take this innovation work forward.

IT will get us started. Remember, getting the recognition and receiving praise is not important; all that is important here is getting the innovation engine started and helping it to scale. The engagement of key business owners is important because these key people know the business well and will have some key insights on behalf of the business and customers.

The triangulation and validation from the key business owners will help to accelerate the innovation process and help it to grow in scale and in depth. This helps to further align both IT and the business around what will be increasingly becoming OUR business.

This is a critical mindset to keep. IT can get the process started but IT can't carry innovation independently from beginning to end. We need and want the participation of the key business owners, the people who drive the business every day.

The alignment and engagement of business leaders is important for several reasons:

Helps create transparency throughout the innovation process

Key business owners have strong opinions and great ideas

Key business owners know the business well

Key business owners typically have good relationships with customers

Key business owners can be advocates for innovation across the business

Key business owners can help guide investments

Key business owners will ultimately operate successful innovations

Key business owners are talented thinkers, exactly what we need

Key business owners can help to secure other resources required for the process

There are many other benefits of involving these stars from across the business. With this involvement, we now have a cross-functional team to help drive innovation initiatives forward and to help ensure the success and impact of key ideas—ideas that will ultimately receive investment and blossom into new solutions. Solutions that are the key to our future.

> *The process of bringing new solutions,*
> *best leveraging the technology we have at*
> *our disposal, never really stops and is a*
> *key to a healthy and thriving business.*

Remember, IT can and should start this process and be the catalyst that ultimately creates successful innovation across the business, but the long service of innovation requires cross-functional engagement and advocacy across the organization. This is too important for IT to do alone.

BUILD THE ENGINE FIRST

The virtual engine of innovation requires some attention and must be in place before any level of sustained innovation is possible. This engine must consist of a number of fundamental elements in order for innovation to be possible over a period of time, and the sustainability of innovation is what brings true value. The ability to innovate consistently over many years must become an organizational competency.

A few things this engine must include:

> *The encouragement of new ideas of all kinds*

> *A culture that continually places value on innovation*

> *A regular forum in which to discuss new ideas and prototypes*

> *A defined process by which new ideas can be taken forward and investigated*

> *The ability to build prototypes and models to prove promising ideas*

> *Leadership support for and encouragement throughout the innovation process*

Time set aside for innovation

Recognition and reward for the top innovation contributors

Each element of the engine is important, which is very much a cultural commitment and a cultural change. Each cultural change, including making time for innovation and creating the forums to discuss new ideas, then clears the way for the next change. Each small element that shifts our culture begins to create a new identity for the business and for the full organization. Every IT organization is either committed to innovation and is creating the right culture and building the right engine, or it is not. This is fully under our control of course, and so is a question we need to ask ourselves and discuss with senior IT leadership.

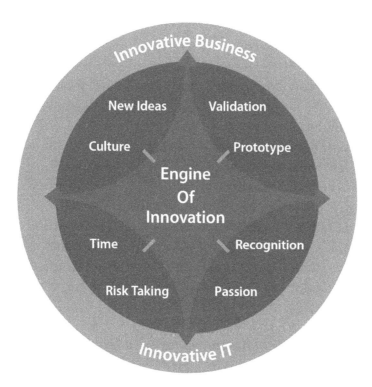

Figure 17.1 Engine of Innovation

This process begins with discussion and with awareness. If the answer is that the teams of IT are not ready to take this on, that is sometimes the case, and it is understandable. Perhaps the time is coming soon and it is just a matter of the timing being right. This is great, and some of the most innovative organizations took some time to rally around innovation and bring the engine up to speed. It just takes some time. It does not matter how we get to the model, only that cultural change begins and IT is able to create the engine.

> *I'm making a reference here to IT creating the engine in order to take forward the idea that IT can be the catalyst for innovation on behalf of the business, a very unlikely catalyst at that, in order to lead the full business forward to a stronger commitment to innovation.*

It is possible that the launch of innovation will come from outside IT, which is perfectly acceptable. It is possible that IT will begin to mobilize around innovation, including building the engine and generating the necessary ideas, and the organization will then decide the innovation center will be located in another organization. This is okay because the only thing that matters is innovation happening, not the how, when, and where. In this case IT has helped to lead the organization forward and raised the awareness that innovation is important and is springing forth from within. Let's not lose sight of what is truly important. Within IT, or outside IT with IT assisting—either model will work, and again all that matters is a stronger commitment to making innovation central to the daily work and thinking of the organization and the cultural change that comes along with this focus.

There are many benefits that come with building an engine of innovation:

Improved focus on strategy in IT and the business

A higher level of organizational energy

Improved competitive success in the market

Improved employee retention rates

Improved ability to recruit new elite-level candidates

Improved alignment across the organization

A more proactive IT culture

Improved employee recognition programs

Creation of new career paths for key employees

A more creative culture throughout the business

Note that an improved commitment to innovation and the creation of our engine for innovation to create a sustainable and scalable process drives many positive changes in the culture and elevates our people, and in particular those creative and talented people who are providing the key ideas into the innovation process and helping to take them forward.

These circles of change grow wider and wider over time and help to change virtually every element of the business.

Of course, there is another vital benefit of a commitment to innovation and the work required to build the engine—a natural alignment and then unity and singularity between IT and the business.

***We discover that innovation is a powerful
and naturally unifying force for IT and
the business, perhaps only exceeded
by an elite level of customer focus.***

A CULTURE OF IDEAS & RISK-TAKING

The process of encouraging ideas, even crazy ideas, and the empowerment of people to take risks is a wonderful and powerful tonic to every organization.

> *Committing to generating innovative ideas is*
> *good for business, strategic, highly productive,*
> *and a lot of fun. How good is that?*

This creates another dimension to how we think and how we work every day in IT and is another great example of how IT can role model for and lead the business into the future.

A cultural change in IT will have a big impact on the teams of IT, and in that alone we will see a lot of value. But this cultural change in IT that leads us to focus on innovation goes far beyond IT. These changes will not stop at any real or perceived boundaries of IT and will begin to move beyond the IT organization quickly and create a strong influence on the overall culture of the organization.

People are naturally attracted to creative activities and want to be part of the brainstorming, sharing, discussion, debate, and overall innovation process. The role of creative skills in IT is growing, and this work will help to nurture these skills and create an outlet that is important and makes a much-needed contribution to the organization.

The beginning of every innovation is very simple—it all begins with an idea. It should be reinforced constantly that every idea is precious, and there are no bad ideas.

Sometimes the idea that meets with some resistance or even outright criticism in the beginning later becomes the single great idea that leads to a big improvement, a new solution, or a new approach that has a meaningful impact. It is therefore critical that we give every idea some support and thoughtful consideration and review. Only after some time will it become clear which ideas should be taken forward and which should be parked for the time being. Then, all ideas should be saved and archived because we sometimes find ourselves coming back to an idea that was raised at some point in the past. The time might not have been right when an idea was originally raised, but with some passing of time and circumstances changing, the idea might be taken out of the archive for a new review and discussion. Remember, every idea is precious and so we treat them as such and none are thrown away.

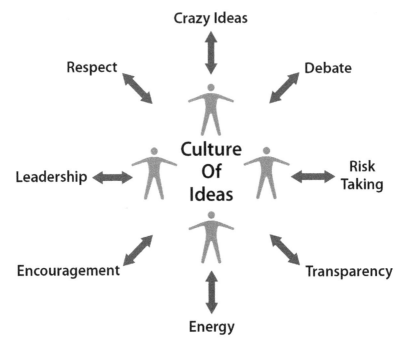

Figure 17.2 A Culture of Ideas

The ideas we need to carry this process forward can come from anywhere at any time, and it's critical that the forum is created to share these ideas openly, to make these ideas visible to the people and teams participating in this process, and to give each idea some time to be reviewed and discussed. Transparency is important for every idea, and we want to be inclusive. Ideas should receive lots of attention and have widespread review and discussion.

> *Another important point is that some spirited debate should be encouraged. We don't need to agree all the time. Our people should never feel that having a different view or opinion is a bad thing.*

We need different opinions and we should never push back on a

different view. Of course, this should always be done profession-
ally and with respect. A healthy debate is a critical process because
sometimes the idea we take forward as what could have the biggest
impact on the business could be a hybrid idea born of a compromise between two different schools of thought. This is a must-have
for the creative and innovation process.

> *A natural extension to the virtual incubator*
> *of new ideas, even crazy ideas, is the ability*
> *to take some risks. These risks can directly*
> *lead to the next big breakthrough.*

The next big innovation could be the result of taking a risk, being
willing to accept some failures and setbacks. This is okay—even
more than okay. Risk-taking is essential to the creative and innovation process. This needs to be a cultural shift and requires some
support and empowerment from management. The message from
IT leadership must be that it's okay to take some risks and we all
understand that we won't always get the result we expect.

Whatever the result will be, we will learn something and get a little better, but this road to learning must include some risk-taking.
Some hesitation is understandable because risk-taking is not natural to IT and is often very much against our traditional IT manner
of operating. Our job after all has included a charter to eliminate
risks from IT and from the business. Traditional IT has been all
about creating an anti-risk organization that brings us as close as
possible to risk-proof. Of course we never fully get there, but this
is where we have come from. Recognizing this, some patience is
required to make the cultural shift to enable and encourage the calculated risk we need.

But the risk-taking we need in the innovation process and living an
innovative lifestyle is different because the context here is creative,
aggressive shaping of new models and concepts. We need to take

calculated risks that can lead directly to a big leap forward and the ability to create a new model, a dramatic shift in the business.

> **It will be necessary to create a platform for**
> **risk-taking that is controlled and with some**
> **secure boundaries in order not to impact our**
> **production systems. We can call it a test lab,**
> **prototype lab, innovation center, innovation**
> **showcase, test bed, or something similar.**

This is a place with the necessary tools and technologies to create a simple, working model of the idea. For the purposes of this discussion, I'm assuming these prototypes or test cases are created by using some form of technology. We are after all IT people, and this stuff is in our blood.

For example, we could be taking forward a new idea for the creation of a new customer-facing portal through which customers can be updated on the status of an order, and access to a knowledge base that answers common questions about products and the use of products. This new idea would be prototyped in our test lab, and then presented to internal people, business owners, and potentially customers for feedback, impressions, and comments. Bringing this idea to life is necessary because when we see anything come to life, it becomes much more literal and creates a new set of discussion points.

The creation of a prototype is taking a fundamental risk, although in this case it's not a big risk but a risk nonetheless. With these two steps of first nurturing an idea and then providing the resources to investigate the idea, take some risk, and create a test case or working prototype, we are able to go to the next level. It might be necessary to create several to many prototypes over time, but this healthy process will ultimately yield the idea and prototype that brings enough value to cross the threshold and get funded to become a real product, a working solution. These new systems and solutions then change the organization forever.

Note that this innovation and risk-taking process can live within IT, within another organization including R&D, or somewhere else. It can be anything, and all that matters is that the ideas are coming to life and we are pushing the boundaries to help identify which ideas will ultimately earn the investment to become a working model. In any case, the innovation process can be started in IT and then staffed and carried forward by talented people from IT and working with other creative stars from across the business. We want to create the opportunity for our best and brightest to shine and to give their priceless ideas a forum to shine and grow.

> *This progression of what started as a crazy idea to a real, working solution is a magical moment made possible by a culture of innovation and our talented people.*

BUSINESS OWNER ENGAGEMENT

Business owner engagement is a necessary part of the growing circle of influence that happens when innovation starts to grow in the business. For the sake of this discussion we will assume the innovation process has started in IT and the engine has been built. We are now encouraging new ideas and have created a forum for the airing of ideas and the discussion and debate that follows. The best ideas then move into a prototyping and testing phase where we quickly build simple working models that show enough capability and capture the idea to enable further discussion and review of the potential innovation.

Most if not all of the process up to this point can occur in IT, but IT can only take this so far without recruiting some assistance and participation from key business owners.

The business owners bring a unique perspective, a unique understanding and insight into the business and its workings. We need this understanding to join the innovation process and provide comments, concerns, and feedback.

This will make a good idea even better, and for those ideas that ultimately won't make it to the next stages, the business owners can help us come to that understanding more quickly—which is valuable and saves both time and money.

Ideas that survive through the innovation process, the initial vetting process, are deemed appropriate for further investment, and make it to testing and prototyping then become part of a select few candidates to be productized into a form that can be used daily and bring value to the business. This can take many forms depending on the industry and the technology. But innovation is naturally a demanding and selective process because the resources for investment will be limited and the standard should be very high. The full process should be competitive to help us identify the best of the best ideas.

A key here is that as we move an idea further through the process, the need to have broader review across the organization grows. This enables us to further validate the idea and the subsequent test model or prototype because we must continually raise the bar. At this stage we should be inviting the most critical comments, the biggest concerns, the biggest risks. These issues should be raised now as a natural part of the process to further qualify the ideas that continue to move through the process and continue to receive additional investment. The resources we put into the innovation process are precious, and should only go toward those ideas that are seen by the teams of IT and by the business owners as the most advanced, the most promising, the most impactful to the business.

> *The best of these ideas and the strongest of the test models or prototypes will rise to the top when we have the extended review made possible by the cross-functional team that combines IT leaders and business owners.*

The IT organization can provide leadership by forming ideas and conducting the initial stages of review, including the elimination of some ideas in the early stages.

IT can be a strategic facilitator in moving the process forward and ensuring the pipeline of new ideas is healthy.

Likely the majority of ideas are eliminated in the early stages, which is necessary to help focus our time and resources on the most promising ideas. IT staff, including IT Business Management, the IT Concierge, and the functional leaders of IT, are very capable of moving us through the early stages of this process and have the expertise to conduct the first few stages of vetting ideas. There is a natural level of technology dependency for this process as innovation will in most cases leverage technology in some form. So within the IT organization itself we want to involve technology experts who are appropriate to the domain within which we are working and who bring valuable insights and will again help validate and identify the best ideas.

The experts will make the best ideas even better.

A certain level of motion is necessary for this process to be healthy. We must keep moving forward and should avoid delays and impasses at all costs.

When needed, we can make assumptions, create new criteria, and be decisive in moving innovation ideas through the process.

The innovation process can only be kept healthy by both bringing new ideas into the innovation funnel, and by sustaining continuous motion in the process. Innovation ideas must keep moving through the process in order to make room for new ideas to enter the first stages of the process. This throughput is critical and we need to avoid ideas getting stuck or stale at all costs—sabotaging everything and disabling the complete process.

The renewal of ideas is a foundation
for successful innovation; the next idea
that enters the innovation progression
could be THE idea we are looking for—
the idea that changes everything.

These great ideas that build our future are there and will come from the talented people of the organization, but they can only come to light by making the room that is required to bring new ideas into the initial review and discussion phases. There must be a natural cadence to new ideas entering the innovation progression, and IT and the organization will determine what this cadence should be. Some number of ideas per quarter is a good metric and should be based on the resources we have participating in the process. This can be complemented by a monthly or quarterly meeting and review of the new ideas, the identification of ideas that will be parked and archived for the time being, and ideas that will move forward into the next stage of the process.

Remember, IT can be the catalyst to help keep innovation renewed and moving forward, but the process can only stay healthy by forming the cross-functional team needed for a more complete and in-depth review of our ideas and the prototypes. This should include the key business owners of course, but can also include leadership in the organization, consultants with a particular expertise, partners, and potentially customers.

We need to surround these ideas with
experts and strong opinions because what
will then emerge from the process are only
the strongest and most creative ideas.
The brightest and richest of the lot.

New ideas entering the process have other benefits, including bringing us energy and renewed excitement.

Each new idea will be seen as fresh and necessary. Every idea will bring a certain boost to our work, and our team will embrace the opportunity to review the next idea.

NEW SKILLS & DIVERSITY

The innovation process is fueled by the creative thinking and energy of our people. Much of this will come from our people today, and that is enough to get the process started. We will discover that given a forum and given the opportunity, great ideas will flow from our talented people. Often we will be surprised by contributions from people we might not originally expect to make them. It is important to provide widespread access to the innovation forums and encourage people to participate. Be inclusive, be transparent, be encouraging, and great things will follow.

If a defined innovation process does not exist today in the organization, it should be started as soon as possible. We don't want to lose any more time because the harvesting of the innovative ideas that will come from our people is precious and we want to get these ideas flowing immediately.

This will carry us for some time, and that is good because starting now is important.

But, to build a more robust and scalable innovation process and more importantly culture, we need to develop and recruit new skills and diversity into IT. It is critical to our future.

This will fundamentally change the IT organization in terms of the daily work we do and at the same time will expand the thinking that drives our innovation efforts. Note this is not just about recruiting; we also need to reassign some of our existing people who have the right skills, provide additional training for staff that extends the skills we have today, and pull people from outside the IT organization into IT and into the innovation process to make the best use of the skills we have in the business as well as in IT today. For example, we might find some of the right skills in marketing, in R&D, in operations organizations, and more. Target these skills and make our people an exciting offer to join the innovation initiative and make a contribution that would help change the future of the company as well as bring value to our customers.

This is after all the destination of all our innovation investments—a significantly improved or all-new solution delivered to our clients.

The opportunity to deliver value to our own business and to our customers will be exciting and highly motivating to our talented people. It is something they will very much want to be part of; we just need to open the door both in IT and across the business. The powerful good in this process will pull people in and in most cases the right people.

Figure 17.3 New Skills and Diversity

Traditionally, IT has not been a diverse organization. Largely made up of middle-aged men with technology and specifically IT experience, we now need to move past this single-dimensional cultural model. Improving the diversity of IT is not just about adding more diversity of people, which is certainly important, but also about adding more diversity of skills. In many cases, both of these things come in the same person. For example, a woman with strong creative or business requirements or customer-facing skills would be a welcome addition to the IT organization.

*We desperately need more women in the
IT workforce, and with every addition of
the right person, we change the culture
and elevate our performance. Never
underestimate the impact of one talented
and passionate person to an organization.*

Another wonderful thing happens when we expand the diversity of the IT organization: It makes it easier to attract the next person, and then it becomes a bit easier to attract the next person, and so it goes. And soon we have made a dramatic shift in the makeup and capabilities of all IT—less like the traditional IT and more like the dynamic and innovative business IT will be. Keeping the heart of IT intact but changing so much in order to line up with what not just the business needs but what our customers need from us.

To continue down this path, a more diverse IT organization also changes the perceptions of IT across the business. This perception is important and will further accelerate the partnership and alignment we must have with the business as well as our partnership with our clients. This is the expanding circle of a unified IT and then a unified business. This force of unification is unstoppable once begun, and the new skills and diversity we bring to IT very much support this unification and singularity.

Skills expansion and diversity are linked to innovation because we come back to the fundamental truth that the seeds of innovation spring from our people. A more diverse and multi-skilled workforce will yield a stronger pipeline of innovation ideas.

By investing in our people and in our culture, including the expansion of skills and a focus on improving the diversity of IT, we are investing in innovation. These things just go together. Similarly, if IT is committed to innovation in terms of success over a period of years and decades but then makes no changes to culture, no expansion of skills, and no improvement in diversity, we will likely not be able to create the scalable innovation engine that is required.

Understand these connections, these linkages between our people and their skills and the sustainable success of innovation, and be prepared to advance the skills and diversity of our culture, and then invest accordingly. This will pay back to us in terms of innovation but in so many other ways as well. The investment will further accelerate the necessary changes in our culture, help support the quality of the cross-functional teams we are building to drive all key initiatives, equip IT to be a more capable and strategic partner with the business, and help to form and then support the direct customer engagement that lies at the heart of unifying IT and the business.

All these primary elements of value, extending to every aspect of the business, are directly enhanced by the expanded skills and a more diverse culture thoughtfully crafted for IT.

CHAPTER 18

BUSINESS AGILITY

While the frantic rate of change of our markets today and the equally frenzied pace of technology advancement create challenges we can't ignore and will ultimately threaten the survival of many businesses, it also represents an opportunity for the Agile Business.

There are many layers of meaning here, so let's explore a bit. Among these layers is the ability for IT to be a center for and enabler of agility. This is both a strategy and an operating model. A select few organizations have discovered this strategy, but the majority of organizations are not yet there, so it's important to begin the discussions and plant the seeds of thought for what can be a transformational and defining moment for the IT organization moving into the future.

> *This is the perfect time to awaken the giant of IT and its ability to drive agility across the IT organization, which then spreads to, influences, and then fundamentally changes the business.*

With the current marketplace and all that it brings, this is the perfect time to drive agility. A significant competitive advantage is there to be taken, but we should all be clear that the un-agile organization will be threatened with extinction. It is likely that most un-agile and lumbering organizations will struggle at best and in many cases will fail and simply go away. Agility enables so much, makes so much possible, brings so much value to customers, creates so much speed—it is thoroughly a powerful and strategic model on every front. The more carefully we study the principles of agility, the more we appreciate the potential of this wonderful strategy.

> *Note that what I'm referring to here is not*
> *a strict definition of agility per the current*
> *framework and best practices guidelines. There*
> *are many published articles and other references*
> *available to address agile in depth and in detail.*

This discussion is with regard to agility in a more technology and business-oriented sense. The framework of agile is very helpful to many organizations, but we will take a different look here.

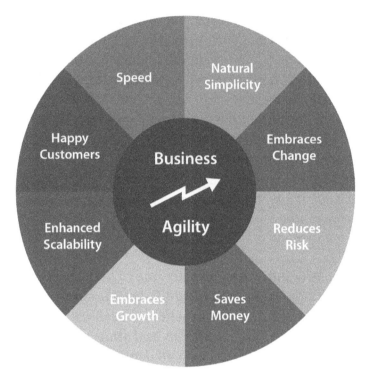

Figure 18.1 The Elements of Business Agility

The previous chapters refer to the quality of agility numerous times because there is so much depth to this strategy and so much of the quality that can change and improve how we think and operate in IT every day.

Note there is a significant intersection between the key performance metrics of the new IT and the strategy of agility, including:

Agility creates speed

Agility naturally nurtures simplicity

Agility embraces change

Agility naturally scales

Agility enhances innovation

Agility better serves customers

Agility creates competitive advantage

Agility saves money

Agility embraces growth

Agility mitigates risk

And this is just the beginning. We are quickly reminded why agility should get much of our attention in looking at the big initiatives we have in front of us—transforming IT, unifying IT, and unifying the business. Although we can describe these strategic steps in simple terms, the changes in IT will define the IT organization for the next twenty years and beyond. Certainly the next ten years will include accelerated change, but this momentum will continue as we push forward to reshape and redefine virtually every action that takes place in IT every day.

But an agile IT does us little good if this agility does not translate fully to the business, which then translates to better serving our customers. Every element of agility, even when born and nurtured in IT, must move quickly to the business and be thoughtfully conceived for the business, so this is no accident. If any investment in agility is purely for IT and does not connect to the business and to the customer, our investments are misguided. Having said this, we should not be confused for a moment and believe the charter for IT is any less urgent or less strategic.

The role of IT in creating agility for the business is more important than ever, and it's even bigger than this—IT must embrace the strategy and responsibility of agility starting with IT and growing from IT. This is critical because in many cases, really in most cases, the business is stalled with regard to improved agility and it needs this boost from IT more than it can understand. In many cases this gap won't be appreciated until sometime later when agility has improved, the model and foundation in IT have been created, and the momentum has grown.

> *Only then will we look back and recognize*
> *that IT has done this wonderful service*
> *to the business by advancing agility*
> *when it was so badly needed.*

Of course it does not matter where this spark comes from, only that it comes, and so we turn to IT to bring this much-needed leadership to the business, for our customers ultimately. Together we can create a new and powerfully agile business like never before.

AGILE FROM WITHIN

Few would argue that agility is a good thing. Agile and its variants are receiving lots of attention, and that is both understandable and a necessary force of change. But we need to look at agility more broadly, as a strategy and model that benefits both IT, development certainly, but the full business as well. Agility has so many desirable dimensions, we can find good stuff everywhere we look.

So, with our affection for agility, the question then becomes where do we start? This is both an important question and an interesting one. Important because we need to get started if we have not already, and there is no good reason to delay because we can make good progress on agility with a reasonable to modest investment. The benefits of agility are just too good and too diverse to put off an investment in this strategy.

If an agility initiative is in place today and good progress is being made, that is great and it is certainly the case for some organizations. But if that is not the case and agility does not have a real focus, something needs to be done sooner rather than later.

We just can't afford to wait. A lack of agility can slow down or virtually disable an organization's ability to move quickly and take advantage of important opportunities in the market.

For example, I have witnessed firsthand the impact of poor agility on mergers and acquisitions. M&A activity is an increasingly common occurrence in many markets today and when executed well is a very effective market consolidation or business expansion strategy. However, when a merger or acquisition occurs and agility is poor, everything slows down and the schedule for bringing the businesses together quickly becomes problematic. Everything is difficult and everything takes more time than expected. Even simple things become complicated and basic integration tasks are painful. It quickly becomes clear when agility is lacking in the business(es) and we are now facing a reactive need to improve agility, which under these circumstances is expensive and will require a great deal of time and resource that were not planned for. This is bad for everybody and there is always a lot of second-guessing and tough questions to be asked. We can all agree this should be avoided at all costs, and that brings us back to getting started now and not wasting any more time.

We never answered the earlier question about where we should start with agility. One possible option and one that is not commonly considered but makes a great deal of sense is starting in IT. In doing this, we are effectively building agility from within.

There are some natural advantages to this approach of creating agility from the inside:

Technology is naturally linked to agility in today's business.

The systems of IT directly enable agility.

Agility should be achieved while ensuring strong security.

Agility is also related to service delivery.

Automation is a significant agility accelerator.

IT efforts to simplify business processes directly support agility.

IT has many of the skills required to drive agility.

> **Considering this profile, IT has a lot of goods needed to drive agility, so an opportunity emerges to create an agility initiative inside of IT and bring the business what is needed more quickly and more proactively.**

This is good stuff and another opening for IT to lead the business. It then becomes a matter of the IT organization recognizing the opportunity and forming a cross-functional team to focus on agility, which quickly becomes a known set of activities to assess the current state of agility and how it can be improved quickly.

Normally we will find two levels of agility opportunities—those that are immediately clear and we can improve quickly and those that are more complex and require a much larger investment. We are reviewing all the primary business processes, technologies, and systems of IT with regard to a current agility grade, and then specific recommendations on how agility can be improved. These are normally processes and systems our people know well and will have a good understanding with which to start, and so the review will proceed quickly overall and we can expect some good recommendations to be raised by the team.

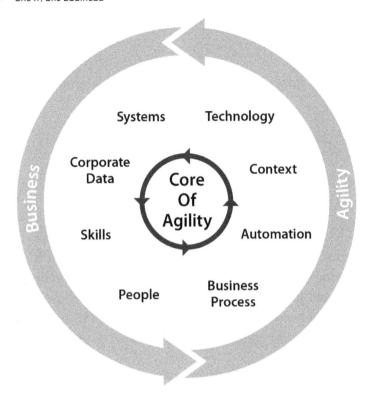

Figure 18.2 The Core of Agility

To clarify, in this context of agility, a review of individual tasks is not normally necessary for the first phase of review, and most agility issues and opportunities will be associated with business processes. Systems can include software applications and any other tools and solutions used by the business like email, calendaring, ERP, HR, procurement, order processing, Security, Compliance, Service Management, Asset Management, and other related solutions. Some will show a strong agility profile, and many will not. These are immediate and valuable opportunities to improve our systems and once again fully under our control.

It is important that the team reviewing the processes and systems for agility is truly cross-functional as this will significantly improve the quality and breadth of recommendations on how agility can be improved. This team should include some of our most experienced and skilled people to ensure the recommendations are impactful and practical.

With the agility improvement recommendations from the team, we can then identify those with the biggest impact and implement them immediately.

Every one of these steps improves business agility and should not be underestimated.

DESIGN FOR RAPID CHANGE

Change is a reality in today's market, and if anything the pace of change is growing. Yet, it is remarkable just how poorly most organizations handle change. This is understandable when we recognize that change is uncomfortable for most people. As such, the organization takes on the natural persona of its people, and so change is something that is avoided as long as possible. When it arrives, it normally arrives quickly and with little notice. Then our people are left to react and to scramble, which creates risk and reduces our ability to be successful.

This is the reality today, but in the years ahead some organizations will equip themselves for change, even to the extent that managing change becomes a strategic strength. This is the case for a select few organizations today, and in virtually every case organizations that create a competency around change will soon enjoy many benefits across the business. Even more, in most cases these organizations that become good and then great at managing change ascend to be market leaders.

The extended process of equipping the
organization to manage change well
creates many positive improvements,
and the business will prosper from these
business process and system upgrades.

In recognizing that so much of managing changes in the market and in the business is related to technology and systems, IT again finds itself in the middle of this multifaceted issue. It is simply not possible to manage change well without a commitment and plan being in place for the enhancement and extension of key IT systems.

A couple of clarifications here—if we are to better prepare for changes in the business, we should assume change will happen quickly and there will likely be little or no time to prepare. The implications of this are significant; the cadence of change creates additional demands and additional requirements. But the good news is that if we build our systems and our processes correctly and with an eye to rapid change, then all classes and tempos of change will be manageable. This is worth our time—considering the implications of rapid change—and from this we will have stronger processes. Stronger processes and systems are more scalable and more reliable as the qualities of these entities are very much in line with change.

> *Creating specific plans to become great,*
> *even world-class at executing small and*
> *large changes in the business is a catalyst*
> *to improving countless things across the*
> *business and has virtually no limits.*

Just a few examples of the kinds of changes to be planned for:

The addition of a large number of users

Merger with another organization of any size*

Acquisition of another organization of any size*

Relocation of a corporate office

Major new audit or compliance requirements

Standing up a new corporate headquarters

Creation of a new sales channel

Launch of a new business line

Onboarding a new strategic partner

Opening of a new regional corporate office

Closing down of a regional corporate office

Start-up of operations in a new country

*We should not assume that M&A activity includes a smaller organization only. It is best to plan for any-sized corporate entity, including a much larger organization. Think in terms of what would be the most difficult, or what scares us the most, and this is where we should begin. If we can manage this scenario, the others will fall into place.

This is not a complete list of course but includes some of the changes that can be disruptive to the business and to the IT organization. For example, doing business in a new country has many implications with regard to currency, taxes, payroll, HR requirements, and new government regulations. This is a lot to consider and any level of planning can make a big difference. It might not be practical to create a detailed plan around each of these items, but even a preliminary plan, a framework if you will, can make a big difference.

Figure 18.3 Rapid Change Checklist

We should think in terms of receiving a notice today that one of these big change scenarios is now real. A few questions we should be prepared to answer and answer quickly and clearly:

What is the first thing we need to do?

Do we have a preliminary plan in place and ready to mobilize?

What are the biggest risks we face?

Do we have a communication plan to help us get started?

What are the costs we need to account for?

What are the key expectations to be set?

Who are the people we need to add to the Change team?

Are we prepared to update the preliminary plan into the real plan?

Do we have a preliminary timeline to work with?

As with all these lists, this is intended to get you started, and there will be many things to be added.

> **There is an IT context to many of these things, but in addition to minding the IT stuff, we also need to watch out for the business. This is perhaps more important than the IT agenda alone.**

With big changes come big opportunities—an idea that should be embraced by IT and by the organization. Once again we come back to the strategy that IT can be proactive in taking a set of actions and performing some forward-looking planning to prepare the business for a big and fast-moving change. With only modest investment we can be ready for the change when it comes, even embrace knowing we are at a reasonable level of readiness, and then maximize the opportunity and help to launch our business into the future.

PLAN FOR SUCCESS AND DISRUPTION

A shift in mindset is an important and powerful thing. Even small adjustments in how we think and how we approach our daily work can unleash tremendous energy in the organization. As we continue to work through the transformation of IT and the further advancement of our strategy through the unification of IT and the business, we should all embrace the wonderful idea of planning for success.

Planning for success underlines everything we do with a sense of optimism. This is a wonderful thing because there is virtually no limit to what a team of optimists can accomplish.

Optimists see the best in everything and see what is possible. Optimists universally have passion and energy. All of this together creates an unstoppable package of good forces.

Conversely, a community of pessimists will underachieve.

Is your IT organization optimistic? It is an important question because it shapes how we think and how we work every day. This is fully our control and it is possible to move a team of people from a negative mindset, or one that is neutral, to a positive mindset. It is possible to cultivate optimism in a team and in a culture where it did not exist before. I have seen it happen and it is a beautiful thing.

This then naturally carries us into a process of planning for success. In order to be thoughtful professionals, while we are planning for success, we will also perform a level of contingency planning to address the major risks in the event any of these risks come to pass. But the majority of our energy will be planning for success, even wild success.

Anticipating success is fun.

Planning for success is energizing.

Expecting success tends to improve our chances of success becoming a reality.

Planning for success creates a common spirit of confidence.

Looking at success brings some swagger to IT—something that is much needed.

Planning for success draws all people closer to us.

Thinking about success is contagious— people are naturally attracted to it.

Let's put a little bit of structure to what planning for success would entail. Success scenarios would normally include growth and expansion to the business, each of which is a form of change and would impact the IT organization.

A few examples of these scenarios would include:

A large increase in the number of employees accessing IT systems

The addition of new corporate offices

Ability to quickly execute a corporate merger or acquisition

A large increase in the number of mobile devices to be managed by IT

The addition of new compliance and governance requirements

The addition of new countries in which the company will operate

The need for IT to manage and secure a significant increase in mobile phones

Each of these items anticipates business success and each item entails a unique number of considerations, but each scenario is created through success, expansion, and growth. Each scenario directly impacts the technology and infrastructure of IT, and as such, the performance and planning of the IT organization directly enhances or slows our success.

It's about IT performing a readiness assessment of its own with regard to our readiness for success. This is a good place to start, and the short list above can be included in the scope of our internal IT success scorecard.

If your organization is one of the few that scores well and would be considered in a strong state of readiness for success, then you should be congratulated for the good work that has already been done. But for most IT organizations, the current state of readiness is not good and there is much work to be done. This is okay because the work can start now, and IT should be proactive in launching this work knowing that when the day comes for a big change, or a big success, IT must be ready. When that day comes, the business will be counting on us.

Even a modest amount of work to create a set of preliminary plans around a few primary success scenarios can make a big difference later and fundamentally change the daily rhythm of the IT organization.

> *We can also turn this theme of anticipating*
> *success back to each of the teams of IT and*
> *ask for their own assessment of the current*
> *state of readiness for success. What is the*
> *single success scenario that creates the biggest*
> *risk? This is a great exercise to go through.*

Then, how do we mitigate this risk? Better us than another organization, and better now than later. This simple approach can make a big difference.

The other topic we want to take on within this section is another simple but powerful strategy. Disruption will come; it is inevitable. So, how do we prepare for disruption but even better, how do we disrupt ourselves?

> *That's right, how can we disrupt ourselves so*
> *this disruption comes more under our control*
> *and the impact to the business can be managed?*

Responding to disruption, particularly big disruptions, is difficult and painful. But we can turn the tables—driven by the business change scenarios we discussed earlier, the success scenarios within this section, or market shifts that have been identified through the market sensors we have in place as discussed later in this chapter.

This is another proactive push to strategic IT, another strategy to take control of the powerful forces that can impact the business. With the work that is being done around planning for big changes to IT and the business, along with planning for success, we can extend that a bit to include this theme of disruption—not completely different, but not quite the same as big change and success.

This set of activities enables IT to become an advanced planning engine for the business, which enables the IT organizations and our leaders, including IT Business Management and the IT Concierge, to become the primary thought leaders in the overall business and drive future business performance. All of these paths for planning and execution are closely related and very much needed.

Whatever form these planning processes take in your business, and it can be very different from organization to organization, the key thing is expanding the scope of our IT planning processes to include more forward-looking content and the scenarios that would not be typical. IT organizations today perform some level of planning, so this strategy is not completely new.

What is new is expanding the scope of the regularly planned IT cycles to include these concepts of big changes, high-risk changes, extreme success, and self-disruption. These processes will then catalyze many other changes and further enhance our alignment with a unity with the business.

Planning scenarios will instantly be recognized as valuable and strategic and serve as a natural force around which our IT leaders and key business owners will rally and unite. These themes are necessary, fun, and thought-provoking. We need more of all of this for the unification of IT and the business.

EMPOWERING BUSINESS LEADERS

The agility of IT, creating the strategy of agility from within, should not be confused with an agile IT for the sake of IT. Any agility we are able to create across IT is certainly important, but make no mistake—this is fully about the business. And it should quickly be recognized that agility for the business is all about being more agile for the customer. This is a critical chain of value and one that we will touch on throughout the book because it is so central to the strategy that is driving the transformation of IT, bringing IT together, and creating a new unified IT.

> **With the vital concept of creating agility for the business, in order for the business to be more agile for and better serve the customer, we must recognize that agility can only come to life through the key business owners and leaders across the business.**

Effectively, agility is inert without the personal fuel and passion provided every day by the leaders in the business, including key leaders in the IT organization. These committed and talented people are the heartbeat of the business, the fabric of the organization.

Agility has a necessary element of structure, of process, of technology. This structure is important because we can't operate an agile model in any sense without the right structure and the necessary architecture if you will. Systems that will scale, technologies that are quickly adaptable, processes that can be changed quickly—all simple examples of how agility is codified into the organization from end to end and from top to bottom.

Then a wonderful thing happens. Our talented people, the leaders throughout the organization, take this model and begin to drive it forward, bringing the model of agility to life and raising its performance to new levels. All of this then gets connected to the needs of our business leaders, who in turn are driving initiatives based on the needs of our customers. A good place to begin our focus on agility is with those key business owners, and they can be in any organization, who are closest to the customers. This is where we can have the biggest impact, and these people will also have the clearest view and understanding of what our customers require.

This starting point and focus then create the leverage we need with agility because we are going directly to the living customer connections, and our people will immediately frame everything in terms of the customer.

This is exactly as it should be and will protect us from driving agility forward based on internal-only or IT-only requirements. There might very well be internal requirements that take a place on the agility roadmap, which is to be expected. But with regard to prioritizing our investments and shaping the overall agility model, it must be tested and validated by customer requirements.

For example, an internal requirement could be related to the ability of the organization to stand up or close a corporate office. This example has been used earlier because it is normally large in scale and a disruptive event for the IT organization. Bringing more agility to this business process will benefit the business certainly and will enable us to improve our speed of execution and help the organization to scale. However, this is not a direct impact to customers but more a second-level impact; it will enable the business to be stronger and potentially add a location where we can better service a specific set of customers in a regional location. All of this is good.

However, a customer-facing entity of the business, perhaps a product-ordering portal or customer support page that is used by our customers every day and has a specific and well-known face to the customer, is more visible. Many organizations struggle with new product or services offerings, content updates, announcements, and other capabilities related to resources, and any improvement in agility that enables the business to quickly improve the user experience and the content used by users in these customer-facing systems is a high-value investment. Both of these examples are important and both would be included in our agility improvements, but we always begin with what directly benefits the customer and provides tangible value directly to the customer. This category or investment stands alone at the top.

Of course, we have a business to run, and the success of the business enables the organization to better service customers as well, so this category can't be ignored. Which brings us back to the daily needs of our key business owners. IT can create agility on behalf of the business. IT should be clear regarding the primary consumers of this agility and use these business leaders to validate and clarify how agility will directly enable them to run the business better and more importantly to better serve our customers.

We must create this circle of value and it must wholly be enabled by IT—the IT organization being the catalyst and architect of agility improvements, including an ongoing agility roadmap, and each element of this plan being targeted squarely at the key business owners who directly support our customers.

As an extension to this and in line with our earlier discussion on direct customer engagement, when we have this channel available to IT, the customers take on a more direct and influential role. Customers bring clarity and specific and real use cases that can help to guide us through the agility roadmap. Customer engagement is always best and will lead us to the best results. This does not exclude the participation of the key business owners because that remains important.

We create a dual path of focus in creating and innovating agility for our business teams and the key business leaders and delivering agility to our customer-facing technologies and systems.

This combination and balance is strategic and maximizes the leverage we create with agility.

MARKET SENSORS

Leading indicators can help provide direction to business agility and enhance the ability of IT to create agility from within. These indicators can be tapped by creating a series of market sensors to be used by the IT organization to get what is effectively an early warning on new market trends and market shifts that are likely to have an impact on the business. IT simply can't wait until these market changes arrive. By that time it is too late. Nor can IT depend on the business to provide this view of the market because it is a fundamentally flawed model—IT must define, create, and then monitor these sensors in order to operate proactively and to manage and then minimize the impact of new market requirements, shifts, and disruptions that will inevitably come our way.

This is yet another theme for the more strategic, proactive, and outside-in IT organization creating connections to the marketplace in order to deliver what the business needs when the business needs it.

Certainly not traditional, possibly even a bit controversial, but it is thoroughly necessary.

Market sensors can take many forms:

> *The formation of, or joining of existing, strategic customer panels*

> *Participation in relevant industry events with strategic market content*

> *Inquiries and advisory sessions with leading industry analysts*

> *Targeted work with strategic periodicals and vertical publications*

> *Feedback from leading industry and vertical-focused consultants*

> *Scanning of relevant social media tools*

> *Review of thought leader blogs*

Much of this is not new for the business, but the monitoring, evaluation, and participation of IT in these vehicles *is* new. Some will object to IT taking on this work, but it is absolutely necessary in order for IT to develop a more objective and independent view of market factors and market changes. We simply can't allow IT to continue operating in a model that relies on other organizations of the business to provide some version of this information, potentially translated or delayed, across the IT organization.

IT must aggressively join these channels and forums where they exist or create them where they do not. These different sources help to balance one another and bring valuable and timely intelligence back into the IT organization on a frequent and unfiltered basis. This is vital to creating a set of real-time market sensors.

Some of this has been done traditionally by organizations, including PR, Marketing, and Sales, but IT now extends this model to support the innovation and agility efforts that are so vital to the new strategic model of IT.

> *Direct engagement, participation, feedback, and dialogue are all necessary for the clarity and perspective IT must have to bring real value to business agility. There is simply no substitute.*

The good news is that we will find sources for the necessary information more available than ever, including open and immediate access to social media forums and online content and blogs. The key is to ignore the low-value content, which does exist, and to identify the high-quality sources that are there for us to enjoy but take a bit of time to identify. This is okay and is a search well spent. Once we find these insightful sources of market information, they are typically updated daily and can be a great sensor resource for IT going forward.

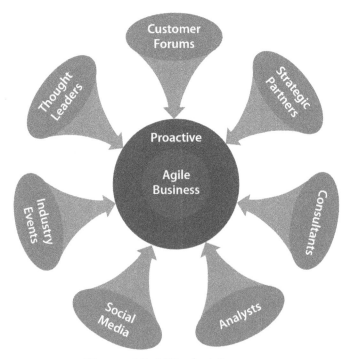

Figure 18.4 Market Sensors

It is important to take a "surround-sound" approach to these sensors—we need to have multiple sources so these sources can be evaluated against one another in order to find the intersection of truth. This helps us to avoid any biases or a limited perspective and bring some balance to our sensor network. Again, time well spent.

It can further help to feed the information we gather into a visible form for our people to utilize as necessary, which can be a set of dashboards, a brief market report, a short briefing at the start of the IT innovation, brainstorming forums, or any other mechanism that works for your organization. Communicate the market information broadly and often.

> *We will be surprised by how many of our IT people are hungry for this information. IT is full of smart people who are often intellectually curious and enjoy learning, so we should feed this hunger with insightful market information.*

The key is to bring this information back into the cross-functional teams of IT that are driving agility, innovation, and other related activities. This should be done consistently and on a sustainable cadence that will keep the feedback and market sensors fresh and on target.

Our talented people in IT will be able to leverage the information to improve the performance of our IT systems and much, much more. This can include engagement with key business owners and executives on strategy and operational discussions to adapt the systems of IT on behalf of the business in anticipation of coming changes. This is IT planning and acting in partnership with key business owners to both minimize the impact of market shifts and to leverage these same shifts in order to improve our competitive position in the market and better serve our customers.

WORK IN PROGRESS

A physical and virtual load of work in progress lives within every organization, and this has always been the case from the very beginning of business. It is fundamental and it is timeless.

What is now new about this work in progress
in the new age of technology and with
the new knowledge worker is the growth
of the invisible element of this work.

To further extend this impact, the invisible work in progress is now far greater than the visible work in progress that has always been with us. In the industrial revolution and the global growth of manufacturing in the past seventy-five years, this work in progress was readily visible—we could find it, touch it, move it, and count it. This work was raw materials, intermediate products, goods, parts, packages, pallets of goods, and much more.

The challenge that comes along with this invisible work in progress is that because we can't see it or touch it, the work can be difficult to quantify and to track. How much of this exists, how much is being completed, and how much progress are we making against this work?

These are important issues for the IT organization in the decade ahead of us because the ability to manage this invisible work in progress will be directly related to our ability to build speed and agility in IT.

> *Because this invisible work in progress represents so much of the load on the IT organization and the business, this weight must be better understood and managed in order to create agility.*

There simply can't be agility in IT or the business if we are unable to better understand and better manage this work. Although it is a fascinating and rich topic, it's beyond the scope of this small section, but my hope here is to raise the awareness of the topic and to then add it to our transformation agenda for the IT organization. If we can't better define this load on the organization and help to better quantify and manage it, the business has no hope of real progress with scalability and agility.

Much of this invisible work in progress is connected to tasks and business processes—the very work units we will review as part of the Simplicity, Waste, Speed, and Automation initiatives, and as such we will gain a number of work-in-progress insights through this work that is already on our agenda. We need to take advantage of this and in the process of advancing these important improvements it should include an improved mechanism for gaining visibility and measurement of this invisible work in progress.

A few questions to be answered around this invisible work in progress:

> *How much work in progress are we loaded with at any given time?*

> *Where does this work sit in the organization?*

How quickly is the work advancing?

Is any of the work in progress currently stuck/delayed?

What is the origin of each unit of work?

How are we performing with regard to our speed improvements?

How are we performing with regard to our automation improvements?

How much of this work is being performed manually?

Are we able to identify the current status of each unit of work?

What is the projected completion date for each unit of work?

Simple questions that we are capable of answering when focused on finding these insights, and with this we can better understand the true nature of the work. What was invisible becomes better understood.

Then with this understanding we can begin to manage the load on the organization. With the ability to manage this load, we can then extend agility, and the invisible work will no longer stand in our way in the advancement of our strategic initiatives and, in this case, Business Agility.

Another extension of this invisible work in progress along with visible work in progress is our ability to maximize the productivity of our people and the organization. This is related to the concept of "flow," and much research and modeling has been performed around the topic in the past twenty years. The same could be said for the Theory of Constraints, a wonderful framework that found much application in the work done on the improvement of Manufacturing and Supply Chain Management. Any student of these concepts will quickly be struck by the intersections that exist in all these models and strategies, and these two examples are certainly not a complete list. To a degree, we could have the same discussion around Agile and DevOps. Good business practices and common sense are timeless and valuable.

> *For the purposes of the framework we present in this book and the unification of IT and our business, there is a clear connection between Flow, TOC and Elimination of Waste, Simplicity, Speed, and Automation.*

Many of the fundamentals are inescapably the same, and we will keep this discussion at a non-mathematical and statistical level in order to keep our ideas connected to the strategy and tactics of IT. These concepts are universal and will be among the building blocks of the new IT organization.

If the IT organization has experts on the concept of flow or the Theory of Constraints or any of the other valuable management or business frameworks, that is a great resource to be leveraged, and this knowledge can be used to advance the strategy and framework presented in this book.

> *We should view this knowledge of business and management principles not as a conflict of any type, but rather another needed boost to the expertise and diversity we need so badly in the IT organization.*

I'm always amazed by the knowledge talented and naturally curious people bring with them to the IT organization every day, and it's something that should be embraced. These same people will take on leadership roles in the future, including IT Business Management and IT Concierge, as well as participating in the innovation forums and process. This is vital to our future and all held by our people and the new culture of IT.

CHAPTER 19

LEADERSHIP OF THE CIO

The leadership of the CIO has always been important, but now it rises to the highest level of both strategic to the business and critical to the future of the organization. In many ways the leadership of the CIO becomes the most dynamic leadership role held in the company due to the unique state of the market and unique stature of technology and enterprise and corporate data. This elevates the CIO to be a trusted advisor to the CEO, the CFO, and the board of directors. The CIO becomes essential to shaping the vision and strategy of the business and in leading it to successful performance in the future.

This new urgency around this unique leadership is due to many factors, including:

The growing dependency of the business on technology

The requirement to better leverage technology to drive strategy

The unique mix of technology and business expertise held by the CIO

Emerging requirements to better leverage corporate data

Increased accountability around governance, compliance, and audit

These key factors and much more shine an organizational spotlight on the CIO, and both the IT organization and the business need the unique skills and insights of the CIO more than ever. The CIO will recognize the opportunity to influence and lead not just the IT organization but the business and to fill what is likely a growing void that exists today around the depth of the business vision and the need for a new and compelling vision for the IT organization.

Figure 19.1 CIO Leadership

The CIO then becomes an agent of change and a catalyst for unification of all teams everywhere. The CIO will have a unique understanding of technology and one that likely far exceeds that of the

CEO and CFO, for example, and positions the CIO to educate other executives on how key technology works in the most basic sense; how the IT organization can better drive the business and our customers; and how every element of the business can better leverage technology and data. This ability is fundamental to the future success of the business. Organizations that "get it" have a bright future and will be in the discussion of the new market leaders; organizations that struggle with this fundamental question will struggle at best and many will not survive the next ten years.

> *This strategic use of technology and data in the context of business strategy becomes a turbulent journey-inside-the-journey of sorts that companies must find a way to cross over into a brighter future or be left behind.*

With this transformational challenge, the CIO is needed more than ever.

The CIO and in some cases the VP IT become trusted advisors to the CEO, CFO, COO, and beyond the corporate leadership team, including the board of directors. With so many questions revolving around technology and with the pace of change in technology accelerating, we will find that IT leadership is called upon to provide expert testimony in a growing number of forums throughout the business and in its many extensions. The business will need the recommendations and insights of the CIO and team in a growing scope of issues and as an input and validation of new and existing strategy.

We should never underestimate the growing influence of the IT organization and the CIO and staff, as so much of what we do every day in the business and so much of the planning processes we rely on every day touch and leverage technology.

We find technology behind the scenes,
propelling us forward in virtually everything.

So, it then follows that there will be a common lack of in-depth understanding for many elements of technology, and in particular the newer elements of technology, and so we then ask ourselves, "Who can we talk to who understands this and can help us?" The organization looks around the room and around the organization in search of precious insights and the experts we need to make sense of it all.

We search in the hopes of finding a new
generation of experts and expertise that can
be valuable resources in finding a unique
balance between understanding technology
itself and, more importantly, how technology
can be used to solve real business problems
and deliver value to our customers.

This is the very essence of business for the next twenty-five years and very much what is driving the transformation of IT and the unification of IT and the business.

The improvement of technology is in itself not what should excite us. Technology for the sake of better technology is tactical and missing the point. Yes, it excites some people who are completely fixated on the features and functions of technology, and this will always be a thread of our culture.

But what is most valuable about the current advancements of technology and a new generation of AI and automation tools is what it means for the improved performance of the business and how we deliver products and services to our customers.

*This is the key, and the right knowledge is
required to leverage this technology fully, to
place technology in the right roles to provide
strategic value and ultimately to provide
what is required to help our customers
meet the daily challenges of the business.*

This is it. This is all that matters and the single thing around which we build the new IT, which brings us back to the CIO and leadership we so acutely need today.

A UNIFIED VISION

A key part of our unification of IT and the business is the opportunity for our people, all our people across the organization, to rally around a unified vision. The vision will transcend the confines of IT and certainly the traditional models and operating structures of IT. The need to transcend is not unique to IT, and we can assign the same call to our business. Every organization must move beyond the current boundaries and structures to rally around a common vision, a common strategy, a common set of goals.

But where will this unified vision come from? Where are we capable of creating it? In some cases it will come from a visionary CEO. The very best companies have this vision, and it will carry them forward for the next twenty years and likely will bring a high level of success for the organization. But these organizations with a unified vision in place today are few, far too few in fact. Visionary organizations do share a few common characteristics, including:

> *A clear sense of how the business uniquely serves its customers*

> *A compelling and simple vision all employees can understand*

> *The articulation of how technology serves the vision in a strategic capacity*

The directional guidance to drive ongoing innovation

A sense of purpose across the organization

A commitment to a dynamic culture and our people

Where we have this vision, it is a powerful and dynamic unifying force across the organization, but in those organizations where it does not exist today, there is a void. A void that might not be understood as of yet, but that time is coming.

In those cases where the unifying vision does not exist, and again there are many of these, a leader in the organization who is uniquely qualified to provide this vision, to fill the void, is the CIO. Yes, I understand this might raise a few eyebrows or cause a few chuckles, but let's think about it for a moment. The unifying vision is now tied closely to the role of technology and the business like never before, which requires a detailed and practical knowledge of both technology and how technology and systems can be leveraged by a business every day. This vision also requires insight into the need for innovation, ongoing innovation as a cultural value and an organizational priority.

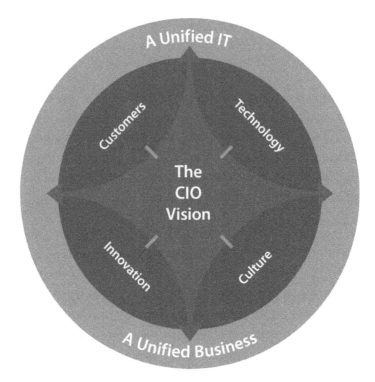

Figure 19.2 A Unified Vision

For most organizations, innovation is closely related to technology. With the technology available to us today, it is about how we take technology and create new solutions that are creatively applied to making business run better and more importantly to delivering a compelling value to our customer. Another increasing role in innovation is that of intelligent technology that has the capability to fundamentally change IT and our business over the next ten years. While we get excited about many things, and new technologies will help us work better every day, only a select few have the capability to create dramatic change in IT—and intelligent technology makes that list.

In many cases the COO, CFO, CEO, and the board of directors will understand at a high level that AI and intelligent technology will have a key place in the future of our organization, but a more in-depth understanding of these technologies is required in order to shape a vision, a strategy, and tactics around how we best leverage this technology.

> *The CIO is likely to have this unique understanding, and so this is yet another opportunity for the CIO and IT to lead our business into the future. If not the CIO, where else can this come from? That is a very difficult question to answer and brings us back to needing the leadership of IT and the CIO and VP IT more than ever.*

We can't wait, we can't delay. It is critical that we take action now and drive this leadership and this vision from within.

IT and our IT leaders can fill the void, and the business will be more complete and will recognize something good when they hear it and see it.

Even in those cases where the vision does not come from the CIO singly, the CIO may work as a trusted advisor and intellectual coach to the CEO, and through this process the vision is born. The CEO may then take the vision forward and give it a face and a voice, but the birth of this new vision would not be possible without the knowledge and insights of the CIO. This model will make the most sense for many organizations, and it really comes down to the people involved, the current state of the organization, and timing. In the end, however, all that matters is the creation of the new vision, bringing it to our people, and rallying our culture around a common cause and alongside our customers.

Don't expect our business to ask IT, the CIO, or VP IT for this vision because that just won't happen. But what *can* happen is the crafting of this vision within IT, because the IT organization needs it anyway. The same vision will shape IT over the next ten years, becomes a unifying force for the IT organization, and helps to bring the daily execution of our people together and focused on a common set of goals. This vision also helps to clarify priorities around investments, application roadmaps, hiring priorities, resource assignments, and much, much more.

Even for the purposes of the IT organization,
this vision should be shaped to align
with key business strategies.

It will slow us down and create confusion if the vision is fully IT-centric, and we then need to take time later to update and improve it to align with our business. We need IT and our business to be equally represented from the beginning, giving us the best possible and most useful vision for the organization.

Our vision should look forward and enable success around our business strategy while at the same time providing the necessary vision for the IT organization where it is often missing today.

For example, an online retailer may have the following vision: **to provide the most convenient and customer-friendly shopping and ordering experience in the market today.**

It is a simple but clear vision based loosely on a real business, and although simple it does contain signification guidance for the business and the IT organization. This is exactly the type of vision needed today in virtually every market segment and for every business.

Although not yet common, it has been done by the leading organizations in any market today. Apple, Amazon, and Google are good examples. These organizations are market leaders, the world's most valuable companies, and have a vision that is uniquely technology- and business-driven. The key is not to create an IT-centric vision that does not address the key business requirements or align with key business strategies, which should be understood from the beginning. When we start with these goals for our vision, the result is achievable and we make the best use of the time we put into the process.

When we are able to create this unifying vision, it will start within IT but will quickly be embraced and seen as useful and strategic to the full organization. This will organically pull our people together and be a powerful and needed unifying force. It is natural and people are quickly pulled into this influence.

It won't be necessary to sell this vision to the organization—that will happen quickly and naturally. Our people will recognize this as something we need and something that provides the clarity that is often missing today, which will elevate the stature of IT and the CIO across the organization—another example of IT leading from the inside and taking a proactive role to move our business forward. This will rally our people around IT and around technology and how it can make our business better for our customers.

CUSTOMER PASSION STARTS HERE

There is no better place to root our focus on the customer than in IT and with the CIO and the IT leadership team. It makes so much sense when we look at the heartbeat of the organization in terms of the systems and data that keep the business running every day. It's all under the stewardship of IT of course, and when we consider that we have account management, sales, services, support, marketing, and other teams working with customers every day and then add the customer passion in IT, we then have the organization surrounded in the best possible way.

This is a critical element of the core influence the CIO and IT leadership can have on the organization, and it will often be the top priority driving a realignment of IT.

> *The good news is this change, this cultural shift, this new elevated passion for the customer, can happen quickly; it can happen in an instant.*

If the CIO displays a passion for the customer and consistently reinforces a focus on the customer and achieving real results with customers every day, the role modeling quickly influences every action we take in IT every day.

To be clear, this is not common in IT today, but if we are to build a new level of focus and engagement with the customer, it is the perfect place to start. By creating this focus within the IT organization, we will see a change in how our teams work every day, and once again, we will see the influence, this leadership, shape the remainder of our business. People will quickly take notice of the priority, which then grows into a consistent passion, and then our best people will be the first to recognize it.

The CIO and the VP IT can both catalyze this focus but are also in a position to bring the customer focus to life. There are strategy elements to the customer focus but many tactical requirements as well. At the strategy level, the customer should be represented in the vision for IT and when we are setting resource priorities and assigning cross-functional teams to staff the initiatives that are mobilized regularly along with priorities. As the CIO and VP IT continue to reinforce the importance of bringing passion for the customer to our work every day, this message will be taken by our teams, and every director-level and manager-level leader across IT will carry this same focus back to their teams. And so this commitment rolls through our teams and reaches every person in one form or another. Making decisions that favor our customers and understanding the priorities that guide us every day become more clear. Once again, it all starts with the CIO, who then demonstrates this focus to his/her staff and management team in every staff meeting, working session, daily work, and the many extensions of communications.

> *Our people will see this clearly, and*
> *the passion will be contagious and*
> *appear in all our teams quickly.*

The CIO is also in a position to hold teams accountable in executing the activities that over time will make the customer focus a success. This includes things like the direct customer engagement model. Where it does not exist today, the CIO and VP IT can make it happen. In some cases it is a matter of making an introduction or requesting support from another team in the organization. The CIO can contact an executive in account management, tech support, or sales to facilitate an introduction or to get the right IT people invited to existing conference calls, an on-site meeting, an escalation process, or something similar that will jump-start the customer engagement. We need the customer engagement across IT to help develop the relationship IT must have with customer staff to clarify and extend our understanding of current and future customer requirements.

At first glance this might seem like a
small thing, but it is a very big deal.

It's important in terms of the CIO helping to build the bridge between IT, through our own organization and to the customer, but also what becomes possible when this connection is in place. So much becomes possible when we build a new relationship with the customer, and a lot of that happens naturally. Good people working with good people will in almost every case make good things happen. But our biggest obstacle in making this model real is the front end—making the right connections and the right introductions. This is where the CIO or VP IT can be a big help. For the CIO it can be as simple as a quick call or text to the VP Sales or the COO or the VP Marketing, and things start to happen. The CIO can raise the issue at his/her executive staff meeting, and once again things start to happen.

Another important point is that this is not just
about the work IT will begin directly with the
customer; the process also further develops IT
relationships with our peers in the business.

These are the roles that currently have a direct engagement with customers and regular communications, reviews, and meetings. The right IT staff simply join these existing forums and work alongside their peers who are working with our customers today. We then find ourselves working together, with an extended team, to better serve the customer. It is not just about making the introduction between an IT staff member and the customer; the step before the introduction will be an introduction to one of our coworkers supporting the customer relationship today. This peer introduction will normally create a quick discussion and planning session prior to the IT staff introduction to the customer, which will include some talking points around how an extension to the team will enable us to better serve the customer. The customer will immediately appreciate it.

> *Customers have a natural interest in working more closely with domain experts and technology people and see them as content experts with valuable knowledge. It's good for everybody.*

To recap, the CIO or VP IT has contacted the appropriate executive in our customer-facing organizations who have in turn made an introduction to the right manager or staff member in their organization; this contact then works with the right IT staff member to bring them into the current running dialogue with the customer along with an introduction at the right time. Once in place, we now have an extended cross-functional team working with the customer and now including IT and likely for the first time. The many discussions and exchanges with the customer now bring key insights directly back into the IT organization.

This is only one thread in our example model, and now imagine this model with a few and then dozens of threads, each of which is a direct connection to our customers, and all of this information is now flowing back into the IT organization every day where the information was limited or did not exist before. The result is truly a hundred-fold or thousand-fold improvement in the understanding of the IT organization of current and future customer needs.

The flow of valuable information, directly from the customer and into the IT organization, has the ability to fundamentally change our perspective and our understanding throughout IT can now improve what is delivered to our business and to our customers. and to our customers.

As this model grows and extends, it is nothing
less than a game changer and all made possible
by the sponsorship of the CIO and his/her staff.

EMPLOYEE NURTURING

Ah, the wonderful people of IT and our business. It is certainly not true that the people of IT have suffered from an absolute lack of development and nurturing, but at the same time, this has not been a natural focus on the organization from the beginning. The DNA of IT was very much formed around technology, domain expertise, rallying to fix problems, and keeping our systems operating. This was born and grown of necessity, and over the past three decades, IT has become very good at each of these.

Today, and with an eye to the future, we are called to invest a greater level of energy and resources in our people. We now understand that so much is at stake regarding the future of our systems and our data, and what technology is now capable of providing to the business immediately calls our attention to the need to better nurture the knowledge workers of IT. Domain expertise, specialized skills, technology mastery, and the like remain vital to the future of IT. But our focus moves to the long-term leveraging of this knowledge and the retention and further development of our people in order to elevate and expand the value these technologies and systems can bring to the business.

The answer to the growing demands and the new stopwatch placed on IT is not to seek more qualified and more talented people outside of IT. The people we have today have the skills, talent, experience, and intellect required to meet today's need and those of the future and more.

> *There are no more talented and committed*
> *people anywhere in our complete*
> *business than the people of IT.*

The answer is to invest more—only a bit more makes a big difference in the development and nurturing of our people in IT—and to then retain our people and grow the average tenure within IT.

This second point is a big one—we know that an experienced person in IT with a tenure of over two years is far more productive than one with less than one year with the organization.

By retaining our key people and growing the average tenure of our people in IT, we accomplish so much, including:

Increased productivity from a more tenured staff

Faster execution of business processes

Improved staff mentoring

Higher quality of service

Stronger pipeline of future leaders

Stronger team relationships and stronger teams

Improved IT employee morale

Higher quality input to the innovation process

Increase in customer satisfaction

As with many good things, this is just the beginning. Our focus on IT staff development and a long-term career development plan is just the beginning of staff enrichment and creates a virtually boundless cultural change in IT.

> *This development of our people is a long-term commitment and a cultural change that impacts the daily motion of the IT organization and is all about consistency. With this direction rooted in commitment, we come back to leadership and the leadership of the CIO and the VP IT.*

This is clearly a case of our IT leadership and likely beginning with this senior team and the clear message that IT will focus on and improve our long-term development of IT staff. The future of IT is in our people. We are prepared to make the necessary investment at every level and make employee nurturing and enrichment something we are great at, which will include creating a few processes and tools where they do not exist, and reviewing and potentially improving what does exist.

A short list of improvements to begin with should include:

Review of IT comp plans and true-up with other organizations

Creation of an IT incentive plan for key staff

Participation of key IT staff in corporate bonus plans

Employee development fund for attending training and key industry forums

Development of mentoring plan for junior and senior IT staff

Partnership with HR to create a new IT staff career development plan

Definition of existing and new IT career path opportunities

Recruitment plan development with HR or outside recruiters

The focus created by this partnership with Human Resources and the extension and enrichment of these employee-related programs send a message to every member of IT and a message that might be long overdue for many.

> **We are betting on our people who are the key to the new IT, a unified IT, and a unified business. While this message will begin with the CIO, it will echo through every leader in the organization and reach every person in IT. With this, the expectations of ourselves will change and the expectations our business has for IT will change as well.**

This is exactly as it should be and a change we all embrace.

THE RIGHT CULTURE

All of us in IT carry a natural affection and affinity for technology. We find technology fascinating, we are in awe of the advancements made by technology in the past ten years, and we enjoy using and exploring new technologies. We welcome the opportunity to discuss technology with our colleagues, friends, and family.

Technology is a natural for us and a natural part of our lives that we welcome.

> *Yet, it is important to recognize and to then embrace the fact that technology, while more powerful and important than ever, is not the single greatest key to our future. Technology does not hold the key to the future of IT and the future of business—this distinction sits squarely with our people and our culture.*

Yes, and it's not even close, my friends. If anything, the more powerful and remarkable technology becomes, the more we are reminded of just how special our people really are. We are reminded of the miracle of humanity and what humanity is capable of providing to IT and to the business that is simply beyond the scope of technology—at least for the next one hundred years or more. That, however, is a discussion for another day.

We touched on this in our chapter on the partnership between technology and humanity. This relationship, this partnership, is truly strategic. In many ways the partnership is the key to the sequence that is the transformation of IT, the unity of IT, and the unity of IT and our business. But this partnership must be enabled by the thoughtful cultivation of the people of IT, and cultivation and nurturing are only possible with the creation of the right culture.

For this discussion we emphasize the importance of culture because it can't be reinforced too often, but even more so the importance of the CIO and IT senior leadership commitment to shaping and encouraging this culture. The full IT organization must live this culture every day, and over time it will begin to influence and reshape everything.

> *The culture of IT will grab the attention of key business owners and business experts who are partnering with the IT team every day; over time it will take root in the business because smart and talented people are perceptive and know something good when they see it.*

By now, after many references to this culture throughout the book, there can't be any confusion around what the culture must be and what it should not be. Another quick summary here can help:

A focus on and direct engagement with the customer as beginning and end

Working in cross-functional teams for virtually all that we do

Encouragement and recognition of passion

Improved communications and transparency

A commitment to and new processes built around innovation

A critical review of IT work to eliminate waste and increase speed

An understanding of the need to unify IT and our business

Proactive outreach and partnership with our business and key business owners

There is much, much more at work here, but these are some good examples. Each of these cultural elements complements the others, and so it is not about a big number of unrelated initiatives that will drain our time and resource. This process holds many natural synergies, and with each change we will find a natural momentum that builds and carries us into the next change, naturally and smoothly in most cases.

This culture is created bit by bit, step by step, day by day. What we really need is a commitment and the discipline to get a little better every day. To move away from bad habits and long-standing biases over time.

It's a journey, and that expectation should be reinforced at every level of the organization constantly, every day. While this is important and with a critical need comes focus and determination, at the same time IT leadership must display a level of patience. Lasting change takes a bit of time.

This is a vital part of the CIO charter, and this is where it starts. The reinforcement needed over time comes from the CIO, and then takes hold with direct reports of the CIO, extended staff, and then director level and manager level. The full chain is important, and we need unity among this group.

While the CIO is a key to this culture, I have been struck by the growing number of talented people in the role of VP IT, including a growing number of brilliant women.

We should expect to see the leadership of IT increasingly promoted into senior roles in the business, and the CIO will become promotable into roles including the COO and CEO. It's all driven by the increased profile of technology in the business, the need for a strong technology-related strategy, including how technology can be more effectively leveraged by the business, and the need for leadership with deep technology expertise. This promotability continues with talented VP IT people promoted into CIO, which will then create a new generation of leadership into the business, but trained and groomed from within IT.

Remember, the culture of IT is changing, and with this new proactive, strategic, and innovative culture increasingly driving and leading the business, it creates a natural pull of the business to bring more IT leadership into non-IT roles. This should be expected and is good for our business.

As a natural extension to this important progression, the growing diversity of IT, including a growing number of women in key expert and leadership roles, IT will prove to be an engine of diversity growing through the organization and bringing what is so needed.

Examples of how IT will lead, reshape, and influence our business by creating a new pipeline of leaders will surprise and shock many, because IT has for so long been stereotyped as something very different.

But we are up to the challenge, and once again are reminded that the very best and strongest leadership can sometimes come from the most unlikely of sources.

Strong leaders are uniquely capable of shaping people and cultures, and so we need this leadership more than ever for the benefit of IT and for the greater good of the business and every element of the organization. Look closely and we will see a void in many companies that desperately needs to be filled.

CHAPTER 20

UNIFYING THE BUSINESS

Everything that comes prior to this chapter is working toward and supporting a single goal—to unify IT and our business and to shape a single organization that is working together, under the same strategy to a single purpose. By now you likely understand exactly what that purpose is: to build strong partnerships with happy and loyal customers.

When we do create strong partnerships and demonstrate unique value with customers and they feel our organization has met or exceeded their expectations, then we are capable of creating customers for a generation, customers for a lifetime. It is more within our reach than ever before because there is an acute lack of great service and value in the market today, and when it appears, it truly stands out. Customers are willing to pay for this, far more in fact than for just the average product or service.

Customers are willing to commit to a long-term relationship, perhaps now more than ever, when they are working with a partner they trust, a partner that delivers consistently to their needs.

The synergies of a unified business are too numerous to list, but what is fundamental of a truly unified business is that improvements are possible and likely to occur in virtually every element of the business. Work occurs faster every day, waste is naturally all but eliminated, the people of the organization are happy and focused, remarkable efficiencies enable the business to deliver products and services at a superior price and at superior value, the quality of people rises in virtually every position because good people and success are a strong attraction for more good people and more success, and the healthy culture encourages the best from every employee and from leadership. This is just the beginning of the performance advantages and the circle of influences created by the unified business.

One remarkable characteristic of the process of unification is that each step we take forward, each step we take toward a more unified business, then enables other new improvements and opens new dimensions to the unified model that we could not understand or reach previously.

> *Everything just works better in the unified business. If we are ever able to create what appears to approach magic in business, this could be one of those times.*

The synergies across the business are magnified when the unity of IT coincides with or precedes the unification of business due to the natural connections created by data, technology, and systems across the organization. These things are effectively the tendons and ligaments of the business, holding everything together and making the motion of the business stronger.

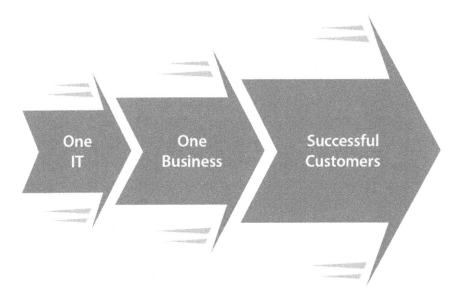

Figure 20.1 Unifying the Business

Regardless of the context—whether it's the military, law enforcement, a government body, or an athletic team—the performance of the entity is far superior when there is unity and a common purpose. Think in terms of sports—the teams that consistently win and the teams that win championships are invariably the teams that play well together and understand a team strategy. The same can be said for the military—the success of a military operation, regardless of scope, normally comes down to the unit working as one and driving to a single mission objective.

Our path in business is very similar—it is virtually identical at its core, although some of the details are a bit different as they must be.

It is a powerful and necessary evolution of the standard business model, but this transformation from a somewhat disjointed and fragmented business can't happen through the efforts of the business alone.

*This model must be enabled, or surrounded
to an extent, by the destination of all
the actions of the business and the
internal enabler of the business.*

In this context, the destination is clearly the customer and our time-less source of clarity and energy, and the enablers are technology and data and the systems of IT. While we can argue that the customer has always been with us and beckoning to those in business who were patient or wise enough to recognize the unique place the customer has and always will hold for business, the enablement of IT and the many inroads IT has in the business has clearly evolved and accelerated in the past ten years. The role of technology and its many variants has fundamentally altered the landscape of business forever and demands our attention as well as underlines and enables the unification of the business.

The more prominent and in most cases strategic role of technology in the business is now creating a powerful force to help drive the business to unification, simply to create a new level of performance, agility, and speed that is not possible without this transformation.

*The force of change that comes with a new
generation of strategic technologies is in itself a
strong agent of change, but when combined with
the unstoppable pull of the customer and the
marketplace, we have before us a combination of
forces unlike anything the market has ever seen.*

Ultimately, and after careful consideration of all the factors shaping business today, we must be left with the conclusion that a unified IT and then a unified business form our only path forward.

The very survival of these organizations is at stake. Those who embrace this strategy and operating model will then have the opportunity to emerge as market leaders and enjoy all the remarkable and exciting benefits that come along with this well-earned status.

OUR BUSINESS

This simple expression represents a significant change in our mindset, and it means so much about how we think about everything and how we act every day. The shift is one from that of seeing the business as a separate thing, as something a bit distant, as another group of people and certainly something we care about, but at the same time, it is simply true there has always been some level of separation between IT and the business.

But as we continue the transformation that began within IT and continues to spread across IT and slowly but surely into our business, this change is a strong force that pulls us together and unites our people in every team around a new and more clear set of goals and objectives.

> *To be clear, we needed to begin the transformation, cleansing, and realignment in IT because we needed to get our house in order first. These big changes in IT give us a much-needed foundation on which to build the forthcoming changes in our business.*

Getting the IT house in order also creates some momentum for new leadership and creates a new set of operating models that have been proven and tested through the work completed in IT. These models can include many things, but among the most impactful are a better ability to leverage data, including customer data, across every organization and recognizing the value of this data and the remarkable insights it holds. In addition to this data as a great asset, other key models include 24X7 access to all company systems, a new generation of automation, including powerful new self-serve resources, and the use of intelligent technology in new and strategic ways.

Each of these examples has been addressed in some detail throughout the book, but we reference them here in a different context—the unifying force these changes and new models bring to our organization. The new models are not just about new deployments of technology; they are about a fundamental change in how we plan, act, and work every day.

These new models and systems, born in IT and brought to our business, become a powerful unifying force, breaking down the old structures and biases that have existed in our organization for the past fifty years, throughout the full history of the modern business.

Figure 20.2 Our Business

Nobody would argue with the good that comes from better team-work, a more synchronized and collaborative organization, and the benefits of unification. What *will* surprise many people is the ability to create these unifying forces through technology and data. This is a powerful strategy—first changing and then unifying the organization from within and through the actions of the IT organization, which is the very reason that IT must take up this mission through our own initiative and without waiting another day.

> *IT must be proactive and take on this mission.*
> *It is critical to the future of our business,*
> *and at the same time, our business will*
> *never ask for this assistance. Our business*
> *simply does not understand and will never*
> *understand that IT is capable of creating*
> *this level of lasting change from within.*

This is not a criticism; it is simply the current state of things. Our business can't recognize these connections and the potential impact of these changes. There is just too much history and rigid structure in place today, so with some context this does make a certain level of sense. Perhaps a few visionary leaders will understand this and quickly emerge as agents of change for these immediate changes, but then will continue forward as the new leaders of our business in the future.

These exceptional people will rise to be our future CIOs, COOs, and CEOs. Look for creative and tech-savvy IT managers and IT directors to be promoted into the role of VP IT, a position that grooms new leaders on a path to the C-Level roles in the future. We need this new generation of leaders who are really good with technology and at the same time understand the business and have a talent for creative solutions.

The grooming and accelerated development of new leaders with a new mix of skills adds another layer to the unification of IT and our business. These skills are very much needed in IT of course, but equally and perhaps more so for our business. This same set of skills become yet another unifying element for the next decade. In the past, the skills we sought in IT leadership could be very different than what we sought in our business, with technology derivative skills often leading the way in the IT organization.

But now a new view is beginning to emerge— that strong technology and systems expertise is only valuable in combination with and when complementing other skills. Technology skills with innovation skills, technology skills with customer-facing skills, technology expertise with communications skills are a few examples of the new model we are rapidly developing an appreciation for.

It is certainly true that this combination of skills is not common but does exist in a number of talented individuals. We likely have some in our organization today, people who should be recognized and developed and invested in. It begins with an awareness of the importance of this skill mix, by recognizing the people themselves and that they are important to our future, and then creating a career development plan that maximizes the value and contribution they can make to the organization. These people are typically wired to be high achievers and will appreciate the recognition and thrive in this culture, which is good for everybody and a remarkable force of renewal.

Years from now we can expect that many people will take some of the credit for the ideas and actions that transformed our business, and that is okay. The credit does not matter; all that matters is making the changes and creating waves that will rock IT and our business and at the same time bring us together like never before.

We bring this full circle back to our business, and all these themes support the remarkable change that is our only future—our talented people thriving in our business with a singular focus on our customers.

It can be no other way.

SINGULARITY OF STRATEGY

Our everyday actions across IT are influenced and shaped by the strategy of IT, and increasingly the strategy of the business, which is a natural model. But because IT is undergoing enormous change and we are working to bring the IT organization and the business together, we should always be aware of things that naturally align our people. One such powerful thing is a consolidated strategy for IT and our business, a singularity of strategy that leads us forward.

But in many ways our timing is good because most IT organizations are in need of an altogether new, or at least a strategy facelift, and looking more broadly, most IT organizations and business don't have a unified strategy in place. This has never been something that was expected, and so most organizations don't have a sense there is a void today. This is changing and none too soon. Strategy is so important today in order to bring to life our ability as an organization to leverage technology, to put technology and data to work in every part of the business in order to better serve our customers.

A singular strategy will help both IT and our business because it brings together the strategy for today and the future that is missing for the business as well as elevates the unique role that technology—the new generation of intelligent technology and the precious data that has grown in our business over the past ten years—plays.

If our strategy does not call out these things, then technology and data are likely to continue to occupy a tactical role in the business, or simply an afterthought. This is unacceptable and not just because we as IT professionals are naturally fans of technology. The businesses that lead the market over the next ten to twenty years will be great at both technology and at business.

Being great at business is no longer enough, however, and it's a critical point to make. We must now be great at business in such a way that strategically leverages technology to perform better than we could with technology in a tactical role—technology simply being technology. This is common and expected, but it is no longer enough. Continuing with the common model today will relegate the full business to being common at best. I make this reference to "common at best" because in many cases—and we have seen some spectacular examples of this in the past five years—the business that is not able to elevate technology to a strategic role or create leverage with technology will fail. These businesses will lose market share quickly to competitors who have created leverage with technology, and they will be faced with a short period of adjustment or failure will come soon.

Several great examples of this failure have come to pass in the retail market, where technology is more visible and more enabling than some other markets.

Remember, this singularity of strategy is not an artificial activity or deliverable we have created to somehow serve the agenda of

IT. This strategy is needed equally by the business for the sake of business performance. If anything, we can make the case that the business needs this new generation of strategy more than IT does.

> *It is a waste of our time to debate if IT needs this strategy more than the business does, and it's probably best to recognize that we all need this new strategy that brings us a common purpose and the clarity that has been missing.*

The full organization can then rally around this strategy and create a set of specific initiatives that will bring the strategy to life. While the business and IT alike need a unifying strategy for the many practical needs across these organizations every day in terms of planning, investment priorities, resource assignments, innovation processes, and much more, the powerful force of unification created by this strategy is compelling.

Figure 20.3 Singularity of Strategy

A singularity of vision and strategy creates a new sense of team-work and collaboration, and a common language for communi-cating. There is no end to the many small benefits created by this singularity of strategy beyond the headline benefits it creates. It's important to not leave this at a high, abstract level and assume that is good enough. It's not. A strategy and supporting goals that have the potential to unify our teams must enable and then be support-ed by a number of operational activities that make the strategy real and help ensure we will deliver the many benefits it has to offer. A good example of a unifying goal would be to improve customer sat-isfaction/renewals by 2 percent over the course of the next twelve months. In many industries this seemingly small increase is a dra-matic improvement and will translate into revenue performance and many other important business results. It is also an indication of a positive trajectory that reflects so much about what a busi-ness is doing every day. Of course, in your organization this num-ber might be lower than what makes sense, but we will use this example for our discussion.

Although a very simple goal, it provides some significant guidance to the IT organization that can include improved communications with clients in the account management organization, special cus-tomer pricing promotions for the sales organization, improved customer training through the training and services department, a reduction in hold times in the technical support organization, and an improved client steering committee forum as managed and hosted by the marketing organization.

Add to this an enhancement cycle for all customer-facing order-ing systems, self-service portals and support portals, as executed by the IT organization, and we now have five or six organizations working in a collaborative way to improve customer satisfaction and loyalty. United by a single and simple unifying goal and strat-egy. Yes, this example is very simple, but simple is good.

*A simple goal is more likely to be successful
than one that is complex, hard to understand,
hard to measure. A simple goal does not
require explaining and all but eliminates
any risk of being interpreted wrongly. A
simple strategy and set of goals are by
their very nature more likely to unify.*

Even better, a simple goal that provides a quantitative result is quickly embraced by our teams and does not require translation or create confusion. Whether it comes from IT or from another organization is not important; all that matters is that we achieve the singularity the organization needs today and will enable us to drive improved business results.

If the organization is stalled and this unifying vision and strategy are not currently present, and the organization is working under an old and stale vision and a set of strategies and goals that are not helping to unify our teams toward compelling goals, IT is ready to fill the void and lift the organization up and take it forward, better than ever.

We can do it as few others can. We are capable of changing our business for the better and with no turning back.

CUSTOMER AND BUSINESS OUTCOMES

A fantastic and self-governing process to create in IT is the focus on outcomes. It is a very simple thing but once again not common in the IT organization today. The wonderful thing about a focus on outcomes is that it naturally creates a shift to measurable and results-oriented performance.

When this happens, it drives a reassessment of our previous metrics, and what we discover is that some of them will not pass the new test and it is no longer possible to verify the value of the previous generation of metrics and measurements. Real outcomes are elevated above what we have measured previously but can't be connected to these outcomes. The outcome can be a measurable result from the business, including things like customer satisfaction and revenue performance. It can also be an outcome provided by customers, including renewal rates, survey results, the purchase rate of additional products, and the like.

These are not hard to find once we begin to look for them.

Target outcomes are everywhere at some level, and we will find our colleagues across the business happy to share them and to join up with IT to better connect our work, our systems, and our metrics to these outcomes.

We will also find customers equally willing to share key outcomes. In my experience a customer has never pushed back on sharing key outcomes and objectives when asked. We only need to ask and this simple question will create a healthy and ongoing dialogue with customers. Customers instantly recognize that it's a good thing for the partnership and that it will enable the IT organization to deliver superior experiences and solutions over time.

We have established that a focus on business and customer outcomes will provide a new level of clarity for the tools and systems of IT—which effectively connects us to the most important element of what we are hoping to provide with all of what IT delivers: happy users and tangible results that improve business and customer performance. Lest you question this conclusion, there is an increasing amount of information available on this topic and increasingly a point that thought leaders in IT and business will agree on.

So with this we have established why focus is important. Now, our attention turns to finding a source for this information and gaining access to the right information. Again, there is good news in that it won't require any convincing on our part. This type of inquiry coming from IT will be an bit unusual for most organizations, but we will get past that quickly. We'll connect with the right people and the right teams, whether they are inside our business or not, and with the key business owners and colleagues who know this information well and provide what IT requires as well as very similar people in our customer organizations.

These connections, inside and outside the business, once established will be a wonderful source of information. Once we have received the initial set of information, a cadence can be established to get updates to the information we have on outcomes and metrics, and to receive new information when new outcomes and metrics are created.

It does not need to be a daily discussion; quarterly updates work well and don't take a lot of time. This process keeps the dialogue going, and we have the opportunity to update the outcomes descriptions and metrics as needed—which keeps these outcomes in synch with our IT efforts and enables IT to keep a fresh view of what is occurring in our business and with our customers. Once that first step is taken to make the connection and start the dialogue, we have natural momentum that keeps the dialogue running.

The focus on outcomes is good of course, but don't underestimate the value of the dialogue IT will carry with our colleagues in the business and with customer teammates. I use the word "teammates" intentionally as that is exactly what will occur with our customers—they will quickly become members of the extended team as we are working together to improve the quality and performance of all, or certainly key IT systems under the guidance of this dialogue. It's a wonderful cycle that is self-governing and self-renewing.

With all this good coming from the results-oriented model for IT, it's hard to believe there is yet more good news, but there is. In creating this model, this focus and dialogue with our business and customers, we are giving rise to another powerful force—a natural unification of IT, rallying around this model and the new dialogues we have created. The unification of IT quickly reaches into every corner of our business and pulls our business people together and then our business people with our teams in IT. This unification could simply not be done by some artificial means or by communicating it as a new priority for the organization. Yes, this communication helps a little but there is nothing with the power to rally our people around a cause like the real needs of our customers.

It requires no help; it is a natural light that our people will respond to immediately. So we are then able to enjoy better performance around the delivery of IT-managed tools and systems with the benefit of these new definitions for business and customer outcomes, which in itself is a great source of value, and in many ways changes how we work every day. Then we also create a unification across IT and bring our business and IT together with a new framework of results to focus on a common mission and terminology.

This complete results-focused model and ensuing lifestyle change is truly unique in its ability to bring lasting change to the IT organization.

ONE

One: a single word that captures so much of what we have discussed throughout the book, in every chapter. It is the ultimate destination in what has become a journey that includes the transformation of IT expressly to improve IT performance and to embrace the digital transformation, automation, leveraging intelligent technology, creating a new culture for IT, building a new engine of innovation, and much more. IT's transformation is critical, but it's not possible to create this transformation without recognizing the natural momentum that is created and where that will take us. This brings us to the understanding and realization that the transformation of IT is only sustainable and only of lasting value when a new initiative extends the transformation itself—the unification of IT.

This unification then complements and enhances all the improvements made in the transformation model and opens doors that are our only path to continued improvements around elements including scalability, agility, and speed—only a few examples of what we can put in the category of strategic IT enhancements that build a fundamentally new planning and operations model for IT. IT's unification and the transparency, collaboration, and teamwork it creates will fundamentally improve how IT performs in every aspect of our work and on every initiative. This level of improvement was not possible with the transformation alone. Yes, the transformation of IT is important, even critical, but the transformation is focused on new deliverables, new system improvements, and leveraging new technology across IT to meet growing business requirements.

> *But transformation alone is not enough. Transformation does change what we do and what we deliver, but not how we plan and work every day. This is fundamentally different and goes to the heart of a unified IT—this is the "how" of the future IT.*

How we work together

How we plan for the future

How we form teams to drive initiatives

How we communicate

How we create transparency

How we align with our business

How we construct a new culture for IT

How we cultivate passion for the customer

How we nurture innovation

The question of "how" becomes everything to the sustainable performance and results delivered by the IT organization. The "how" is both the hard part and the important part. We know *what* we have started and we have taken the first step, but until we know *how*, we can't be successful.

Just as the momentum of change through the transformation of IT does not stop with the transformation alone, and this momentum carries us into the unification of IT, the force does not stop with IT—the growing momentum and cultural change then continue into the unification of our business. This is both unstoppable and very necessary.

> *The new models that lie at the heart of IT are first proven in the context of our transformation, which includes important elements like innovation, automation, and our engagement with the customer. It is clear that while these initiatives are necessary to address the immediate needs of our IT and digital transformation, the good does not stop here.*

A core strategic and tactical model along with the supporting priorities is necessary for our IT transformation but provides so much of what we need to create a new and unified IT. Note that virtually every component of the transformation model directly drives or encourages a more unified IT and a more unified business. It is easy to focus on the immediate results and deliverables, and this is certainly important. But what we are creating is the process of delivering to these immediate needs and changing how we plan, act, and deliver every day. Each of these principles is unifying, and they include better communications, transparency, working in cross-functional teams, accountability, diversity of skills, employee development, and public innovation forums. The influence each of these creates for unifying IT is striking.

Then, taking this one step further, we can draw the same conclusions with regard to the boundless ability of a dynamic and unifying IT to unify our business and create what becomes increasingly difficult to separate IT and our business. It all simply becomes our business and our people working together to drive the right results across our business and with our customers.

This is exactly as it should be.

> *We are building something timeless, something*
> *we can be proud of, a legacy that will stand*
> *the test of time and the many challenges*
> *that come the way of our business.*

We simply can't build this powerful and timeless model that will in turn create business success and customer success if we are divided.

We can only do this as one, every team and every person in IT and our business working together. As one, anything is possible.

This is One IT and One Business.

FINAL THOUGHTS

It has been a true pleasure crafting this book and sharing my thoughts on the continued journey we share as brothers and sisters of IT. I sincerely believe the next ten years will be the most dynamic and most important decade in the wonderful history of IT and in many respects of the business as well, because as we have explored, it is no longer possible to separate IT and our business.

We are now joined as One, as we must be to ensure every person working in the organization has a bright future—a future that offers the opportunity to build great businesses where the strategic leveraging of technology is fundamental to our everyday work and the everyday success of our customers. These shared successes are simply not possible without the bridge that technology and data can uniquely provide. This is a living connection, one made possible by a new generation of technology and strategy, born in IT, that now brings the IT organization and our business together as One.

Depending on the organization, a unification of IT will be necessary first in order to groom IT for the broader unification, and a similar action might be required in our business, but this is all a necessary passage before we can create the One of IT and our business.

The union then becomes the ultimate evolution of these organizations, and no further distinctions of this organization and that organization are necessary in the future. It is simply *Us* working together to drive customer success as the only path to business success.

The greatest force underlying these unifications will surely be the customer—unique and boundless is their ability to bring us clarity and further unify us in our quest to rethink and transform virtually all we do. This can only be possible with the shining light of the customer as our guide.

Although there are many things that come together to create the remarkable tapestry that forms the future of IT and our business, a few things really stand out. If you have read only a few pages of the book, this will come as no surprise. If you have skipped to the end, well, I don't blame you, and I will share those highlights here for your brief enjoyment.

First, it can only be the customer who brings IT and our business together as respective unified organizations and then as One. As many elements and organizations and people before, we become One in order to serve our customers better and create relationships and partnerships for life. This is the ultimate test of any business, and when we are able to be successful in creating these relationships, everything else falls into line.

Next is nurturing and developing the talented and passionate people of IT and our business by creating a culture thoughtfully designed to encourage our people and our teams to be the best they possibly can. This culture then becomes self-directing, self-governing, and self-guiding through the principles and leadership models we create. Our people are able to make the right decisions quickly, enforce the right priorities, and take the right actions every day because the culture we have created generates such a strong context and such strong teams, we know what we must do. The many difficult choices of business become more clear—we are now more focused and far more capable of separating the distractions from what is truly vital.

Finally, we described and embraced the leadership of IT as an organic source of much-needed direction and strategy with regard to how and when the organization can leverage technology, tools, systems, and increasingly intelligent technology for the greater good of our business and customers. This includes many elements, including an engine for innovation that creates ongoing value for our customers and competitive advantage in the global marketplace—a marketplace filled with shrewd consumers who demand so much of us. This leadership has been called unlikely at times, but is critically needed, and we have seen countless examples of why today, IT is uniquely capable of providing this leadership both directly when needed and as catalyst and facilitator when appropriate.

These elements all come together today to set us on a journey that in the decade ahead will see the IT organization unify and then quicken the rate of change and draw together every thread of our business into One with singularity of strategy and action. The result enriches everything we do and lifts our business to new heights simply not possible today.

Regardless of your history and experience in IT, your history or experience in business, we are all fortunate to be part of this remarkable journey that will carry us through the adventure of the next decade and beyond. This journey will be equally demanding and exciting for those new to IT and those who have been in IT for twenty to thirty years as many of you have.

Our exciting unification and the many improvements it entails will hold remarkable learning and growth opportunities for each of us—opportunities that are virtually boundless when we consider this will reshape not just IT but virtually every small and large action alike that occurs in our business every day.

It will be fun, my friends. Thanks for listening and I look forward to hearing your stories when our paths cross.

Kevin

@kevinjsmith4IT

REFERENCES

The Practical Guide to World-Class IT Service Management. Kevin J. Smith. The Anima Group, 2017.

The IT Imperative. Kevin J. Smith. The Anima Group, 2018.

World Class IT. Peter A. High. John Wiley & Sons, 2009.

NOTES

NOTES

NOTES

NOTES

NOTES

NOTES

NOTES

NOTES

NOTES

NOTES

NOTES

NOTES

NOTES

NOTES

NOTES

NOTES

NOTES

NOTES

NOTES

NOTES

NOTES

NOTES

NOTES

NOTES

_____

_____

_____

_____

_____

_____

_____

_____

_____

_____

_____

_____

_____

_____

_____

_____

_____

_____

_____

_____

NOTES

NOTES

NOTES

NOTES

NOTES

NOTES